Suggs is a s~~i~~n~~g~~e~~r~~, ~~s~~o~~n~~g ~~w~~r~~i~~t~~e~~r, D~~J~~, actor and TV presenter. He is perhaps best known as lead singer with Madness, who have had twenty-four Top Ten hits and continue to tour. Suggs lives in Camden, London.

'Brilliantly nutty . . . gloriously irreverent'
Mail on Sunday

'Beautifully recreates the memories of his early years'
Sunday Express

'Wonderfully evocative'
Scotsman

'His early life would make a novel in itself'
Ian Rankin

'Really well written . . . Gripping'
James Brown

OR A RIOT

WARWICK UNIVERSITY ARTS
FEDERATION

deaf school!

AT TIFFANY'S, COVENTRY PRECINCT
THURSDAY, 24th FEBRUARY, 1977

SKETCH

Allegorie
uncertain

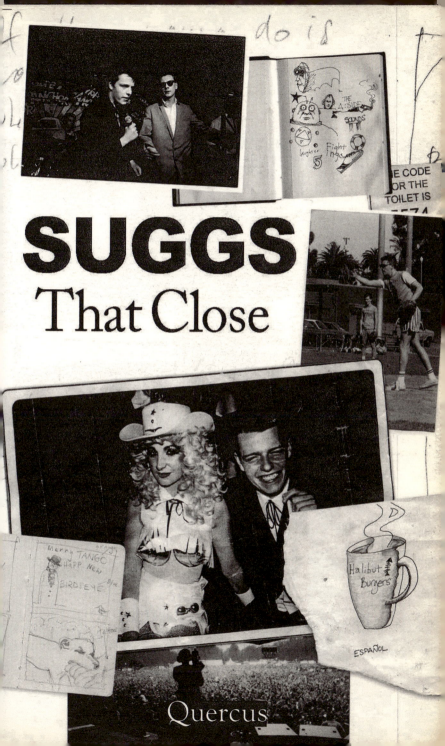

SUGGS
That Close

Quercus

First published in Great Britain in 2013 by Quercus Editions Ltd

This paperback edition published in 2014 by

Quercus Editions Ltd
55 Baker Street
Seventh Floor, South Block
London
W1U 8EW

All images taken from author's private collection, except for the following:

Text: pii–iii *left* Clare Muller, p156 REX/EUGENE ADEBARI, p189 REX/Andre Csillag

Plate section: pvi Chalkie Davies/Getty Images,
pvii *top* Virginia Turbett/Redferns, *bottom* Clare Muller,
pviii Chalkie Davies/Getty Images, px Clare Muller, pxii Clare Muller,
pxiii *bottom* Clare Muller, pxiv *top* REX/Andy Rosen, *bottom* Clare Muller,
pxv *top* Rex Features, pxvi *top* Rex Features *centre* Rex Features

'Baggy Trousers' Words and Music by Graham McPherson and
Christopher Foreman © 1980,
Reproduced by permission of EMI Music Publishing Ltd, London W1F 9LD

'One Better Day' Words and Music by Graham McPherson
and Mark Bedford © 1984,
Reproduced by permission of EMI Music Publishing Ltd, London W1F 9LD

A CIP catalogue record for this book is available
from the British Library

ISBN PB 978 0 85738 955 8
ISBN Ebook 978 0 85738 954 1

10 9 8 7 6 5 4 3 2 1

Text designed and typeset by Ellipsis Digital Ltd, Glasgow

Plates designed by Rich Carr

Printed and bound in Great Britain by Clays Ltd. St Ives plc

Anne, Scarlett and Viva

THAT CLOSE

we're that close
It's scary.   ready for love?

we are so close
I couldn't get nothing between us.
I cannot tell you

we are that close
to getting it right
                "
to making it perfect...
and then
everything changes
oh no - everything hinges
   - on how I feel about you now,
because no one else could know
what made me we dare 2nd seen.
What no one else can see
and I know it sounds sad
and it might make me look bad it's all a hazy dream

'I don't wanna be seperated from you
I don't want no-one between us
I would kill to be with you

So many people tell me
So what the fuck do they know

and then you
left.
I felt bereft

like Hughie Green
on opportunity knocks.
(came to an end)
the clapometer stopped,
The audience went
home.
(You left me alone)

It's like morcambe without wise,
It's like the your sake telling lies,
Tommy Cooper without a fez,
The Happy Mondays without Bez,
Like the trees without leaves.
It's like not being able to sneeze
with pepper up your nose
- Lady Godiva wearing clothes.

Left me in the lunch
posted me off my
              perch.

All the vices, in moderation.

It's like Punch
without Judy,
It's Oliver with no
Ron Moody.

CONTENTS

Once upon a time. A long long time ago.
When time wasn't of the essence.
When time waited for no man.
When time wasn't money.
Time just flew.
Time took a cigarette.
Time was an irrelevance.

Time, gentlemen, please.

Time flies like an arrow.
Fruit flies like a banana.

INTRODUCTION

I've been asked a few times over the years if I fancied writing my autobiography. But I never felt the time was quite right. A few years ago, a very nice publishing house offered me a more than fair amount of dough for the rights to my life story. They offered it on the proviso I worked with a ghostwriter. A meeting was duly set and I met this rather charming ghostwriter woman at the Bar Italia, in Soho, one sunny morning to see if we could get on.

The publisher told me she was the best-selling ghostwriter around. Over coffee we had a nice chat and she was taking notes, but as the conversation drew on, I noticed her pen hovering motionless between the less juicy bits. I could tell, unsurprisingly, she was searching for the more sensational end of my market. It turned out the reason she was cited as Britain's most successful ghostwriter was that she'd penned the hugely best-selling David Beckham biography. Well, no disrespect to the great man, or the writer herself, at that time a monkey could have written a best-selling book about old Golden Balls.

Well, for me, what tipped me over the edge into thinking now is the right time was a set of converging circumstances.

On the eve of my fiftieth birthday I was standing on the balcony of an old music hall in Wapping called Wilton's, one of the last of those great palaces of working-class entertainment, surveying a room full of friends and foes who'd come from all over the world to join me on this auspicious occasion. I was having the party the night before my actual birthday as the venue had already been booked on the night by Marc Almond.

Wilton's is an amazing place. Just over a century ago the writer and theatre critic Henry Chance Newton said that 'without its Palaces of Variety and its Music-Halls, living London would only be half alive.' All of which makes it rather surprising that today just a handful of these places survive. So here I am surveying the scene on the eve of my fiftieth birthday, having a toast to Mr Wilton and his magical music hall, and it's beautiful just looking round the room. Even my cheapest friends have dressed the part. It's a room full of Victorian dandies, all top hats and mutton chops and girls of every shape and size bursting out of bodices left, right and indeed centre. And you don't get many of them to the pound, missus!

The crazed, the lunatics and the thieving toerags had all turned up, and even people who aren't in Madness. Boom boom. It was brilliant.

Anne (Bette Bright), my lovely wife, much to my surprise, had organised a whole music-hall show. There were sand dancers dressed as Egyptians dancing in hieroglyphic fashion. A burlesque singer, dressed, albeit briefly, as Vera Lynn. A pearly king making a ladder out of a rolled-up newspaper, whilst singing:

Oh it really is a wery pretty garden,
And Chingford to the eastward could be seen,

Wiv a ladder and some glasses, you could see to 'Ackney Marshes,
If it wasn't for the 'ouses in between.

Lee Thompson, Madness sax player extraordinaire, did a tremendous Max Wall routine. He actually came on the Tube in the full outfit. Clive Langer, Madness producer, and his son Johnny, performed a stirring version of 'My Old Man's A Dustman'. My two lovely daughters, Scarlett and Viva, in giant nylon bee-hives, came on singing 'Sisters'.

At the end of this fantastic night a giant birthday cake, I mean huge, was wheeled into the middle of the stage, and bang, out of it leapt this gorgeous woman as a finale to the show. I thought, Phwoah! I'm taking her home tonight. Ooh missus. It was my fiftieth birthday after all. It was my wife, Anne. It was a truly unforgettable night.

So there I was the following morning, on my actual birthday, lying in the bath, amongst the bubbles and ducks, mulling it all over. Feeling somewhat worse for wear but deeply content. Thinking about all them faces I saw at the party. People I grew up with on the council estate. People I went to school with, my family, my two lovely daughters all grown up and moved on, but only to within walking distance of our fridge.

Like a movie of faces floating past. People I've known since they were kids, whose lives splintered and fractured in a million different directions. Poets, painters, criminals, fruit and veg wholesalers, record company executives, dealers, dustmen, butchers, gardeners, lawyers, accountants, cocktail waiters, social workers and of course the band. The band Madness.

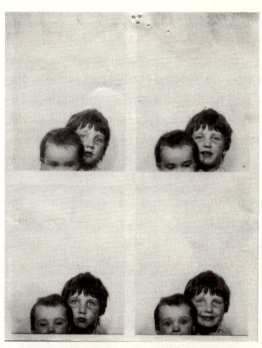

Scarlett and Viva, photobooth stool at its highest

Mike (Barzo) Barson (Mr B)
Lee (Thommo) Thompson (Kix)
Chris Foreman (Chrissy Boy)
Cathal Smyth (Chas Smash)
Daniel Woodgate (Woody)
Mark Bedford (Bedders)

So many memories attached to each and every one of those faces I've known, on and off, down half a century.

When BANG, I hear a terrible crash, and I turn round to see my favourite cat, Mamba, lying motionless on the bathroom floor, surrounded by shards of glass. What's happened here? Has he been fired through the window?

He looks perfect, there's no blood coming out. But I sort of know he's dead, I just can't believe it. Hold on a minute – the glass shelf above the sink's gone. Maybe he jumped up on it and it broke. But cats can't die from a fall of four feet. Cats got nine lives. Cats can fall from eight-storey buildings, I've seen it on YouTube. But there he is, lying motionless on the floor. Maybe he just didn't have time to right himself from such a short fall. Maybe he bashed his head on the sink on the way down.

But I just can't believe it. My Mamba dead on my fiftieth birthday? The cat that caught eight mice in one day. The cat that saw off the horrible cat from next door that used to come in our house and spray on my shoes. The cat that used to climb up the ivy at the front of the house and knock on the bedroom window when he wanted to come in!

He was my best mate.

I get out of the bath, dripping, and feel his pulse. I feel his chest – he's definitely getting colder. How can you do this to me, God, on my fiftieth birthday? Now I'm not gonna go on about pets. It's a bit like people going on about their babies. Mine's the prettiest, cleverest, etc. . . .

But I did love that cat.

We're having a load of people around for dinner that night, including my kids. I don't want to ruin the evening by telling everyone that the cat's dead, and I'm half hoping he's not. So I spend the entire night running up and down stairs to the top bathroom in the forlorn hope he's only been concussed, that somehow he'll wake up and stroll off. But he doesn't.

The following morning I break the terrible news. There's wailing and gnashing of teeth. Real sadness; he was a real character. We follow the usual procedure of trying to find poor old Mamba a vacant plot in the pet cemetery that is our back garden. Amongst the other cats, mice, gerbils, hamsters, rabbits, guinea pigs, the lizard and that goldfish that have come and gone through our house over the decades.

I even get my daughter's boyfriend round for a bit of moral support. And to help with the digging. He was a big old cat.

He's buried with all the usual formality, it's sad, we all loved him. His big brother Voodoo looking down from the roof of the garden shed. After the funeral and a short wake in our local pub I'm off to see my mum. I didn't get much of a chance to talk to her at the party. I jump in a black cab and direct the driver to Soho. After a couple of minutes the driver turns and says: 'Here, Suggsy. You all right mate? You look a bit glum.'

I explain.

'Well, actually it's my fiftieth birthday today. I know it's only a number, but it's sort of just hit me. I haven't really thought about it before. Fifty years, half a century of my life, gone!'

'You don't want to worry about that, son, I'm fifty-two, look at me.' He glances in the mirror and carefully runs two fingers through his comb-over quiff, while I take in the back of his fat bald head.

'Yeah right. Well, to tell you truth it's not just that. My two lovely daughters have just left home, which has left a big hole in my life.'

'What! Couldn't wait to see the back of mine.' He drives on.

'Right . . . Well . . . OK . . . What's really tipped me over the edge, and it might sound a bit stupid, but my cat died this morning.'

There's an awkward silence. The cab slows and pulls into the kerb, and I hear what distinctly sounds like sobbing, crackling through the intercom.

'My cat, Bubbles, died last week . . . I know exactly what you mean, mate.'

We get chatting about how I ran up and down stairs to see if Mamba was still alive. He tells me his Bubbles got run over in the street and he had to carry him in the house in a bin bag. And everyone in the street's asking: 'What's in the bin bag?' And telling me this sets him off again.

He tells me his next-door neighbour's a vet, and the vet says to him: 'Are you sure it was dead?' and he says he thought it was, but he's buried it now.

The vet says: 'Well, if you've buried it, even if it wasn't dead, it certainly is now.'

And that's it. That's what gets me going. I'm fifty. Life has changed dramatically since the kids left home. They've been at the centre of our lives for twenty-five years. I've suddenly found I have got time to reflect on my own life, now I'm not so busy with theirs. But it's Mamba's sudden death that's really done it. He's buried now.

Fate and chance, never knowing what's round the corner. My whole life has been directed by so many quirks of fate, chance encounters that could have led me down so many different paths. It was often that close. That close to people, that close to success, that close to disaster.

We were that close, it was scary,
We were that close, I couldn't tell you.
Ready for love, we were that close,
To getting it right, or crashing and burning.

Skidding on the surface, with the brake jammed down,
Slow motion sliding, head-on . . . we were that close.
Remember them summer days, when we took whatever came
* our way,*
Getaway, hey, but not too far, took a spin round in your broken-
* down car,*
No one else could know, what we done and seen,
No one else could see, it's all a hazy dream.

I spent quite a lot of time on my own as a kid, being an only child of a single parent. Mum worked long hours in the clubs of Soho. And I got used to, and still enjoy, my own company. When I first met the rest of the band, in my teens, they were all very independent characters. A number of whom shared a similar background. A group of very strong-minded individuals. A band of loners. Joining the band and rehearsing in Mike's bedroom in Crouch End of an evening, was, for me, a great alternative to running round the streets causing trouble.

I am often asked why I think it is that Madness are still as popular thirty-odd years on and, apart from the obvious fact that we had a lot of hits, I think it's because we have always ploughed our own furrow and have rarely, if at all, been in fashion. That gave us an independence from the fickle business of show. And given that in the early days there'd be ten or more of us and our friends, often a lot more, on the road together, we could create our own crazy world, style and sound, which for some peculiar reason still resonates today. And I honestly feel that amongst all of our great achievements, the greatest is that we are still friends today.

Well, eyes down, boys and girls, here goes. After a few half-hearted attempts over the past few years, what is left of my befuddled memory is now down in black and white. Of course I have written before, and have always enjoyed writing, it was one of the few things I was any good at, at school. In fact, apart from art, the only thing I was any good at.

I've written another book, about London, called *Suggs and the City*, and jolly good it is too, but I did that with a lot of help from the people who worked with me on the *Disappearing London* TV series.

And of course I've written songs, loads of them.

Writing a good song isn't easy, by any means, but the discipline is completely different. You're more often than not collaborating with other people, and to be perfectly frank if you get a couple of good lines for a song, real good ones, it's a productive day.

But this book-writing lark is quite a different fish. Hours and hours in front of a laptop, and if like me you have the brain of a deranged butterfly, it's more than a small challenge.

Trawling through the backwaters, searching through the undergrowth (amongst the used condoms and syringes of life). To the furthest corners of my unruly mind, for a minute nugget of info that may unlock another long-forgotten anecdote and help in the almost impossible task of trying to piece together the mostly unfathomable nonsense of my life.

I'm very grateful for my life, for many reasons, not least the opportunities it has given me to meet some of the most incredible characters. Without whom I would be as naught. And to be honest it's not all there, maybe I'm not all there, and factually it may not be completely correct, but I do hope that these snapshots give you some sense of how Graham McPherson became Suggs.

To infinity and (one step) beyond!

CAVENDISH MANSIONS

'Cavendish Mansions', thundered the bearded Victorian philanthropist, to the crowds of excited townsfolk, on a bright spring morning about four million years ago. His watery eyes glittering, he cuts the billowing yellow ribbon and throws his top hat in the air. Signalling tumultuous cheering, the flutter of ticker tape and hats of every shape and size flung skyward. Hordes of semi-naked children and ragged men and women, fresh from the Clerkenwell Workhouse, flood into the courtyard. Covering their heads from the falling hats and clutching shiny brass keys they crowd up the various stairwells and into their posh new abodes.

It must have looked pretty smart back then, through the great arched entrance into the courtyard and eight floors of shining red brick Victoriana. Bright white window surrounds on every floor.

I wonder what Mr. Bearded Philanthropist would have made of it today. Unspoilt, all original features. Fixtures and fittings untouched by regular maintenance ever since. En-suite toilet off tiny kitchenette, sink and ascot. Mum asleep on her bed in the living room and me in the bedroom. He probably would have approved, unfortunately the rest of the world had moved on somewhat in that time.

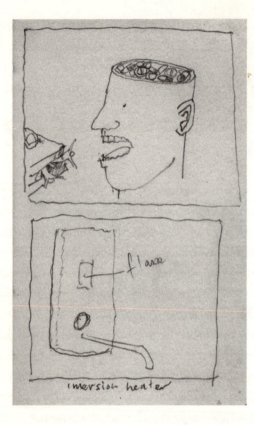

Mum was working in a bar in Soho and she didn't get back till late. She was out for the count. I slipped past her bed and straight into the gas rebate stacked neatly on the table, three cardboard 10ps, a couple of Chinese coins and two pounds fifty. I took thirty pence, four fags from the packet of Player's Navy Cut and headed out. The landings were open to the elements. The stairs were deadly, completely worn down. Smooth and hard as marble. Only drunks or babies could survive a fall down these.

We lived on the seventh floor. I gazed out over the balcony across the rooftops of my kingdom. Wet and grey, and winter.

Down in the courtyard Tiger and my best mate, Andrew Chalk, who everyone knew as Chalky, were kicking around a soggy leather football, to no great avail. Chalky was born on Halloween and I was born on Friday the thirteenth. A right little pair of nightmares we were too.

Bong! The ball slammed into the enormous metal bins that lined the outside wall.

'Go on there, Jeoorjie Best!'

'Piss off . . . come down and play!' exhorted a puffing Chalky.

It's almost impossible to get an exciting game of football going between two players, but when one of them is Tiger (who'd just come over from America and hadn't really got the hang of 'saccer') it never gets going. His mum and dad were even more American. I'd no idea why they were here, I think it was something to do with Speakers' Corner.

I gingerly slid down the rest of the slippery steps and out into the courtyard. The ball squirted in my direction and I booted it as hard as I could. Jesus, the soggy thing was like concrete, and even though I didn't connect properly I felt like I'd broken my foot. I sliced it at a right angle smack against a basement window and down into the area.

The area was about five feet deep and three feet wide and ran like a moat around the entire building. Maybe it was something to do with the war. Although who or what we were being protected from I could never work out. Maybe it was to keep us in.

I climbed resignedly over the railings and down. It was dark and spooky and no one liked going down there. Every twelve feet or so a bridge to one of the stairwells ran overhead and plunged the whole thing into complete gloom. It was knee-deep in years' worth of newspapers and rubbish, and as I kicked through the debris looking this way and that for the ball, one of the basement windows behind me burst open.

I nearly jumped out of my skin. It was one of the mad old geezers of which the flats had more than their fair share. Most probably driven mad by the smacking of soggy footballs against their windows.

'Want yer ball?' he said, none too kindly, making moves to climb out of the window. He had a face like the dad from *Steptoe and Son*, only with fewer teeth. He was wearing a red and white striped bobble hat and looked ominously sprightly for an old darzer. With one hand on the sill he leapt through the window and landed in the rubbish, grinning maniacally. He was about ten feet away, and the ball was in the space between us. I was weighing up the chances of grabbing it and running, when he suddenly hopped forward and from behind his back produced a Second World War bayonet.

The drizzle drizzled, and I backed away. 'Here, take it easy,' I mumbled. 'Want it, dooooyer, yer Jerry bastard.' He lunged; I stumbled backwards and fell into the rubbish. Through a closing curtain of chip wrappers I saw him lift the bayonet above his head with both hands and plunge it down.

AAAAAAAHHHHHH!!! BANG! HISSSSssss. He'd killed the ball, stabbing it to death. 'Oi, you old bastard,' shouted Chalky from above. 'Leave it alone. He still thinks he's in the trenches!'

I scrambled to my feet, the MOG (mad old geezer) brandishing the ball on the end of his bayonet, grinning, toothless and victorious. I turned and ran, churning through the knee-high rubbish. 'Go on, English Tommy,' shouted Chalky, laughing. I scrambled round the corner and out of sight, frantically looking for a way out. As I waded forward the rubbish in front of me was mysteriously jumping up and down. I scooped off the top layer to reveal a pigeon flapping around, unable to fly. With the fate of the hissing football still fresh in my mind I scooped it up, stuck it through the railings, and clambered up. The MOG had given up the chase.

The pigeon had a broken wing, and a plume of feathers sticking out the top of its head, like it had been got by a cat. I carefully picked it up and wandered round the corner to see Tiger and Chalky leaning over the railings, still ranting and raving at the MOG who'd already gone back inside with his prize.

'The guy is crazy,' said Tiger, in his stating-the-obvious American kind of way. 'Yeah, and that was a good ball,' ranted Chalky. 'My ball, you old bastard! I'm gonna get you for that, you old git!'

'Never mind your effing ball, he nearly killed me!' I said.

'What the hell is all the noise?' shouted Mrs Pirimaldi from the window above.

The Pirimaldis lived on the second floor and owned the news-agent's over the road. There were seven of them.

'It's Saturday morning, you bloody hooligans. A day of rest. Have some flippin' consideration. Some of us have to work the rest of the week.' And BANG, down came the window.

On each landing of the Mansions there were two flats, and somehow Mr Pirimaldi had contrived to get both of them allo-cated to him. On the inside, unbeknownst to the council, he had knocked them through. He had installed a cupboard in the hole with doors at the front and back, in case the council came round. This cupboard didn't lead to Narnia, just to the second half of their illegally enhanced council flat. They had the most palatial pad in the whole building, and two front doors. Whenever I knocked for Alex, the eldest son, I never knew which one would open.

SOHO

'I must have been eighteen or nineteen. I was working in Manchester for a chap, they called him Bill "Man Mountain" Benny', Mum said.

'He was a wrestler and gangster. I sang in his clubs. Sometimes four in one night. I had a good voice. I had a great voice. Got "Best Jazz Newcomer" in *Melody Maker*. Eighteen. Eighteen! I was young, I was naïve. Bill used to slobber over all the girls. But I stood up for myself. The clubs were full of gangsters. I was going out with a burglar at the time, although I didn't find out till later. They were amazing times, they were amazing people, they really were.'

And she laughs.

'They found Bill naked on the dance floor of one of his clubs. Dead. He'd had a heart attack. There was this terrible screaming for what seemed like an age, before they discovered the poor girl trapped underneath him. They had to get a winch to get him off her!

'I even sang at the Blue Angel Club in Liverpool, where Cilla Black and The Beatles used to come after sessions at the Cavern. The carpet there was so sticky the house band stayed for thirty years. One night this really nice fella starts chatting to me and he gives me his card. Says I'm too good for Liverpool, said I should try my luck in the bright lights of London.

'You should have seen his face when I knocked on his door in Soho.'

'So what? That was my dad?'

'Noooo. That's when I got a job at the Colony Room Club.'

There's a lull in the conversation and I hear myself say, 'Mum, what did happen to Dad?'

'What do you want to know?'

'Er . . . anything?' He left when I was a baby, is all I knew.

She looks at me for a second.

'He was jazz mad. I met him in a coffee bar just round the corner.'

'In Soho?'

And she starts to tell me stuff she's never told me before.

The 'wicked lady' heroin destroyed him. He had so much potential. He was passionate about music, about jazz, but even more passionate about photography. He used to work in a photography shop in Hastings. They'd lend him the cameras, and he'd take arty pictures around town.

He worked as a smudger on Folkestone beach down the road, to make ends meet, but he had greater ambitions in photography.

'Hold on a minute, Mum. You knew Dad was a heroin addict?'

'No, not until after we were married. We started living together very innocently. But I came back from work one day and found him with a needle hanging out of his hand. So I took it out, broke it, and poured all his stuff down the sink.'

'He ended up in Tooting Bec asylum. He tried to inject himself with paraffin.'

'Mum, what?'

'Look, I fell in love with him. He was the nicest man I'd ever met. He was a very talented, funny, bright man. He was a beautiful person. He was just like you.' I was stunned not by the heroin but my Dad was a 'nice man'.

'He turned up when you were probably twelve years old. He'd got out of the asylum and wanted me to help him stay out. I went to see the doctors. They said there was nothing I could do for him. I am afraid I could not afford to have him back in my life with you to bring up.'

The sixties Soho that Mum arrived in from Liverpool was an extraordinary place, perched on the edge of Covent Garden fruit and veg market, where the pubs opened at 5 a.m., and the magic of theatreland, filled with tinsel, glitter and greasepaint. It was a run-down area and the rents were cheap. You could find queues of musicians carrying their instruments heading to the Musicians' Union in Archer Street, looking for work in one of the big bands. Gangs of sailors on a big night out. Girls in feather boas making their way from the working women's hostel to one of the big shows. Coffee bars that stayed open all night. In the sixties drinking hours were highly restricted and gambling and homosexuality were illegal. Small, discreet, so-called members' clubs were springing up all over Soho.

The Kismet, where my mum worked for a period, was one of the more famous. It was also known as 'Death in the Afternoon'. In fact George Melly was asked by a friend, when opening the door to go in, what the strange smell was. 'Failure, dear boy,' he said, as he swept down the stairs.

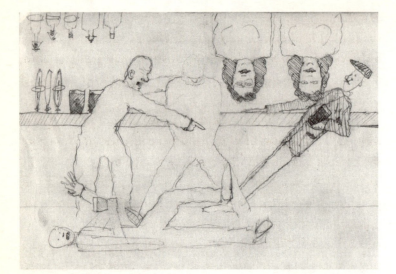

Having made sure the pigeon was safely in the cardboard box in which I'd hidden him on top of the cupboard in my bedroom, I headed up west to get some money off my mum for tea. She was working in the Colony Room, bang in the middle of Soho. What went on in the Colony, as they say, stayed in the Colony. They just seemed normal to me, my mum's mates.

You could be anything you wanted in there, anything except boring. The place was run by Muriel Belcher, a redoubtable old Hungarian bird, who shrieked and swore at every new customer. She didn't care if you had no money, but if you were boring you were out. No questions asked.

I got off the bus and walked down Denmark Street. I love Denmark Street. It's where all the music shops are and you can get any kind of musical instrument. It's also where songs are written, and sometimes you'd hear the strains of a piano and the voice of some young hopeful drifting out the window. It was also known as Tin Pan Alley. The story goes that in the olden days budding songwriters filled every floor, and so that their competitors couldn't hear a new hit composition they were playing on the piano, they'd employ a kid to stand under the window, in the street, and bang a saucepan to drown it out.

I stopped for a coffee at Bar Italia. Going there as a teenager in the mid-seventies was a real treat, proper coffee with froth, cocoa, the lot. I sat outside and watched the world go by.

And what a world! Man, you wouldn't even get this stuff at the pictures. Maltese fellas standing about in ground-length camel-hair coats smoking cigars. Girls milling on the corner in stilettos and tatty fur jackets – 'That was never caught, it gave itself up' – chatting and laughing loudly, eyelashed eyes out for tricks. Old chaps in bowler hats and rain macs ducking in the doorway of a shop that just says 'Magazines'. Blond-haired teenage boys, about my age, wearing lipstick, heading for Piccadilly.

Aldo, the owner, came out, put his espresso down and sat next to me. 'How's it going, son?'

'Not bad, Aldo. How's yourself?'

'You know, times are hard, son, but we're doing OK.'

Everyone knew Bar Italia did more than OK. Cash business, small denominations, it was the envy of every trader in Soho. But they worked very hard for it, it was open twenty-four hours a day. Aldo's dad was interned during the war. Yeah, they just came one day, made him take down the sign and took him away to a camp on the Isle of Man. Aldo's got pictures of it, his poor old man up a ladder taking down the Bar Italia sign, and then to the fucking Isle of Man. No wonder he felt angry.

One of his uncles ended up in a camp built on Peckham Rye Common. Eight Nissen huts with a fence round them in the middle of the park. But the security didn't last long. When the locals realised there was more fun going on in the inside than the out, they left the gate open so the Italian POWs could come and go as they pleased. More importantly, the locals could get a bit of what the interns were cooking up from their vast and well-tended allotment.

Aldo took a sip of his coffee. 'Your mum tells me you got nicked last week.' Here we go I think, everyone knows your business in Soho. That's the irony, as it's the place people come to for anonymity, to get on with what they wanna get on with, away from prying eyes, yet it's really a village. Bar Italia was the post office.

'I didn't get nicked.'

He took another sip. 'Mum tells me she had to come and get you out of West End Central the other afternoon.' He put his cup down.

'I wasn't nicked. We were just messing about with a fruit machine, and the nonce police or whatever they're called came in. You know, that new lot, the protecting minors from dirty old men branch, or whatever. They took us down the station for our own good. They wanna get down Piccadilly.'

'Why'd they take you to the station?'

'Well, from what I could make out, so's the chief inspector could give us a lecture on the dangers of marijuana. Didn't know what he was on about. He opens the blinds to point out a squat across the road. "See them hippies?" he says. "I know what's growing in them window boxes. D'you understand what I am saying to you, boys? You'll go nowhere, like them grubby hippies, if you don't. Do you understand?"

'We all nodded, but we didn't, we just wanted to get out of there, obviously. What it had to do with us I don't know. Then he spent another half-hour umming and ahhing round the delicate subject of kindly old men in raincoats with sweets in their pockets. We weren't nicked. They just called Mum. Who had to come and get us. She took us all for an ice cream; she wasn't bothered. The other parents went ballistic, they'd read about Soho in the papers. I've never felt unsafe here. I feel safer here myself than on the Tube. A packed compartment, that's where the old bastards grab your arse.'

'Your mum's a good woman. She works hard. Don't be upsetting her,' said Aldo.

'Honestly, Aldo, she really wasn't bothered. It was nothing.'

'How long you got left at that school of yours?'

'Two years.'

'Well, you stick at it, son, you get yourself some qualification, get some of them levels, make your mum proud.' He ruffled my hair. 'You're a good kid, bright. Don't waste it.' He got up and went back inside.

Two butch fellas came past with a poodle. I finished my coffee, paid, and headed round the corner to Dean Street. The entrance to the Colony was a small green door. I pushed it open and went up the dingy staircase, past the giant tins of Cyprus potatoes and into the tiny club on the first floor. The whole place, floor to ceiling, was decorated in bilious green. The walls were covered in various pieces of art, from cartoons to oil paintings. Donated in return for unpaid bar bills. It was basically just a small shabby room with a toilet and telephone at one end and a battered upright piano, but full of the most incredible characters.

A thick fug of tobacco smoke hung permanently across the bar, just above my head. Mum was singing at the piano, Muriel, the owner, sitting, as always, on her throne, a stool by the door. 'Hello, it's little cunty', she said, as I wandered in. Every new entrant would be greeted with a barrage of good-natured expletives. It was a rite of passage that not everyone could deal with.

A test, because the crew could get a bit rough of an evening on the good ship Colony and the conversational sea very turbulent. One poor chap wandered in one afternoon to be greeted with: 'I don't think you'll find any of your friends in my bar.' He replied: 'But I'm here to meet someone.'

'She's not a pretty little lady, is she?'

'I've never been so insulted in my life.'

'On your way, Lottie, or I'll give you a fourpenny one.'

There's a story about Muriel, where one night at closing time she spotted four red eyes glaring at her from under the bench in the corner. It was two rats. 'You two can fuck off.' But being a kind woman, she explained, 'You see I've called last orders, and anyhow you're not members.' She opened the door and the rats left without argument.

There was always a colourful mixture of characters in there, swearing good-naturedly, smoking and knocking back the whiskies. As I say, you could be anything you wanted in there, it was a haven for every kind of social misfit: jazz musicians, writers, painters, toffs, artists, poets, coppers, strippers (often still in their feather boas), gangsters, transvestites and plain old drunks. There was no need for a bouncer in the Colony, Muriel's razor tongue would slice any would-be opponent to shreds.

But she was a kind person, the regulars were like family, she called Francis Bacon her daughter, and if you had no money it would go on the tab, until you were flush again. Whereupon you would be ordered to 'Open your bead bag, Lottie.'

Amongst the minor villains, strippers, theatrical types, toffs and coppers you'd find the likes of George Melly holding court in the corner, the writer Jeffrey Bernard leaning on the bar getting progressively more aggressive, and one or both of the champagne-drinking painters Francis Bacon and Lucian Freud. Francis had originally been employed by Muriel to bring in gay clientele when homosexuality was still illegal. He got a fiver a punter, in those days good money.

My head just below a thick fug of tobacco smoke, which hung permanently across the bar, I navigated past a series of fishnet-clad knees. And that was just the fellas!

Occasionally a giant hand would reach down through the tobacco cloud and ruffle my hair, or better still proffer a two-bob coin. I couldn't really see or hear what was going on at adult level, which was probably all for the best.

I stood at the bar and ordered a Coke – the Colony was the first place I ever tasted Coca-Cola. Coke with ice and lemon. Bill Mitchell spotted me, came over and looked down, his watery eyes and big smiling face framed in a black Stetson, which glided through the tobacco cloud like a shark. Bill was American and was the voice-over king. He had the lowest voice in the world. Every time you heard a deep voice trailing films at the pictures, it was always him.

He always wore black, head to toe. Although legend has it that when a pal of his went to pick him up from the airport in Ibiza for a holiday, Bill was dressed completely in white, even the Stetson.

'What's going on, Bill?' his friend said.

'I have no enemies here,' replied Bill in his gravelly drawl. 'How's it going, son?' Bill made John Wayne sound positively effeminate.

'All right.'

'You seen the new Bond movie?'

'Er . . . No.'

'It's good.' He pulled out a big wodge of notes – he was pissed. 'Here you go,' and he handed me a ten-bob note. A whole ten bob. The note was the size of a cigarette coupon in his hand and a tea towel in mine. I folded it carefully and put it in my pocket. Ten bob!

All the same, I got two bob off me mum for some chips. I was a rich man. I headed out and down the green staircase just in time to hear Muriel screeching: 'Peanuts, Peanuts! You boring dreary little cunt. This is the Colony Room Club, not London Zoo. Now fuck off.'

On the pavement outside a wino was shouting: 'We are living like kings, and these days will last for ever!' He promptly tripped over and fell flat on his face. I had other issues on my mind, I had the opportunity to live like a king, albeit briefly. If I could just manage to get past the arcade on Old Compton Street and my old chum Mister Fruit Machine. 'Must not stop at the arcade. Must not stop at the arcade,' I repeated. I'd gone home hungry more times than I care to remember chasing the elusive three bells in a row.

I made it past the arcade and on past the Sunset Strip. The door was open and I could see one of the girls bent over while a couple of punters played bongos on her arse. Outside the French, Jenny, a dancer pal of my mum's, was skipping about on the pavement with a glass of wine in her hand. The French was another watering hole favoured by Soho bohemians.

All the legendary Soho drinkers were regulars at the French, including Dylan Thomas who, before he went into that dark night plastered, left his one and only manuscript of *Under Milk Wood* under a table in the bar following a night on the lash. Amazing he managed to misplace it, as that's where he ended up most evenings. Apparently, Gaston, the guvnor, retrieved the script and kept it safe until the grateful head of BBC radio drama came to collect it.

The French was originally called the York Minster, but everybody knew it as the French. This had something to do with the Resistance during the war. The Free French used to meet upstairs, and allegedly it was the location where Charles de Gaulle drew up his Free French call-to-arms speech. Although what use they'd have been defending Paris against the Nazis in the upstairs room of a boozer in Soho, I wasn't quite sure.

Gaston was standing in the doorway, hands on hips and resplendent with huge curly moustache. He spoke in a broad French accent but although his dad, Gaston Senior, was definitely French, no one was sure about Junior, because his accent slipped into broad cockney every now and then. Gaston Junior, who was born in an upstairs room shortly after his father took over the pub in 1914, was a master of diplomacy when it came to ejecting troublesome customers: 'I'm afraid one of us is going to have to leave, and it's not going to be me' was his signature line when such action needed to be taken.

Yeah, the new Bond movie. Why not? I had nothing else to do. I headed on down Berwick Street market towards the picture house in Piccadilly. The market was still in full swing, the stallholders calling out and advertising their wares, fruit and veg mainly. There was one fella shouting: 'Pommygrannies! Get yer pommygrannies!' He was holding up what looked like a big cricket ball, really red and shiny. I was intrigued. He had one split in half on the front of his barrow, and it looked like it was full of small red jewels. I bought one, it was rock hard, I put it in my pocket and headed for the cinema.

On the way I stopped for a piss in the public toilets. The white-tiled walls were sprayed with what looked like black ink, which I would only later discover was, in fact, dried blood squirted from the syringes of junkies, so as not to put air bubbles in their veins.

I tipped up at the box office and bought a half-priced kid's ticket. I found a seat on the left of the cinema, on the smoking side. It always struck me as odd that cinemas were divided into the two sides, smoking and non-smoking, as the cigarette smoke didn't know which side it was supposed to be on and just happily drifted about all over the place.

The lights went down, the curtains drew back, and the screen flickered into life. Bill's voice boomed, 'Kia-Ora, in the foyer. Now.' A giant plastic carton of the orange stuff floated magically in the middle of the blue screen, with a really skinny straw sticking out of its tinfoil lid. I got out my pommygrannie and tried to get a nail through the skin. It was like leather. I was digging in with my thumb so hard it shot out of my hand and disappeared under the seat in front of me. Shit, it had gone down the pitched floor. Bollocks, but I certainly wasn't about to start crawling about on my hands and knees in a dark cinema in Piccadilly Circus.

The film was good, with all the usual gear, birds getting slapped then snogged, car chases and explosions. I was really getting into it when I felt the usherette's torch flashing in my face. 'You paid half price,' she hissed. 'Kid's ticket. You can be a kid, but you can't be a kid and smoke. Out!'

Outside, back in Piccadilly, it was dark and raining with feet shattering neon reflections and taxi wheels spraying diesel rainbows. There was a huge flock of starlings, swooping and swirling as one, like a black cloud across the purple sky. I pulled up my collar and headed up Shaftesbury Avenue. I wasn't mad on the West End at night, the pavements thronging with out-of-towners, all starry-eyed and wondrous. Made you wonder if they'd ever seen shops or electric light before, the way they just stood about pointing at things, filling the pavements, taking photos of nothing.

On the way back from the pictures, as I strolled up the avenue beyond the brightly illuminated theatres, to where the streets reverted to their natural dull sodium, I came to a long line of bedraggled hippies. All shivering, skinny, greasy hair, pulling their army great-coats tight with long nicotine-stained fingers. John Bell & Croyden, the chemists, was involved in an initiative to hand out free heroin to registered addicts.

One of whom, it would turn out, was my dad.

THE WALES

I remember walking for the first time
Into an open field,
South-west Wales in 1968,
I'd never seen anything so huge,
I walked, and I walked and I walked,
Toward the curved green horizon,
And the sky.

I sat down by the track,
I never felt so sure,
I lay down on my back,
Felt like nature pure,
The grass beneath my back,
The sky has never been so blue.

The sunshine and the haystacks,
Wide tall ochre sails,
Rows of potato picking,
A ploughed field in south-west Wales,

Swimming in the river through the trees,
Climbing saplings in the woods,
The bungalow my uncle built,
The weather's ever-changing moods,

The quarrels and the cloud formations,
In south-west Wales,
The hymns and the sailing boats,
Wide tall ochre sails.

Every summer I'd go to my aunt's in Wales for the holidays, and this one was no different. As usual, me and Mum got the train from Paddington. It was a long journey but I liked the train as I could read comics whilst eating crisps from that funny little trolley that came up and down. Eating crisps and just staring out the window, it was hard to believe there was so much countryside, miles and miles of the stuff, green fields with tiny stations that seem to be in the middle of nowhere. Who lives in these places, and what do they do? I wondered.

We changed at Cardiff Central for the second leg, which was about as long as the first. A rickety old train on a windy track which ran right down to the furthest corner of south-west Wales, stopping about a million times at stations with unpronounceable names. My aunt was there to meet us in a school minibus. She was a pillar of the local community and she taught tennis and shared the rota of driving the school bus all around the countryside, picking up and dropping off kids for school.

When we got to the house my three cousins were waiting and waving. I'd spent most of my holidays with them. Hector, Sarah and Jane were like brothers and sisters to me. My uncle had had a house constructed by local builders. A bungalow. It was smart and white and had a huge panoramic window with a clear view down across the fields to the river. The family joke was that the plans were the wrong way round, as the front door was at the back of the house.

Mike was a jolly man, always telling jokes and drawing cartoons. He had a good job at the oil refinery in Milford Haven. I dropped off my things and we went straight outside to mess about. When I first came to Wales the enormity of the place was a bit of a shock, the field in front of the house seemed to go on for ever and stuff was growing everywhere. No buildings, just nature, sprouting up untamed in all directions. I felt that if I went too far from the house I'd never find my way back, I'd just be wandering in the countryside for ever. No one to ask for directions and no distinguishable landmarks. 'Oh yeah, I must remember, turn left at that tree, on past that enormous field and just right at the sheep.'

The back garden was like a jungle, the grass at head height, it needed a combine harvester to mow it. There were four trees, one in each corner, and we had one each. We'd spend hours just sitting in the highest branches of our own trees shouting rubbish at each other. All day, every day, was spent outdoors, come rain or shine. And south-west Wales had more than its fair share of rain.

Mum stayed the night but headed back to London in the morning, and my holidays commenced. The sun was shining and we trooped off down the lane to the river. On the way was a strawberry farm, with long rows of plastic sheeting covering the irresistible prize. It was a dangerous business as you had to crawl in to get them and once inside you couldn't see out, but you could be seen within. You had to crawl on your hands and knees, so inevitably some red juice would end up on your clothes. If you were caught it was impossible to deny the crime and there would be merry hell to pay back at my aunt's. Sarah kept dog as Hector and I ran the gauntlet. We squashed as much of the juicy treasure as we could in our mouths and backed out with a few for Sarah and Jane.

Running beside the river was a huge newly planted pine forest. We headed in but it was dark and spooky, dense with bracken and brambles. It was almost impossible to walk through, but climbing to the top of one of the twenty-foot saplings, you could then make it bend over enough to be able to leap on to the next one, and so on and so on. It was like climbing across the roof of the sky with the river below, surrounded by hills.

At the top of the nearest hill was the Thomas's farm, and there were five or six brothers and sisters, a ready-made gang. Me and my cousins, and a few others from the lane, formed our own gang and called it The Black Panthers. It was something I'd heard off the telly. We'd have wars in the woods with bows and arrows. Then we'd go swimming and skimming stones in the river. I had my first kiss with a girl called Vanessa under an upturned boat down there.

The summer flew past. Jane and Sarah made me get married to Mary Rowland from down the lane, in the back garden. She wore a tea towel on her head and I sported a bow tie made from a dock leaf. My aunt led the proceedings and we celebrated with lemonade out of wine glasses.

We made dens, dammed streams, scrumped apples till we got stomach ache. We went on walks for hours to far-flung farms across the fields. The Scale's farm where we'd make tunnels in the warm haystacks, shoot rats in the grain store with air rifles and go on torch-lit processions in the woods. All that Van Morrison stuff. We'd skip round in circles staring at the blue sky.

There were animals everywhere, dogs, horses, cows, sheep. I got to recognise birds and trees and plants. I rode my first horse on the Scale's farm. It jumped the gate and I promptly fell off onto a pocket of conkers. There was food and fresh milk aplenty. The kitchen door was always wide open, even in the winter, and the log-fired stove permanently glowed.

I had a pet fly who followed me round. His name was Jim and he'd always find me at some point during the day. It never occurred to me that it might have been a different one. I spent afternoons lying in the middle of a field amongst the dried cowpats, staring up at the vast blue sky, where I could literally feel planet Earth beneath me, roaring through space at (I then discovered) about 66,000 miles an hour. I'd close my eyes for as long as I could and open them in the hope of seeing some inquisitive cows staring down at me with their giant eyes, which I often would, chewing and licking their nostrils with them big pink tongues.

At harvest time everyone came up from the village to the giant field in front of the house to help move the bales of hay. They were heavy and the string cut into your hands. They would all be carried bit by bit into the middle of the field and arranged into a giant stack so the farmer could get them onto his lorry in one go, and transport them to a dry barn. At the end of a long day everybody sat about on bales happily exhausted, passing round bottles of cider.

It was a couple of days before the farmer came for his hay, in which time we'd castellated the top of the twelve-foot stack and, via a ladder, loaded it up with wheat stumps. What the combine left made perfect ammo – a four-inch stump which, when pulled out of the ground, came with a big clod of earth. Nature's hand-grenades.

The war with the Thomases went on all day. Kings of the castle and the dirty rascals went home every night, covered in scratches and bruises and happy as Larry. There was a jam sandwich and a Tupperware beaker of squash when we came in starving, until tea was ready at about half six. In the evening we'd sit round in the living room while Uncle Mike told jokes, drew cartoons and made up exaggerated stories about his exploits in the war.

I remember one night he was telling us about, and drawing diagrams, of himself flying a biplane that was being chased by the Germans. They were catching up. He looped the loop and while flying upside down back over the German plane, he dropped a spanner on the pilot's head. Aunt Diana told him to stop talking rubbish.

The summer was drawing to its inevitable close and the city beckoned. Uncle Mike suggested we should take a walk in the woods.

'How d'you like it here?' It seemed like an odd question.

'It's great, Uncle. You know I love it.' I thought he was gonna tell me off for playing in the building site up the road. We'd been told not to, and I had been in trouble already for it.

'D'you fancy staying on for a bit longer?' Now I was totally confused. 'Staying with us for a few months. A few months while your mum gets some proper accommodation sorted.' The penny dropped. Mum had said something about staying longer, but I wasn't sure. We had moved probably eight times in my life already that I could remember.

'Mum's not coming back?'

'No, she is, but not just yet.' He threw the stick he'd been tapping the ground with into the undergrowth.

So it came to pass that I was nine years old and heading for my first day at the local primary, Houghton VC, I think there were about a hundred kids in the whole school. As my aunt drove the bus up and down windy lanes picking up kids, I knew most of them from the summer days running about in the fields. The school was so small that my class had eight- to eleven-year-olds mixed. They were mostly farmers' kids, as the whole area was agricultural. The headmaster was Mr Pound, and he was strict. He had an unerring talent for being able to hit you in the earhole with a piece of chalk from twenty paces if concentration was deemed lacking.

'McPherson, McPherson, MCPHERSON!' Whack! Chalk in the earhole. The kids there were great, and although it was strict the school was filled with a real sense of inspiration. I was thriving, doing well both academically and at sports. The fresh country air was infusing my brain and body. The farmers' kids were fit as fleas, and days running around and climbing trees had had an impact on my puny city body. On sports day I would sometimes win things, competing with my mate James Scale, admittedly not so difficult to win things when there are only five kids in your age category.

But I was entered for the all Wales county trials in

Swansea. It was serious, and held in a proper sports field with an enormous red-ash-covered running track. I had only ever run in the field behind the school before. The first event was the two hundred yards. I was given a pair of running shoes with spikes. Bang, the starting pistol went off and it felt like I was running backwards as the rest of the field shot off in front of me. It was like one of them nightmares where you feel like you're running in treacle. It set the tone for the whole day and I was last in pretty much everything.

But I did pass my eleven-plus. They'd phased it out in England but forgot to tell the Welsh. Diana said she'd get me a Polaroid camera if I passed, but it was a bitter-sweet experience. I discovered half of my mates would now be going to a different school, the secondary modern at the bottom of the hill, while the rest of us would be going to the grammar school at the top, to learn about grammar. Secondary modern, modern but secondary. I couldn't work it out, but it split brothers and friends and the last day of term was sad. But soon I settled in and was doing well at the grammar school. Halfway through the first term my Aunt Diana told me I was going back to London, Mum had found somewhere for us to live.

THE WHO, CAMDEN, CLOTHES AND PUNK

I arrived back in London from Wales in 1972. The original skinhead thing had mutated into the suedehead look, the hair had got a bit longer and Crombie coats with red hankies and Solatio shoes, loafers with a kind of basket-weave upper were all the go. At the football the boot-boy look was on the rise, feathered haircuts, à la Bowie/Faces, Levi jackets with the sleeves rolled up, and half-mast baggy trousers and DMs, gangs going round in *Clockwork Orange* gear. Scarves were worn round the wrist or through the belt loop. Proto-glam rock had come over the horizon; Bowie, T-Rex, Slade, Roxy Music, Cockney Rebel.

In the mid-seventies The Who brought out the album *Quadrophenia*. I loved it. It followed the story of a West London mod heading for Brighton and eventually doing himself in. The songs were full of all sorts of teenage angst, which I could identify with. It had a gatefold sleeve and inside a booklet of photos of a mod in his Levi 501s and his highly decorated scooter, knocking about the streets of London with his tasty mates. I thought it was a great look.

I found a Lambretta Li 150 in *Exchange & Mart* for forty quid in New Cross and bought it from a woman who lived on a council estate. It was cream with royal-blue side panels. I'd never seen anything quite so beautiful. I think it had belonged to her son.

I worked out how to kick-start it, and it started fine. I'd never ridden one before, and you didn't need a helmet in them days. I rode it back north on pure instinct, kangaroo-leaping up and down the back streets of South London in first and second gear, with no idea where I was going, until I hit the river, but I got it home.

In the summer of 1976 The Who played at Charlton football ground and we all went down to see them. I was fifteen, and it was my first gig. We all piled off the train and headed to the ground. When we got there we found out it was two quid to get in, and we only had about 50p between the lot of us. The security were out in force. Gangs of chaps had already been repelled from steaming through the gates; the place was buzzing. The streets were swarming. There was absolutely no way of sneaking through the main gate. We wandered off, out of sight of the security round the entrance.

The wall around the ground wasn't actually that high. Probably about seven foot-odd. It looked like with a running jump it might be possible to scramble up, and hopefully over. Some way down the road I had a go.

Yes! I got some decent purchase on the top of the wall, but just as I was pulling myself up, scrabbling away with my legs, a spanner whanged in the space between my hands. Shit, I let go and dropped back down. The security had manned the wall on the other side and were whacking encroaching fingers with a variety of metal objects. We tried again a bit further down, with the same result. Just before we were about to give up, some way down the wall we spotted a kid clambering up and over, and successfully disappearing into the ground.

Well, they couldn't man the whole wall, maybe they'd given up down there. We jogged up to the spot. I jumped up and hung on, no spanner, fingers intact. I scrambled over only to find myself going head-first into a urinal, it was an open-air toilet block.

I just missed a big fella having a piss as I rolled down onto the floor. A couple of the others followed me over in quick succession. The three of us had barely made it to our feet when four security guards clutching a variety of weapons burst in. I jumped up and in one movement turned towards the urinal, making out I was having a piss. 'Right, you lot, out!'

The big fella I nearly knocked over turned and said: 'Fuck off, they're with me.' What a gent. We were in. (If I ever see Roger Daltrey I will repay the two quid.)

It wasn't like the festivals of today – food concessions from around the world, showers, portable lavs – it was mostly blokes. Blokes who'd brought their own beer. Watney's Party Fives and Sevens. Tins that held five or seven pints, and they were proper tins, like giant baked-bean tins. The atmosphere was tense and fights were going off all over the place. What security there was were preoccupied with trying to stop people bunking into the ground from outside its perimeter.

First up was The Sensational Alex Harvey Band, and sensational they most assuredly were. Alex Harvey burst through a giant brick wall, dressed as a rocker in leather hat and jacket, and sang 'Framed'.

We were standing next to a big gang of geezers, including our mate from the bog, who were all wearing blue and white striped shirts and swigging away on their giant tins. Alex threw his hat and jacket into the crowd to reveal a blue and white striped shirt. Our new mates went mad. One of them launched an empty Party Five into the air, and it seemed to fly for ever before a terrible clang cut through the music. That would have hurt.

Alex Harvey was brilliant, from his peculiar take on 'Delilah' and the incredible 'Faith Healer' to his dramatic version of Jacques Brel's 'Next'. It was an extraordinary show. Another band came and went before the main act – I think it may have been Little Feat. The drummer bounced his sticks off the drums and into the crowd.

It was dark as the synthesised pulse of 'Baba O'Riley' began ringing round the stadium. Not only was it my first-ever gig, but I was about to witness the world's first laser show. An announcement had been made, warning us not to get the laser in our eyes.

As Pete Townshend's first earth-shattering chords rang out, a single green beam shone from the top of the stage and bounced off mirrors attached to the top of the floodlights. A lone hippy was cheered as he clambered up the stanchion, followed by three security men, towards the laser beams to burn himself a third eye.

The 'oo were great and *Quadrophenia* became album of the month at school. I don't know if it was because of the pictures of the mod on the inner sleeve exactly, or a documentary on mercenaries in Angola that had been on the box, no one can remember, but one lunchtime a few of us went up to a barber's in Kilburn High Road and got our hair cropped. I remember straight after I went into an Oxfam shop and nicked a pair of straight white trousers and a stripy Ben Sherman shirt.

It was easy, you just took a load of gear into the changing room and put what you wanted under your own clothes and bowled out. In the middle seventies second-hand clothes shops still had a lot of great gear from those days, what they now call vintage, even antique. Over the next couple of years our little gang got more and more immersed in the gear and music of the sixties. You had to have some bollocks to bowl about in that sort of gear in the mid-seventies. Me and Chalky began to collect old ska and reggae records. We'd write 'S+G' on the labels and had an agreement that the first person to get their own pad would inherit our collection. It was me, and every now and then at home when I pull out one of them old 45s with our initials on, it takes me straight back.

NAUGHTY BOYS

My new school, Quintin Kynaston Comprehensive, was an amalgam of the local secondary and grammar schools, a huge social experiment. And a huge sprawling place, made up of two glass-clad mini-tower blocks now connected by covered walkways. It was so big you were allowed ten minutes to get between some classes. Ten minutes in which anything could, and often did, happen. You ran the gauntlet every afternoon in that walkway – 1,700 boys from the roughest estates from Kilburn, Maida Vale, north-west London and beyond. We were all squashed into a multi-storey greenhouse which hot-housed trouble.

It was what they were calling 'progressive' and it took the excluded kids from the whole area, so there were some real cases. To get expelled from Quintin I think you actually had to be certifiably insane.

So there I am, halfway through the first term in 1972 with a slightly Welsh accent and a grammer school blazer. Neither of which lasted very long. During my time in rural Wales my harsh cockney tones had softened, as had the colour of my vocabulary. I'd lost the swing of the quick-fire sarcasm, the machine-gun pace of insult, and the ever-changing slang of a huge cosmopolitan

London comprehensive. But it wasn't long before I was soon back in the swing, fast-tracking my re-uneducation by hanging around with the wrong crowd. Hanging round with the lot I did was also a form of self-protection.

Comprehensive Quintin's certainly was, especially where language was concerned. Kids of every ability from the top to the very bottom. Every cultural background: West Indian, African, Pakistani, Indian, Chinese, Greek, Turkish and, given the school's proximity to Kilburn, a huge proportion of second-generation Irish. But only one, yours truly, with a Scottish name and a slightly Welsh accent, which he was gonna lose fast.

Quintin's had more than its fair share of tough kids, but I always felt the toughest were the four or five down the front who actually wanted to learn, kids whose parents imagined them becoming professionals – doctors and lawyers. Trying to concentrate was a more than tricky business while doors slammed, fights ensued and kids in balaclavas steamed in, hitting people indiscriminately over the heads with locker doors.

I met Patrick Brown an old school mate recently, he was doing security at a gig we were doing in Minehead. He was big even back then, and he had brothers; he'd enjoyed his time at school. Not that he didn't have the odd moment. We were reminiscing, and I recalled a fight between a pupil and the PE teacher. It happened in the gym, which for some reason had windows at ground level, so we were all lying on the ground trying to see what was going on. All we could see were feet flying up and down. It was the days of Bruce Lee and kung fu fighting. It turned out the protagonist was Patrick. The teacher had called him a spear-chucker, Patrick invited him into the gym and as he put it, 'ironed him out'.

The headmaster, Mr Phillips, was an amiable/forward-thinking/

enlightened/balding man from Manchester. He would patrol the vast boundaries of the school perimeter in the afternoon, hanging out the side door of the school minibus, which was driven by the deputy head, shouting forlornly into a squeaking loudhailer: 'Get back into schzzzool, I can see you boyzzzzzzzz', as pockets of kids drained over the school fence and into the surrounding streets.

It was chaotic at the best of times, anarchy in the UK all right, there was this song on the radio at the time, something about 'Teacher, leave them kids alone'. At our school I used to think it was more like 'Kids, leave the poor bloody teachers alone'. We drove the woodwork teacher Mr Pringle so mad he used to chase us round the classroom with a huge metal ruler, like a madman with a machete in the jungle. When we got hold of it and snapped it in the vice, he went berserk. The thing was, his name wasn't even Mr Pringle – we just called him that to drive him mad. Which it did.

Our science lab had a brass door handle, and five minutes before class it would be heated by half a dozen Bic lighters so that when the teacher came to open the door – sizzling flesh, etc. Teachers were having nervous breakdowns left, right and centre, and only the really thick-skinned survived. Witless supply teachers would be thrown through the school gates like meat to the lions.

But the last day of term always took the proverbial Rich Tea biscuit. Even the kids who'd been expelled turned up, often wearing crash helmets and clutching bottles of cider. They came to observe the only true school tradition in this relatively modern establishment, the all-inclusive end-of-term scrap with the slightly posher St George's down the road.

We gathered throughout the day under the eaves of the purpose-built loitering area, so favoured by your sixties architect. It was the only day I ever remember seeing a full contingent at school. God knows how, as half of them hadn't been there for any of the other 364 days of the year. How they even remembered where it was, never mind when the last day of term fell . . . no mobile phones, no Facebook, no Blackberry messages, hundreds of us all just turned up on instinct. Like some great natural wonder, salmon swimming upriver to spawn, birds migrating east in the winter, or whatever. The last time I took part in this piece of traditional school history, I'd spent the morning in geography watching a film. It was about the production of rubber somewhere in the Commonwealth. It seemed like the most laborious task in the world, really made you wonder why they bothered. Young men were chopping away at rubber trees in the baking heat, cutting grooves that ran the entire length of the trunk.

About a week later a teaspoon of the white sap would run down the groove into a tin cup tied at the bottom. There was barely enough for a jolly-bag, never mind a mackintosh. It was warm and dark in the classroom and I drifted off. I dreamt I was made of rubber and was bouncing down the road. I woke to see tyres being put on a car on a production line in Birmingham. The lights flickered on and we filed out. It was lunchtime. We trooped over Finchley Road to the grocer's. The school dinners were diabolical, mince, just mince, every day – a grey sludge of minced meat of some description, the occasional diced carrot and sometimes a topping of either potato or pastry. You'd honestly rather starve than eat that stuff. We were given a lunch token every day, which with any luck you'd sell for a few pence to one of the greedy beggars who actually enjoyed that swill, so's they could get two helpings.

Outside the shop Fred Moynihan and his crew were taking the piss out of Frank, one of the school's glue-sniffers. Frank was swaying wildly from side to side, with a half-puffed crisp packet in one hand, his livid spotty face staring skyward and dribble coming out of the corner of his mouth. It wasn't a great look.

'What you seeing, Frank?' Fred leered, laughing. Frank tried to fix his lolling head, his eyes wild and rolling. 'Wha?' He couldn't focus. Fred kicked him. 'I said, what you seeing, you ugly spotty wally?'

'Wha, man, there's fuckin' elephants, tons of 'em, flying.' Frank was quite obviously hallucinating and didn't have a clue where he was. Fred kicked him again. 'Ow.'

'Here, leave him alone, Fred,' I said. Fred turned to me – he was big, he played rugby. 'Mind your own business, you flea-bitten tramp.' Life at Quintin's was nothing if it not volatile and unpredictable. I went into the shop and ordered my lunch from the set menu of cheese roll and a bottle of milk. We all then converged on the wall of the flats opposite, eating our rolls.

Pigeons swooped down after the crumbs. One landed at my feet and I squirted some milk at it through my teeth and it flapped off. Fred marched across the street. 'What you do that for? Poor pigeon never done nothing to you,' and he punched me. I ducked but he caught me on my forehead. He was wearing a big sovereign ring which left a perfect indentation smack bang in the middle of my forehead, and for the rest of the day I wore Fred's royal seal.

A glue-sniffer-hating pigeon-lover – like I say, life at school was volatile and unpredictable. You only had to say the wrong thing at the wrong time to the wrong person to find yourself flat on your arse. Only problem was, you never knew what the wrong or right thing was where psychos were concerned. It was all just part of the rich tapestry of school life. Ironically, some afternoons I'd bunk off only to hang about at Chalky's school, Hampstead Comprehensive. A slightly less volatile institution.

As Fred walked away I half-heartedly booted him up the arse. Whoops! He turned round, glared at me, and time stood still before he started lashing out wildly. 'Fight! Fight!' The cry went across the street immediately.

I spent the next twenty minutes dancing round a parking meter, having milk thrown at me by the baying crowd, trying to avoid Fred's kicks and punches. Fortunately Fred was employing what he thought was the most dangerous weapon in his arsenal, his 'donkey kick', which basically involved him turning round and lashing out backwards like a wild horse. This was enormously destructive if the target was static and unsuspecting, what with them rugby player's legs of his an' all, but not so effective with an agile one dodging around behind a parking meter. The donkey kicks were slowing but one hit the meter and nearly took the top off. The ground shook. The meaninglessness of these things meant they would fade as quickly as they flared. Fred got bored and drifted off.

A line of teachers dolefully trudged across the playground heading for the pub. The feedback from Mr Phillips's loudhailer filled the playground from the top-floor window as he tested the batteries. 'Testing ... Bzzz ... tezzzding ... one ... tzzzz.' Sending out a signal that he knew, we knew, would be received but not understood.

Football had been banned in the playground, and all we'd been told was that it was something to do with inclusiveness. Me, my mate Terry and some of the others were playing twos up the wall, which involved standing at a predetermined distance and lobbing twopence coins at a wall – the one that landed nearest to the wall took the lot. That and the other lunchtime sport, blowing smoke rings, something we spent hours practising. Legend had it that if

you went to the offices of Peter Stuyvesant and managed successfully to blow one smoke ring through another, you'd be given a
free supply of fags for life.

Terry was a bright kid but, like me and the rest of our little gang,
bored by a lack of respect for authority that had left us all some way
behind academically. One lunchtime, Terry had been sitting with
his trilby on in the dinner hall (he was the first to turn up to school
in the full Ivy League look) when Mr Phillips came up to him and
said, 'Terry, you're going to have to take that hat off.' He said 'Why,
sir? I'm Irish and it's religious, sir.' Mr Phillips said, 'Don't be stupid,
Terry, take the hat off.' Terry said, 'Look, sir. Over there there's a
Sikh with a turban on, over there there's a Rasta with a tam.' Mr
Phillips said, 'Come to my office after lunch, Terry.' Terry flicked
the peak of his hat and said, 'Not now blue eyes.'

The world-weary deputy head broke ranks from the pub pil-
grimage and headed our way. Terry dropped his fag and casually
stood on the pile of coins. 'Listen, boys, just a quiet word in your
shell-likes.' He was well meaning, but always sounded like he was
rehearsing for a later, more important, conversation. 'This inter-
school thing. It's got to stop.'

'What, not the cricket as well, sir?'

He stared into space and sighed. 'You know exactly what I'm
talking about, the fight with St George's, and I'm telling you it's
not going to happen.'

'What, have you lost the balls, sir?'

'Macreanor, just shut up, I'm saying this for your benefit. It's
got out of hand. Mr Phillips has informed the police. Arrests will
be made.' We all knew, including him, that was bollocks, because
we were all minors.

'So if I get the slightest whisper, d'you hear me, the slightest whiff that any of my year have been involved in this stupidity, I shan't hesitate in handing you in. D'you hear me, boys?'

'Yes, sir, the slightest whiff.' Terry started laughing. The deputy had drifted away to perform his now-rehearsed piece in the pub. 'Here, sir, sir! I think McPherson's just whiffed.' The deputy plodded off towards the school gates without looking back.

Terry scooped up his winnings, a princely 12p, and we drifted across the playground towards the loitering station. Four mopeds buzzed past like wasps, Suzuki 125s. 'The cavalry's here.' Two minutes later they buzzed back again, parping their insect horns.

'Get bzzz into schzzzchool! Wheeeee!' Mr Phillips had the loud-hailer on overload, and was starting to sound like Jimi Hendrix with his face all purple haze as he hung out of the top-floor window. The mopeds were already leading a phalanx of the more dedicated school traditionalists at walking pace down the road towards St George's. The odd cider bottle flew through the air and smashed on the pavement like an impotent Molotov cocktail.

Steve New, wild-eyed, stood on the wall with his long blond hair blowing in the breeze. He was playing 'Children of the Revolution' on an acoustic guitar. He was really good. Last time I'd seen him play that song was at assembly one morning. Steve came in with his guitar, and a nun. She proceeded to strip in front of the whole school, while he gave it some Marc Bolan. She liked an audience too. She was a stripper he'd met in Soho. It didn't half liven up a dull assembly. I reminded him of this some years later. He looked blank. 'Did I?' he said. 'How on earth did you remember that!?!?' He led a colourful life, did our Steve.

He wasn't interested in the fighting, he just turned up cos he knew there'd be an audience. And what an audience – there were about two hundred of us by now, all cheering and jumping up and down.

Steve stamped his foot and serenaded skyward, as the rebels without a brain flooded out of the gates and trooped off behind the mopeds, down Carlton Vale in the direction of St George's. Mr Phillips was chocks away, throwing himself in through the sliding door of the minibus. 'Get down off the wall. Now!' Hanging out of the side he put the magic hailer to his lips. 'Go . . . bzzz . . . squeak . . . gzzzz!' The deputy promptly kangaroo-leaped the bus into the school gates.

St George's was only five minutes down the road, and we were being escorted by a patrol car, but by the time we got there it was already like a medieval siege. There were volleys of bricks and bottles as the first wave of infantrymen scaled their school wall. I launched myself at it, clambered up, and sat on the top, surveying the scene and calculating whether I could get back up again if I jumped down. But my presence wasn't required in the affray. On the other side the St George's lines were already broken and scattered. The rout was completed in a matter of minutes. St George's was a mixed school and one or two of our foot-soldiers, bored with fighting, were chatting up the girls. By the time the second panda car arrived everyone was drifting off.

Right next to ours was an even posher school, the American School. Wow, well that was another world. Tales were told from some who reckoned they'd sneaked in there, that they had Coca-Cola machines, a disco and a cinema. And they had girls, pretty girls with long blonde hair and fresh, healthy faces. I don't ever remember talking to anyone from that school in all my time at Quintin's, even though we passed it pretty much every day. It really was another world, all confident young people, smiling and chatting, and doing normal things. Talking – to each other. It was like watching a different and superior race. They took their lunch break up the posher end of St John's Wood in restaurants and that.

Strangely, we never attacked their school. This might have had something to do with the three burly, CIA-looking fellas, with their earpieces and Ray-Bans, who permanently stood guarding the school gates. Legend also had it that the huge smoked-glass window above their entrance was bulletproof. After school one night, someone got half a brick to test the theory, and guess what? It fuckin' wasn't.

There were some great teachers at Quintin's and my form teacher, Mr Thomas, was one of them. He was Welsh and took me under his wing, but the battleground was pretty much the same every day. Given a strong desire to catch up socially and fit in, it wasn't long before things went rapidly downhill.

My Welsh academic successes were wilting at an alarming rate. I had an aptitude for English, and art, but was constantly distracted by the urge to be a clever dick. I was bright but was becoming increasingly uninterested and, let's be honest, falling behind. Ultimately and inevitably, I became disruptive.

Here's a school report from my third year:

SUBJECT/FORM TUTOR/YEAR TUTOR REPORT

NAME G. McPherson		FORM 3S
DATE February 1975		
SET/GROUP	EFFORT E	ATTAINMENT E

McPherson seems to be incapable of understanding the simplest of procedures, questions or instructions. Together with the apparent lazy attitude that he exudes, it is, therefore, highly inevitable that he should obtain the above marks.
He is extremely slow and is, it seems, even incapable of copying a sentence correctly from the blackboard. It goes without saying that any other form of work seems totally beyond him.
I even wonder if I can hope for an improvement.

SIGNATURE

MJP

Can't wait to show that to my mum! The funny thing was the report book I found these in only had four reports in it. I used to tear out the bad ones.

But I also found this maths report, which was a surprise:

SUBJECT/FORM TUTOR/YEAR TUTOR REPORT

NAME G. Mc PHERSON   FORM 3S

DATE 6/2/75   SUBJECT MATHS.

SET/GROUP   EFFORT B   ATTAINMENT B

Works quite well in class.

SIGNATURE

MJP

'Works quite well in class.' What? I was useless at maths. But then I remembered that I was so disruptive that the maths teacher told me he'd sign me in if I promised never to turn up at all. And I didn't. There was so much to be getting on with out on the streets for me and the other four-thirds of the maths class.

Up to this point, writing on walls at school had amounted to not much more than scribbling 'Mr Pringle is gay', 'Man Utd are shit', and 'I like cock' (then, obviously, writing your mate's name and phone number underneath). But a book from New York appeared on the scene, *Subway Art*, which was full of dramatic photos of huge multicoloured three-dimensional nicknames or tags, which kids were spraying on the subway trains of New York. It looked incredible and I was keen to get started right away. But my name, Graham McPherson, wasn't quite right, and it wasn't a great idea to deface private property with your own name. However the only nicknames I'd managed to get from my highly imaginative classmates so far were Grey and Mac.

And Flea-Bitten-Jock-Welsh-Bastard was going to use up far too much spray paint.

I needed to find my own nickname, my own tag, but how? Time was of the essence as this exotic street art was starting to appear all over North London and legends were being born. Mr B, who had done a huge train coming out of a corrugated-iron fence in Hampstead, Kix, Dare-devil, Sha-na-na. Multicoloured wonders on the walls, bus shelters and train stations were sprouting up all over North London.

But where to start in my quest for a distinctive tag? We didn't have a lot in the flat, but Mum always had books and she was always giving me things to read, like Anthony Burgess and Graham Greene, and reading books like these really was my saving grace, as my school education drained rapidly down the plughole.

I was sitting in the flat one evening when I noticed on the bookshelf a fat tome called *The Encyclopedia of Jazz Musicians*. I don't know why but I got it down and opened it, and in the index I saw all sorts of weird and wonderful names like Satchmo, Jelly Roll Morton, Bird, Thelonious Monk. Hang on, I thought, this could be it – a positive treasure trove of diverting nicknames. But which one to go for? Given the mind-boggling choice, I decided I would leave it to fate. I would pick one at random, and it somehow felt more real, that I would feel more ownership of this borrowed tag, if the gods had a hand in it.

I would give it one go and that would be it. Russian roulette. No matter what happened I would stick to my side of the bargain and forever more be known as . . . ?

I opened a page at random and held a pin aloft. Now what nom de plume did fate have in store for me? No more Jock, no more Haggis. I closed my eyes and thrust the pin downwards. I opened them to discover the pin stuck in the middle of the letter 'e', of the word 'Peter'. Peter. Pete . . . Well, that's no good! What sort of kudos was I gonna garner from my contemporaries by spraying 'Peter' on the wall? None.

Bollocks. So much for my deal with fate. I was just about to close the book and start all over, when I noticed his second name . . . Suggs. Peter Suggs, a jazz drummer from Kentucky.

Suggs?!! Hang on, Suggs. It was weird, and not really the kind of New York street thing I'd imagined. But Suggs, yeah, well, that was the deal. It was certainly different, I was keen to try it out straight away. Having acquired some tins of spray paint from the car parts shop via Chalky's old man's coat, which had holes in both pockets, I got going that night on the wall of a disused factory off Theobald's Road. It looked good, and there was something about the double Gs. I liked it. That was it – Suggs.

At school the next day I announced my new title to my mates and for the whole week made a point of not answering to anything but Suggs. After a while it caught on, and now I was Suggs. I was diligently spreading the good news on the private property of the good people of North London – their walls, their garage doors, their bus shelters and stations. I was really putting in the hours.

The proclamations becoming more and more preposterous. 'Suggs is our leader.' 'Suggs is everywhere!' 'Who is Suggs?'

> *Naughty boys in nasty schools,*
> *Headmasters breaking all the rules,*
> *Having fun and playing fools,*
> *Smashing up the woodwork tools,*
> *All the teachers in the pub,*
> *Passing round the ready-rub,*
> *Trying not to think of when*
> *The lunchtime bell will ring again,*
>
> *Oh what fun we had,*
> *But did it really turn out bad,*
> *All I learnt at school*
> *Was how to bend not break the rules,*
> *And oh what fun we had,*
> *But at the time it seemed so bad,*
> *Trying different ways*
> *To make a difference to the days.*
>
> *Headmaster's had enough today,*
> *All the kids have gone away,*
> *Gone to fight with next-door's school,*
> *Every term that is the rule,*
> *Sits alone and bends his cane,*
> *Same old backsides again,*
> *All the small ones tell tall tales,*
> *Walking home and squashing snails,*
> *Lots of girls, lots of boys,*

Lots of smell and lots of noise,
Playing football in the park,
Kicking pushbikes in the dark,
Baggy trousers, dirty shirt,
Pulling hair and eating dirt,
Teacher come to break it up,
Back of the head with a plastic cup.

Oh what fun we had,
But did it really turn out bad,
All I learnt at school
Was how to bend not break the rules,
And oh what fun we had,
But at the time it seemed so bad,
Trying different ways
To make a difference to the days.

BUTCHER BOY

I looked at my watch. I was late. At the weekend and in the holidays, I worked in a butcher's in Chapel Street market in Islington.

Mum was asleep. I climbed on a chair and put some bread and water in the cardboard box inhabited by the pigeon, who I'd christened Sultan due to the plume of feathers sticking out of the top of his head, turned and ran, slamming the front door behind me. I didn't stop till I got to the bus stop halfway up the road.

I just managed to jump aboard a number 19 as it was pulling away. There were no seats, so I went upstairs. The air was clogged with fag smoke. All the windows were steamed up and shut. Panting, I flopped in an empty seat near the front.

I rolled the loose Player's Navy Cut cigarettes around in my pocket and thought about lighting up myself, but decided I probably had about twenty fags' worth of smoke in my lungs already. The top deck was full of the hungover, the living dead. Buses in the morning are always the most melancholy, but better than the Tube, where you had to sit facing the miserable bastards.

It was perfectly obvious to everyone at the butcher's that I was not apprentice material. I got all the most menial tasks, the ones whose instruction barely needed communicating, apart from a boot up the arse. The day normally started with cleaning the congealed fat out of the metal trays in the back yard. There was only a cold tap, and the water was cold, really COLD.

It was so cold, it turned your hands blue instantly, and that's how they stayed for the whole day. You could chop off one of your fingers, wrap it in a packet of sausages and not notice till you got home. And fat is impervious to cold water – that's why ducks wear it.

Everything about butchery is cold. The display units, the walk-in fridge, the freezer cabinet, the meat . . . and the manager, Mr Althroppe. He hated me with a lust and took the fact I hadn't left school to become a full-time apprentice as a personal insult to his trade. You could say I wasn't one of his 'boys'.

'Ho ho, it's yzal', said Geoff, top apprentice (and definitely one of Mr A's 'boys'), in one of his many unamusing derivations of butcher's slang. In this one you just said the words backwards, in another you put 'thg' after the first letter of every word, and in another the first letter at the end of the word. They were used, mistakenly, with the idea of insulting people without them noticing. Or maybe just to protect the butchery trade from avaricious green-grocers.

Geoff was an unpleasant character whose genetic line had done away with the vulnerability of a neck, or more like years of humping huge carcasses around had left his head flush on his shoulders. The butcher's was his life.

'Go stuff yourself,' I hit back in plain Queen's.

'Oothgoo, gthget hthgim!'

'Where the hell have you been?' A red-faced Mr Althroppe

burst out of the cold store, eyes bulging out of his frosted bottle-end glasses. 'You know this is our busiest time. I wouldn't bloody employ you if it wasn't. Now get out the back and scrub them soddin' trays!'

Mr Althroppe had a big red face even when he wasn't angry – it was in the butchers' constitution. I made as if to go out into the yard, but slipped right and up the stairs instead. On the second floor was the toilet and a rudimentary office where the tea and coffee were made. On a Formica shelf stood the company kettle and some grubby mugs. I made myself a coffee and tried to get a spoonful of sugar that didn't include any mice droppings from the lidless Tupperware container. Under the window was an old wooden table covered in green dockets and a Bakelite phone and a clapped-out office chair. I sat in it, put my feet on the table and sparked up, imagining I was the boss of the firm. I picked up the phone and dialled Chalky's number.

'Hallo,' came his dulcet tone, eventually. 'What are you doin'?'

'Nothin'. Did you get the ball back?'

'No, the silly old sod wouldn't come to the door. It's knackered anyway.'

'No it's not. It could be fixed, it's real leather.'

'I'll get the old bastard. What are you doin'?'

I blew a smoke ring in the direction of my feet. 'I'm working, aren't I.'

'Not coming to football later?'

'Nah, can't. The tips get shared out today. I can't afford not to be here.'

'Well, we're meeting at the King's Head at one thirty. We've got to get over to Charlton, wherever that is.'

'Nah, I can't. Maybe see you after.'

I got straight back into wallowing in the luxuriousness of the first cigarette of the day. I gazed out of the office window and down onto the market. It was bustling to bursting point with Christmas shoppers. So many that the ebb and flow was almost at a standstill. Most of the stallholders were wearing them red nylon Father Christmas hats, bobbing up and down as they filled and whirled brown paper bags.

The market was mainly fruit and veg with the odd stall selling plastic buckets and mops, pet food or, at this time of year, Christmas decorations. All of them bedecked in tinsel, baubles and lights. In the dim early-morning light the whole market was twinkling and swaying like a gigantic Christmas tree that had just fallen over.

The nicotine was sliding in. Player's Navy Cut tasted most foul but were so strong they gave you a brief high. Curling round your brain and down through your legs, inducing a kind of dizziness. I was almost drifting off when the door burst open. Wordlessly Mr Althroppe strode across the floor and pulled me to my feet by my collar, and projected me through the doors and down the stairs.

Taking my blue hands back inside it was all hands on deck. The shops were only closed for four days over Christmas but people were shopping as if a nuclear holocaust was imminent. The queue went out the door, past the window and down the street. My presence was required behind the counter. The pecking order was thus: Mr Althroppe fretted up and down behind the serving staff, tut-tutting and redoing the things he felt needed redoing. Absent-mindedly chatting to the regulars while checking their raffle tickets, finding their turkeys from out the back and, 'not-minding-if-he-did', having the odd shnoofter from the sherry bottle that had been set on the counter.

Next came Ted, who was very old and a master butcher, which meant he mooched about at the back doing the specialist cuts. Then Geoff, the top apprentice and top bore. He and Andy took turns to man the till while I fished about in the display cabinet, my dead fingers searching for chipolatas and chops, as well as the hamburgers, a new line from the States.

Hamburgers, like sausages, had to be constructed in the hours of darkness, and definitely not in front of the customers. I made them and they definitely didn't require any specialist cuts, more like all the bits of a pig with hair on, the ears, the snout, the bollocks and the bum hole all went in the hand mincer.

And there way up high, next to the till, in pride of place, stood the holy grail. Yes, ladies and gentlemen, if you would . . . The Christmas Box! It literally glowed as Mr Althroppe's missus had dressed a cardboard box in gold flocked wallpaper and written on the side, in wonky felt pen: 'WISHING ALL OUR CUSTOMERS A VERY MERRY XMAS'. It was already groaning with a good few quid and with every new handful of loose change, all eyes turned towards it.

Lunchtime. We had to take it in shifts and me and Andy were given the first break. I liked Andy, he was the youngest and friendliest of the lot. Nearly all his family worked in the market. One way or another he knew just about everyone and had the easy confidence of someone from a big working family. We whipped off our aprons, threw on our coats and headed out into the madness of the market. Jesus, he said, as we pushed our way through the crowds, it was rammed. We normally went to the café, but Andy struggled on past it. 'Come on, it's Christmas, ain't it?,' I just about heard him say over his shoulder, as he pushed on down the road and into the pub. Inside it was crowded, smoky, and the talk was loud. It was only 12.30 p.m., but pubs in the market were always busy and some of the stallholders had been at it since 4.30 a.m., so this was evening to them.

Not being quite the required age, I lurked at the back while Andy went to get the drinks. The continuous roar of convivial conversation and shrieks of laughter mingled with Christmas chestnuts blaring out of the jukebox. The ceiling and bar were a riot of shiny decorations and paper chains of every size and colour. In the middle of the room a large group of revellers were drunkenly hokey-cokeying in paper hats. It was Hogarthian, people falling about all over the gaff. The Christmas spirit was driving people to drink more, and faster, than ever.

I felt cold beer slop down my back. I turned to see two extremely drunk fellas, swaying backwards and forwards, eyes slowly opening and closing. 'Oi, mind yer beer,' slurred Number One, 'yer wasting it.' I brushed my shoulder and moved away. It was the only option.

Andy pushed his way back through the crowd, with two miracu-lously full pints over his head. 'I needed that,' he said, wiping his mouth, having guzzled nearly half of his in one go. 'You here for Christmas?'

'I dunno,' I said truthfully. 'We sometimes go to my aunt's in Wales.'

'Well, if you're around we're having a big do, Christmas Eve. At the Gunter.'

Drunk Number One stumbled backwards, fell into a woman behind him and they both crashed to the floor. While she was being pulled back to her feet some irate hokeyists started cokeying drunk Number One on the floor. Drunk Number Two went to launch himself into the affray, and in the process of trying to free himself from being held back, elbowed me in the nose. The star of Bethlehem twinkled and I sank to the floor.

The next thing I remember I was sitting on a bar stool clutching a damp bar towel to my nose with one hand and a huge brandy glass in the other. People were buzzing and swarming in and out the pub like a beehive hit by a stone. I downed it in one.

'You all right?'

'No,' I mumbled through the towel. By the time I finished my drink the flow of blood had stopped and all the participants in the rumpus had been carted away. I stood looking at my face in the Watney's mirror. I felt giddy, but my nose looked OK. Not broken, at least.

We went out into the crowds of oblivious shoppers and back to the shop. My legs felt a bit wobbly. When we got there the sherry bottle was empty. Mr Althroppe was half pissed and getting in everyone's way. 'What's up with you? Sheen a ghost?' My face was white.

'Leave him alone. He got clobbered by some idiot in the pub.'

'Shouldn't be drinking when there'sh work to do.'

Mr A threw me a lump of braising steak, much to the amusement of Geoff. 'Slap that on it an' get behind here.' I caught it smack in the middle of my hand. I suddenly felt violently ill. I stumbled out of the shop, past the queue, and started throwing up on the pavement. Andy came out.

'Listen, you go home, mate, I'll take care of fat-face.'

'Ere, yzal, you haven't dropped that bit of shteak?'

I hadn't, but I was half way up the road before I realised I'd missed out on the effing Christmas box.

CHARLTON AWAY

On the bus I was feeling dizzy, so I stood on the platform and let the cold wind blow through me. Back at the Mansions a small crowd was gathering in the courtyard. Today's foray was far into enemy territory. Charlton – but nobody could remember where it was. Their ground was called The Valley. Someone helpfully suggested it might be in Wales.

Chelsea had been shamefully relegated to the second division last season, 1975–6, and we were now having to find out where such exotic places as Leyton, Luton, Croydon and Charlton were. South-east, east-south or something. We'd managed a foray into deepest South London a couple of weeks earlier to Millwall, and as we got off the bus at Cold Blow Lane we were met by a Chelsea fan lying on the pavement, blood coming out of his head. Things went downhill from there. Gangs of chaps were milling about outside the ground, but we couldn't see anyone we recognised. We walked past a group of fellas wearing donkey jackets and flat caps, who we presumed were Millwall. To get to the entrance we had to walk down a muddy track. No one was saying anything. The noise growing louder and louder, when we got to the fence it was at a crescendo.

As we made our way through the turnstiles, the people on the inside were screaming and shouting at us through the bars. Chalky took the impulsive decision to swerve left and head for the Millwall end. I followed as the others got swept towards the away section. Mad or genius? Well it didn't seem like such a great idea when we got in there. We were definitely the only Chelsea, the whole end was roaring for Millwall and even Chelsea weren't gonna try and take the Den. But as we took our places in the stand and looked back down the pitch at the away end there was a full-scale riot going on. I swear you could literally see bodies flying through the air, the Chelsea section was being attacked from all sides.

When the game kicked off it looked like all our players were standing in a line down the middle of the pitch. There was no way our winger Ian Britton was going anywhere near the touchline and the baying mob. Our striker Steve Finnieston didn't come out for the second half, I didn't blame him. Millwall scored and our end went ballistic, so we pretended to cheer. Millwall scored a second, and half-heartedly we cheered again. In the second half their striker took a long range shot which hit the crossbar, the ball bounced back and hit Peter Bonetti on the back of the head, rolling into the goal in front of us, Chalky sat down. People were starting to stare, the game was up, we left.

Anyway, today the plan was to start at King's Cross, get to the station and try and get hold of some red and white scarves. Charlton played in red and white, and the scarves would help us gain entry to their home end, as was the form in the pecking order of this occasion. This was proving increasingly difficult in the mid-seventies football climate, with hooligans the tabloids' top topic of the day.

Chalky strolled over.

'Ya coming?'

'Nah.' I still felt ill.

He came right up to my face. 'Jesus, what's happened to you?'

A huge shiner was forming under my right eye. Others started to gather round. 'Who the fuck was it?' I gave them the details of what had happened in the pub.

'Well, come on, you need cheering up,' he said, having lost interest in the details now there was no definable enemy in my story. I didn't need cheering up. This sort of match could play havoc on your nerves, and mine were shot. Even if Charlton weren't up to much, all away games were like the Wild West. Narrow streets you didn't know, hostile pubs, a possible ambush round every corner and Old Bill, who'd been wound into a frenzy by the tabloid hysteria, determined to restore law and order on the terraces by whatever means. A rite of passage set in the twilight zone.

I felt even sicker at the thought of it. Chalky turned and began leading the troops out of the flats. I started to watch them go before a keen sense of loyalty, where these things were concerned, dispelled my queasiness. That, and not wanting to be seen as a bottler. I followed.

There were about eight of us from the Mansions and the first stop would be the King's Head to meet the others. Outside the pub the overspill stood on the pavement wrapped up against the cold, chatting and trying to light fags in cupped hands. Right! We set off in that striding walk that I've only ever seen at football. Purposefully in the direction of an enemy as yet unseen.

I really hate the Tube. A hatred, and a fear, to be honest. King's Cross underground station is a maze where a myriad of tube lines connect to the overground station. You can easily get lost, and on match days no one could pretend it wasn't scary. Turning every corner in those winding tunnels could lead you into a foaming gang of hooligans criss-crossing town to get to their various games.

There are eight active teams in London, any of whose paths you could cross. Plus the thousands of northerners piling down the Tube heading east, west, north and south across town to Arsenal, Chelsea, West Ham, Tottenham, QPR, Fulham, Millwall and Charlton.

We started stalking the winding passages of King's Cross station, in search of red and white. All the senses on full alert, we strode purposefully on, with every distant roar of a train rushing down the tiled walls a jolt, a sound, a frequency, that could easily disguise the roar of a crowd of geezers coming our way. There were four London teams playing at home that Saturday, a handy fact to know. This meant up to eight different firms, of varying size and ferocity, could be scouring the catacombs of King's Cross, like us, in search of easy pickings.

We were getting close to the huge escalator that would take us up to ground level to the main station when there was a huge roar that could not be mistaken for a train, and as we turned the next corner we were greeted by the sight of a dark puddle, a very dark puddle. It was blood. Some of it was running down the grubby white tiles. We'd found it – red and white – but not the sort we were after.

For the first time in an hour we slowed. We stopped and peered in the puddle, as if hoping to see a glimpse of the future, until someone spat their chewing gum in it, we stepped over and strolled on. The roar was at crescendo as we turned the corner into the main hall, and the giant escalator that stretched up to the sky was swarming with hooligans. One lot was steaming upwards while the other mob was backing up the stairs, lashing out at the oncoming marauders. The whole thing was juddering and rolling slowly

towards the surface like a line of battling soldier ants. At the top
the silhouettes of clenched-fisted arms filled the horizon, and the
noise was amplified tenfold by the cavernous space.

In all tribal activity magic and myth go a long way, and this was
Millwall, who had plenty of both. And, oh yeah, they were also
really hard. It was Nottingham Forest who were backing up the
escalators, no mugs themselves, but given what they faced, they'd
all but disappeared over the horizon.

Millwall were taking the steps two at a time. An eerie silence
descended and bemused tourists hugged the walls, boggle-eyed. We
tumbled out of the tunnel into the hall and stood in a semicircle,
all eyes following the spots of blood across the floor and up the
now empty escalator, to God only knows what.

We didn't run up the escalator two at a time. In fact we didn't
move at all, we just stood for what seemed an age as the old wooden
thing rumbled and groaned to the surface. When we reached the
top the station was swarming with Old Bill, some with their hats
off and puffing, kids in headlocks, some lying face-down on the
floor. It was hard to take it all in – small pockets of kids skittering
to and fro while wild-eyed coppers stood with truncheons drawn,
prepared to pounce. Fear was in the air, but it looked like the bulk
of the affray had been and gone.

A football mob has its own way of walking – it wants to be
inconspicuous, but is always in a hurry. Adrenalin strolling. One
mob can always spot another and we were spotted as soon as we
stepped off the escalator. Amongst the now disparate carnage a
largish crowd were gathered outside the station pub. Some of
them were pointing and gesticulating at us. They were starting to
make moves in our direction, when up went the roar, 'CHELSEA!
CHELSEA!'

We looked at each other and realised that it was our mob. We clapped along and, smiling, headed in their direction. We were greeted by a fat bloke I recognised from the Shed (that's all he was known as, the Fat Bloke). I remember him because he had this amazing knack, when the Shed was being invaded by opposing fans, of shouting 'Come on, let's have 'em!' and making to charge forward. You'd go with him, only to find yourself in the front line and him mysteriously some way behind. I think it was maybe where Michael Jackson got the moonwalk from.

'Are you Chelsea then or what?' said the Fat Bloke. 'Of course we are.' He was a bully as well as a coward, but had a good few followers. 'Yeah, I seen this lot before,' said one of his spotty lieutenants. What, from behind? I thought. Fatty looked disappointed. 'Really?' 'Yes, really!' He then turned and disappeared back into his mob.

Apart from the odd character being frogmarched out, we were the only mob left in the station. I grabbed a red and white scarf from a passerby, and before he had a chance to see where it had gone I disappeared past the thirty-odd coppers who had formed a cordon round the pub. Still, worse places to be stuck. I stuffed the scarf down my jacket and we got some beers in.

'What happened to the Millwall?' I asked the spotty one.

'Did you not see?'

'No, I didn't see, that's why I'm asking you.'

Spotty's eyes lit up. 'Forest tore up the escalator. There must have been at least a hundred of 'em, their top boys, tooled up and everything. Well, it turns out some idiot's stabbed one of Millwall's top chaps on the underground.' The Dark Puddle.

'So we're stood there, bracing ourselves, expecting Millwall to come flying off the escalator any minute. Don't get me wrong,

Forest regrouped, they didn't run, but they knew what was coming. Then, nothing, before cool as you like, the leader of the Millwall drifts up and over the top of the escalator, wearing a panama hat, bright green bowling shirt and silver-grey Oxford bags. Like he was in a movie and, get this, a black chick on either arm! Two beautiful birds on either side! Where the hell did they come from? Well, Forest took one look at that, turned and just ran!'

Magic and myth. Oh yeah, and being hard.

There were about a hundred of us in the pub now and it was obvious, given the amount of coppers, that we weren't going anywhere but straight onto the football special that was leaving from Victoria. The specials were trains that were designated to ferry fans to and from away games without stopping, in the hope of segregating rival teams along the way. The only special thing about them was that they were the oldest stock available, cranky, rickety old things that belonged in a museum. They were falling to bits, and normally were in bits by the time they delivered their precious cargo of testosterone-filled youth back into town.

We settled on the antiquated seats as far away as we could from Fatty and his mob. The train was packed, which was a blessing in disguise as the draughty old thing would have been freezing otherwise. It was a crisp, clear winter's afternoon and London's grey boroughs flew past the window like a film. Looking down on all the chimney stacks and the backs of broken houses, a view you only get from a train: bricks – millions of them. The Victorians loved a brick, and I must say, so do I. Red clay, the very fundament of the city. From the bottom of the canals to the top of the chimney stacks. Earth to sky. London.

We spent the journey playing cards, drinking warm beer and trying to avoid paying taxes to various Chelsea faces walking up and down the aisle, taxes that would supposedly go towards paying fines for captured miscreants. Someone started singing some old song about Bobby Tambling and the whole compartment joined in, chanting and clapping. Jollity abounded.

The kids on the next table couldn't have been more than twelve or thirteen. Never mind Bobby bleedin' Tambling, they'd probably never heard of Peter Osgood, the king of Stamford Bridge.

The door to our compartment swung open and it was the Fat Bloke. He waddled through and everyone fell silent. He was one of football's many self-appointed leaders. He didn't really like anyone who wasn't part of his subservient mob, most of whom came from out of town somewhere. Though admittedly they were impressive in numbers, we thought they were suburban divs.

Waving his sweaty flat cap, he shouted: 'Jeff Connelly, collecting for Jeff!'

'Who's Jeff?' muttered Chalky, shuffling the deck. There were faces you'd recognise but also faces you may never have seen with names you'd recognise, like the legendary Babsy, a black geezer with one arm who I'd probably only seen twice but was a whirling dervish of magic and myth. There were a lot of names which had entered the annals of hooligan history with acts of derring-do, stories of bravery beyond the call of duty in the field, tales passed into myth and legend amongst the ranks. Some faces that would one day, in the distant and unfathomable future, turn into best-selling authors and film-makers.

But the Fat Bloke wasn't one of them, and neither was Jeff effing Connelly. 'All right chaps, hands in yer pockets,' he said, waving his cap under the noses of the kids on the next table whilst his spotty lieutenants peered over his shoulder. The kids looked bewildered.

'Collecting for Jeff. Big fine. Come on, boys, put your copper away, let's see some silver.'

'Never heard of him,' said Chalky, still shuffling.

The Fat One turned and said, 'Not talking to you.'

'Leave 'em alone.'

Fatty's crew was squeezing through the door. 'Why, what you gonna do about it?'

Chalky stood up, but before he had a chance to say anything a huge bloke from the table behind us turned and said, 'Yeah, leave 'em alone and fuck off.' The whole compartment fell silent. Fatty surveyed the scene, the veins in his neck bulging. He stared daggers at our table, did his famous about-turn and left.

The train pulled into Charlton station and we all piled off. 'WE ARE THE FAMOUS, THE FAMOUS CHELSEA!!' We weren't famous, we were infamous. When we arrived all the usual faces were milling around, trying casually to extract themselves from the huge police cordon and find the home end. We did, and I donned my red and white scarf. As we approached the turnstiles Chalky was stopped.

'Where you going then, son?'

'To support my team, Officer.'

'Who do you support then, son?'

'The mighty reds, Charlton.'

'Who's your reserve keeper then, sunshine?' It was stuff the coppers learnt, stuff it was important to know.

'Reg Morris,' came Chalky, quick as a flash.

I pushed forward with my red and white scarf to the fore. The copper looked at me, with my fresh black eye, and eyed us both up and down. He knew the Chelsea special had just pulled in, but there was nothing else he could do with the limited espionage he'd been given. He stood on my foot. 'No steels.' Unfortunately they weren't and he nearly broke my big toe. 'All right, in you go,' he said, tapping his truncheon on his leg. 'But any trouble and, believe me, there'll be hell to pay.'

Hell indeed, but not the one Plod had anticipated. Within minutes the antiquated Charlton end was on fire. Smoke billowed across it. Scarf carefully stuffed back in my jacket, I waited. We waited for that very specific moment. A very specific moment that only happens in the home end when it's been infiltrated by an away team. Standing next to some recognised faces, it didn't take long. The minutes passed, then a lone voice we were waiting for shouted 'CHELSEA!' That was the signal, the moment when, if there wasn't enough of you, the home fans would steam in, followed by the coppers, who took no prisoners. You could never be sure.

But there was enough, there was more than enough, and soon the chant spread across the whole end. A small pocket of red and white regrouped in one corner. A phalanx of Old Bill hastily formed a line to keep the two sides apart and the stewards looked up anxiously from the pitch. A few marauders tried unsuccessfully to breach the thin blue line, but it stood firm and the whole thing was over in a matter of minutes. A feeling of anticlimax descended.

The ground was full of expectant marauders with nothing left to maraud. The lot in front of us had made a space and were throwing handfuls of loose change onto the terracing. It was starting to form quite a pile until it became irresistible to some foolhardy soul, Chalky, who made a desperate lunge at it, grabbing as much as he could while being booted from all sides.

To make matters worse, moments later Charlton scored.

Bollocks! The Charlton contingent were in the air and going mad. I got swept off my feet as our lot surged towards them and I heard a familiar cry, 'C'mon, let's have 'em!' Lo and behold, the Fat Man was moonwalking backwards, while directing his troops forward in the direction of the enemy. He backed straight into me and nearly knocked me over.

'Hang on, there's Charlton here.' Some of his squaddy-headed mob turned. 'You're Charlton,' he squealed, eyes alight.

More of his firm turned and we squared up. 'Of course I'm not.' He knew exactly who we were, he smiled, and a space opened up around us. 'Well, what's this then?' He yanked the red and white scarf that was protruding from the bottom of my jacket. 'What d'you call this then?' He knew what it was.

The tension crackled, hundreds of faces turned, now straining to hear. Fatty held up his prize, victorious. 'Come on, let's have 'em!' But before he had the chance to retreat behind his on-coming troops, I snatched the scarf from his fat hand and waved it aloft. 'Come on Charlton, come on Charlton,' I chanted. Silence, the Fat Man's eyes bulging in confusion, then laughter. Our gang joined in, 'Come on Charlton.' The atmosphere cracked and someone piped up: 'We want Fatty for our leader, 'cause he's so big and fuckin' daft. Fuckin' daft!' Even some of his own crew started joining in. There was a loud 'Shut it!' and the Fat One disappeared.

Things were going from bad to worse on the pitch. Mike Flanagan had scored a hat-trick and with twenty minutes to go we were 4–0 down. The fire had spread to the back of our stand and part of the perimeter wall had come down, bits of masonry flying in all directions. Chalky and I looked at each other, yeah, time to go. Outside the ground it was obvious we weren't the only ones who'd decided to retire early, as every other car in the street was either on fire or turned over. Smoke billowed from the ground and whining meat wagons disgorged yet more coppers. It was like Beirut.

We weren't the first to get to the train either and by the time we did every window and light on the thing had been smashed. Not the greatest idea, seeing as we now had a draughty hour and a half, on a cold December evening in the pitch black, back into town.

I was freezing my nuts off, literally teeth-chatteringly frozen by the time we pulled into Victoria, half-hungover and knackered. The joys of teenage hooliganism were waning fast. As the light of the station platform beamed through the broken window, illuminating shards of broken light bulb swimming in beer and piss, I really started to think that there had to be better and more useful ways of spending my time. Really.

The alternative to the football special. Pompey here we come!

PARMESAN WHEELS

Back at the flats there was only time for a quick pint before Mr Draconian and his licensing law saw us back on the pavement. Backslapping and exaggeration concluded, I headed up the draughty staircase home. Home, which consisted of two rooms – my bedroom and the living room Mum slept in. We didn't have a bathroom or fridge. I called Chalky posh because he had a bath, albeit in the kitchen. If they put a door on it, it doubled up as a dining-room table.

I grabbed some milk from the windowsill, put two bob in the gas meter, put the kettle on and turned on the two-bar electric fire and headed into my room. I'd papered one wall of my bedroom with covers of Marvel comics, which were getting increasingly scratched as Sultan scrabbled up the wall, flapping his way back to full health. I loved Marvel, especially Spider Man. He always seemed to have problems in his head, but when he put his gear on he became a super hero, and I could relate to that. I had some nice gear but it was all over the room and I needed to go to the laundrette. This was one of my household chores, as Mum often did two shifts and she very rarely got home before 3 a.m. But I didn't mind going to the laundrette, especially in the winter. The warm dry air and smell of cleanness, I don't know if it was the soap powder or what, but it always smelt nice, and pulling a pile of hot clean clothes out of one of them giant driers was always a great feeling. Sometimes if it was pissing down I'd even put my DMs into the drier.

I went into the living room (it was warming up) and turned on the radio on the music centre. It was John Peel and I liked his show – it was weird but you'd often hear things you'd never imagine could be recorded, let alone put on record. I was starting to get into music you actually wanted to own.

When we moved into Cavendish Mansions, the flat was fully furnished, if you can call two beds, one chair, a table and a cupboard fully anything. But strangely, on the top shelf of the cupboard in my room were two albums and one single, with no covers, presumably left by the previous occupants. One was the Rolling Stones' *Around and Around*, and the other was Manfred Mann, which had that song 'Five, four, three, two, one'. I don't know why they'd been left there but I liked them, especially the single, which was 'Papa Was a Rolling Stone' by The Temptations, which had the most incredibly long and dramatic intro and continued on the b-side. It had the line 'And when he died, all he left us was alone.' I was never sure if Papa left them alone or a loan.

Mum had quite a few records, mostly jazz. She was a good singer and I'd often wake up to hear her singing along to Billie Holiday or Morgana King when she came home from work. I liked jazz too, but it always sounded kind of sad. One record in her collection which I really did like was an album of Burundi drumming. It was a French LP recorded somewhere in Africa, with literally hundreds of drummers all playing the most amazingly complicated rhythms.

I smoked my last fag and went to bed. I fell straight asleep – it had been a long day. A very long day. I woke at about half three to hear *Sketches of Spain* by Miles Davis, one of my mum's favourites, the theme of which I can still recite in my head, note-perfect, even though I've never played it since.

In the morning I woke with a start. The butcher's was shut Sundays, but I helped out the Pirimaldis in the newsagent's over the road. Outside my window it was still dark, but the lights in the shop were on and Mr Pirimaldi was shifting bales of papers into the shop. I was late, as per. I stuck my head under the tap, threw on some clothes, and headed out.

In the shop Mr Pirimaldi, fag on the go, was standing next to the till scribbling a set of figures on a scrap of paper. Alex, his eldest, was cutting the string on the bales and arranging the newspapers on the shelf. He looked up slowly and peered at me through the fag smoke in his eyes.

'Whadda the hell is up with you kids today?'

'What, sorry, I'm not that late, am I?'

He went back to his figures and, without looking up, pushed a copy of the *News of the World* in my direction. Pictures of the Charlton riot were all over the front page.

Alex turned and just laughed. 'What happened to you?' I glanced at my face in the Wills tobacco mirror – Jesus, the black eye had gone green and purple.

'Hooligan,' grumbled Mr P, flicking his ash on the floor. 'Fang! Kill! Get him.' A small kitten trotted through from the store room.

'Look, I had nothing to do with that bollocks. I got this' – pointing at my blackened eye – 'in the pub yesterday.'

Before I got a chance to continue, Mr P butted in. 'Fighting and smashing up the places, you should be ashamed. Fang. Attack.

Kill!' The kitten meowed. 'They wouldn't get away with this shit at Juve.'

Alex laughed again. 'Yeah, should bang the lot of them up.'

The day was off to a flyer. First in was old Granny Groodle Carpet Slippers and yapping dog. 'Ooh, it's disgusting,' she said, reading the front page, still occupying the front of the counter.

Mr P rang the till. 'Tell me about it, missus.' Warming to his theme, 'I've got the leader right here.' He pointed his bookie's pen at me. 'The hooligan's *numero uno*. I'm just holding him here till the cops arrive.'

She looked at my bruised mush and took a step back. 'Ooh dear.'

I went downstairs for a carton of Number 6. There must have been a thousand different varieties of fag down there – in those days smoking was good for you, and everyone smoked. Number 6 were small but Number 10 were even smaller, barely worth wasting a match on. I don't know how the numerical rating worked, as I never saw a Number 11, or any other number but 6 and 10. You could get five Park Drive, they were actually smaller than a match.

The basement was like Aladdin's cave, stuff piled up everywhere. The spare time Mr P had left between the shop and the bookies was spent buying job lots at auction, water-damaged goods from the docks. It was pot luck. The stuff was in containers, and your only clue to its contents was its place of origin. Mr P tended to go for anything from Italy. I don't know if it was a sense of national identity, or business nous, but that basement was piled from floor to ceiling with everything from damp straw-covered Chianti bottles to Bella Donna underwear. According to Mr P everything made in Italy was better, more stylish, more beautiful. Sophia Loren, Ferrari. '*Bellissima*.' I couldn't quite see where the mouldy Chianti bottles fitted in.

ABOVE: Dad developing photographs.

ABOVE: Mum singing with Kenny Clayton.

RIGHT: Bill 'Man Mountain' Benny (*left*). 'Anyone lost a shoe?'

LEFT: Auditioning for the Chippendales.

BELOW: Aunt Diana takes a photo in the Preseli Mountains.

RIGHT: Me and my cousin Hector in Haverfordwest.

BELOW: Last of the international bootboys, trousers supplied by Laurence Corner, the soles of the Dr. Martens – white.

Me and Clive Langer in the luxurious kitchen at Swanky Modes.

Window of Swanky Modes with Scarlett.

Theatrical and brilliant – Deaf School.

ABOVE: Another quiet night on the 2 Tone tour.

ABOVE: The songwriting process – another cracker from the Madness hit factory.

OPPOSITE: Pauline Black, Me and Neville Staple.

LEFT: James Bond and Dr No.

BELOW: Double-decker 'Nutty Train'.

Back upstairs the place was buzzing, if you can call a room full of old codgers chatting and smoking a buzz. Sunday mornings were the busiest time in the newsagent's. Newspapers and tobacco products were flying out. Alex had the radio on and Diddy Hamilton was chatting jovially between Christmas crackers. Mr P slammed down the phone and winked at Alex. He put his fag back in his mouth and rubbed his hands together.

'Hold the fort, *ragazzi*. I'll be back in a shortly.' He clapped, triumphantly. 'It's a big one. The big one!'

'What, like the last three-legged nag? Please, Dad, don't make me laugh.'

'I'm not talking about the gee-gees, *ragazzo*,' Mr P said, grabbing his tweed coat. 'The-Big-One.' He winked again, threw on his tweed cap, and he was off.

'Ho, ho, ho. Merry Christmas, *a tutti*!'

The bell-tinkling door slammed behind him and he disappeared up the road. Alex plucked a packet of Rothmans from the shelf and ripped the cellophane. 'Mum's gonna go mad.'

About elevenish the shop began to quieten and soon we had it to ourselves. We sparked up and carefully leafed through some porno mags that weren't wrapped in cellophane, in silence. Mr P still wasn't back at one o'clock when the shop shut, so me and Alex piled up the returns, pulled down the shutter, and closed up.

Lunch at the Pirimaldis' was never anything less than a celebration, and there were rarely fewer than nine or ten people. Today, apart from Alex and his three sisters, there were a couple of aunts and uncles who had come over from Covent Garden. They were all perched on stools round the dining-room table. Even though they had the two flats knocked together, it was still a tight squeeze.

Mrs P appeared through the cupboard door from the kitchen

and squashed past with a huge steaming pot of pasta. She wasn't overly happy that Mr P had disappeared, which usually meant that the day's takings had gone too. She tossed the pasta vigorously in the sauce with two miniature wooden rakes and splashed a generous glug of olive oil over the top. Lunch was served with big glasses of damp straw-covered Chianti, and we all tucked in. Silence descended, the kind you only get with good food.

One of the front doors clicked open and slammed in quick succession, and in came Mr P, cap on the back of his head. Without looking up Mrs P said: 'Did you get any *Parmigiano*?' There was a very sorry-looking crust on a saucer in front of her. I'd never seen real Parmesan cheese before I met the Ps. I'd only ever seen the powdered variety that came in a little cardboard tube, which seemed to have more in common with the dry skin my mum used to file off her feet with a pumice stone. Olive oil was something you got from the chemist, in a dropper, for earache.

'Have I got the *Parmigiano*?' He was sweating and puffing. He took off his coat and threw his cap on the couch. 'Have I got some *Parmigiano*? Take a look,' he gestured at the window.

'What are you talking about, you fool? Sit down and eat before this gets cold.' She started grating the sorry-looking nubbin.

He was having none of it, snatched the rind of cheese out of her hand, opened the window and flung it out. 'Da-da!' he said, pulling back the net curtain with a flourish.

'Have you gone completely mad?' Mrs P's voice was serious.

Maria, the youngest and nearest to the window, peered out. 'Oh. My. God. Mum, look.' Mr P took Mrs P gently by the arm and led her to the window.

'*Mamma mia.*' She swooned slightly in his arms and we all crowded round the other window. There in the street below was an open-backed truck, filled with what looked like giant yellow lorry wheels.

One of the uncles started jumping up and down, clapping his hands. '*Parmigiano, Parmigiano autentico!*' He stared at me wild-eyed but I didn't have a clue.

Even Alex looked impressed: 'What, Parmesan cheeses, whole Parmigiani?'

I was still bemused. 'What, that's cheese?'

'Yes,' said Alex, smiling. 'A small fortune's worth.' Mr P was already back out the door. '*Il grande uno!*' We all piled out behind him down the slippery steps, out the archway and into the street. And there it was. A small truck piled high with whole Parmesan cheeses.

It was cold but the sun was shining as me and Alex clambered onto the bumper and into the back of the truck. Mr P and the clapping uncle climbed into either side of the cab. The heavy doors slammed, the horn honked and the clapped-out diesel engine revved. The idea was, Mr P explained, to get out and about as soon as. Clerkenwell boomed on a Sunday afternoon, Leather Lane market was teeming, and St Peter's, the big Catholic church, would be tipping out the majority of Clerkwell's big Italian community after Mass. Also all the local delis and restaurants would be full of expats chatting the afternoon away.

No time to waste! Mr P ground the truck into first gear and swung into what ended up a laborious, grinding, three-point turn in Clerkenwell Road. First stop the church. HONK! And we were off. I don't think there can be many more pleasurable experiences for a young chap than sitting in the back of a truck, wind in your hair, sun shining, ten feet off the ground, flying along and waving a fag majestically at the passers-by.

We were at the church in a matter of minutes. It really was like a scene from *The Godfather*, the men in their smart suits and hats, the women in all their finery. Mr P pulled up wildly on the kerb and a well-dressed couple had to jump out the way, smartly. HONK! Mr P climbed out of the cab and he and Uncle Clapper clambered up in the back with us. 'Roll up, roll up.' Mr P lowered one side of the truck and sat, feet dangling, over the edge.

'Wass up, Giuseppe?' said the man in the camel-hair coat who had been nearly run over.

'Wass up? Wass up? I show you wass up. Here, *hooligano*, pass me one of them precious babies. Careful now.'

There were a good forty of the giant cheeses lying on their backs. I went for the nearest. Now the thing about a water-damaged good is that it's wet. And cheese when wet, I now know, becomes slippery. Really slippery, and it must have weighed twenty kilos. I wasn't weak, but I just couldn't get any purchase on the soddin' thing.

The shouting below grew. 'Here come on, hand it over. Don't be shy. There's customers waiting here.' A small crowd was gathering, trying in vain to peer over the side of the truck. 'Yes, just wait till you clap your sorry eyes on this lot, my Italian *cugini*.'

I'd just about managed to get the slippery bastard in the air, with my knee under it, when Uncle Clapper decided to hurry things along. With Mr P gesticulating wildly behind his back, saying, 'Something very special indeed!', Uncle Clapper grabbed me, and the thing shot out of our collective arms and out the back of the truck. Much to the amusement of everyone, it bounced off down the hill towards Farringdon Road.

'Well, don't just stand there, get after it!' Mr P stood, hands on hips, as we scrambled over the back and chased after our slippery escapee. 'That's a small fortune there!'

Fortunately there was no oncoming traffic as the twenty-odd-kilo lump of cheese bounced down the tarmac, hitting a lamp post and exploding into Farringdon Road. The rest of the afternoon didn't go a whole lot better; in fact the only big one we got was a big eff off from the owner of a local trattoria. Even the deli wouldn't take one – a dry one would be hard enough to shift, never mind wet ones. A lump of cheese that size, eating a shaving at a time, would take a lifetime to get through.

At about half four we gave up and drove the cheeses back to the newsagent's and rolled them down into the cellar. Mr P thought if they dried off he might have a better chance of shifting them. I can only presume they're still there. If you are in a tobacconist's in Clerkenwell and amongst the aroma of old shag you get a faint whiff of cheese, you'll know why.

SULTAN, THE FLYING DEAD PIGEON

I went to the Jewish deli in Leather Lane, bought some liver sausage, matzos and a small jar of gherkins, and headed back to the flat. I was met by a thick fug of tobacco smoke as I went in. Mum was sitting up in bed smoking a fag and Chalky's dad, Peter, was sitting in the chair chugging away on his Boar's Head roll-up. I think they were having a scene. In fact I knew they were.

Peter must have lived somewhere with an open fire once, cos whenever he'd finished a fag he'd flick the butt into our electric fire, where it would just bounce off and fall into the hearth. The six brown tiles were completely covered in dog-ends and matchsticks.

Peter was a site foreman, bright, and a communist who earned good money. He liked to redistribute his wealth amongst the bookies, women and booze. The rest, as they say, he just frittered away. I liked him – he took me to Chelsea for the first time and taught me to play chess.

I ate my tea in my bedroom and gave Sultan, who was perched on the end of my bed, some of my crackers. His flying was definitely improving. He could get halfway up the wall now before giving up and frantically scratching back down the wallpaper into a forlorn heap on the floor. After a while Mum put her head round the door.

'D'you fancy going out for a drink?'

'What? Out out?'

'No, not out out. Just for a drink.'

I carefully put Sultan back in his box and put it back on top of the cupboard. They were heading up the Merlin's Cave, a pub off Pentonville Road, to see George Melly and The Feet Warmers. George was an infamous Soho character who played the Merlin most Sunday afternoons, singing his lewd trad jazz business. I wasn't mad on the music, but it had a certain *joie di vivre*, and he was funny.

Opposite the pub was the Merlin Street Baths, a proper old wash house where women did their laundry by hand and squeezed sheets and pillowcases through giant wooden rollers. For a shilling you could have a bath. Yes, a proper bath. A whole fifteen minutes on your own, to luxuriate in three or four inches of hot water with a bar of carbolic soap in one of the twenty or so cubicles, serenaded by happy people singing and whistling to the left and right. The tap was turned on and off with a spanner so you couldn't have any more than the 6 inches of hot water provided. A sharp rap on the door would break the reverie and tell you your time was up.

When we got to the pub, it was packed with all sorts of Soho crazies. George was kicking up a storm in a bright pink floral zoot suit and yellow fedora, Humphrey Lyttelton and John Chilton's Feet Warmers all parp-parping and stamping their feet. Ironically they weren't so flexible with the under-age drinking in the Merlin. I think they had quite enough to deal with, what with the goings-on inside. A disparate gang of kids would gather outside eating crisps and drinking pop. Some of them were all right but I was very pleased to see Chalky turn up.

'Seen my old man?'

'Yeah, he's inside with Mum.'

Peter brought us out a couple of light ales and we chatted about Mr P. I popped my head round the door and Mum and Peter were right into it, down the front waving their drinks in the air, singing and dancing. We decided to head off; we played street golf with two sticks and a stone all the way back. Chalky won, he always did.

We stopped at the mini-market to get some fags, and other things. Chalky had his old man's magic leather coat on. The pockets had gone, and his hands would appear to be inside the coat when they weren't. He came out with priceless riches – a Fray Bentos steak and kidney pie, a packet of Smash, a tin of baked beans and a packet of digestive biscuits. The big one, indeed.

Having finished our gourmet supper we were luxuriating in an Embassy Regal like a couple of swells, when I heard a bang from my bedroom. I went in to find Sultan's box on the floor – it had fallen off the top of the cupboard. I opened the box. Shit, he wasn't moving, I picked him up. He was dead.

I was sad, properly sad. I liked that bird and I'd really bonded with the scraggy little thing. I thought I could bring him back to full strength and release him back into the wild. Like you see in them David Attenborough programmes, you know, that moment of truth after months of nurturing when the bird is released back into the wild and everyone's looking on nervously through binoculars. Would it adapt again once in the wild, albeit an urban wild in poor old Sultan's case? Still, the city is the wild for these ratty pigeons. You never see the skinny ones with deformed feet in the country. They're all chubby and shiny. Some people pay good money to eat them. You wouldn't want to eat Sultan. He's bony and cold in my hands. And them wood pigeons make that horrible, depressing, whooo whooo noise, over and over, like a broken record. Sultan never made a squeak. His plumed head lolled over my hand.

Moping about and feeling sad wasn't going to change anything and it wasn't long before I got over it, and made new plans for Sultan. Next thing Chalky and I were tying Sultan to a wire coat hanger with some fishing line. I carefully wound the line round his neck, his head fitted perfectly to the neck of the hanger and then the tips of his wings to the ends. He spread out beautifully, exactly the same size as the coat hanger. Brilliant – he really looked the part of a bird in full flight.

The obvious next step was to tie some wire to the hook of the hanger and lower him out of the window. Never mind woo-woo. This was whoo hoo! I started swinging him gently to and fro as he went down towards the pavement. He was turning slightly, but otherwise, in the fading light, he looked like a proper flying pigeon. A kamikaze flying pigeon!

I started swinging him harder and harder, higher and higher. It was great, and by the time he reached ground level he was coming down really fast. It was getting dark and the pedestrians couldn't work out what was going on – we clocked some geezer and knocked his hat off in a puff of feathers. Go, Sultan, go! The rest were all ducking and diving out of the way as he swooped down, again and again. Alfred Hitchcock eat your heart out.

The thing was flying better than it had when it was alive. Sadly, on about his fifteenth mission Sultan became detached from the hanger and went flying off down Farringdon Road in a cloud of feathers to join the exploded Parmesan.

IN CAMDEN TOWN

Mum had managed to get us rehoused from Cavendish Mansions into the 21st-century delights of a new council flat above Maples, the carpet shop on the corner of Tottenham Court Road. A brand-spanking-new flat, it had two bedrooms, a bathroom, a fridge, everything, it was like a palace.

It was a lovely flat in the most amazing location. A ten-minute walk to the left and you were in Soho; ten minutes the other way and you were in the heart of Camden Town. And a very different place that was too, in them far-off days. Impossible to imagine quite what it has become, if you were one of the hippy overspill from psychedelic all-dayers at the Roundhouse who, in the sixties, first pitched their stalls in the old stables, selling patchouli oil and joss-sticks.

And it was in fact outside this flat that I first heard tell of the band. I bumped into Chas Cathal, a sharp dresser and a cool geezer, who I'd seen around and about in Hampstead. He was wearing a Prince of Wales suit and he had short hair which, in a sea of Kevin Keegan lookalikes with big flares and even bigger hair, was hard to miss. While we were talking he told me he was playing bass in a band with Mike, Lee and Chris called The Invaders, and that they were doing covers of Kilburn & the High Roads, some old reggae and Motown. It sounded great and I was intrigued. Little did I know that one day I would also be involved.

Crossing Euston Road and heading in the direction of Camden, the first thing you would encounter was, and still is, the wild wind whistling round the Euston Tower, the crosswind down Euston Road, where you still occasionally see old people literally being

Fags flying, frozen fingers,
matches wasted,
in the crosswind down the euston road.

Fingers frozen, fags flying,
wasting matches,
in the cross wind down euston rd.

I'm losing the thread

bragging the
smoking a joint
you're making you
losing the point,
I'm losing count of the conversations
Half the words get cast like
the leaves in the wind,
I nod and we carry on walking.
you're leaving me behind,
philosophically - ... speaking.
but the trees are doing the talking
we're doing the walking,
kicking thru dry autumn leaves

lifted off their feet. Euston Tower was, amongst other great and modern new things, the HQ of the sexy new independent radio station, Capital Radio. I was wary of walking past it, as one afternoon on my way to nowhere in particular I was chased by a load of scary, screaming teenage girls. The Bay City Rollers were making an appearance at the station unbeknownst to me, and dressed as I was, in my half-mast white trousers, DMs and blue and white scarf stuck in my belt-loop, I was mistaken by the hordes for one of the lads.

'B, A, Y. B, A, Y. B, A, Y. C, I, T, Y. With an R, O, double L, E, R, S. Bay City Rollers are the best!' is indelibly printed in my mind.

The next port of call, Camden-bound, was Laurence Corner. I don't know who Laurence was but his shop was on the corner of Drummond Street and sold army-surplus gear, the very place I bought my white bags, in fact. They had everything in there, and should really have a blue plaque as the costumier of most of the teenage fashion of the time, from the hippy/Goth greatcoats, boot-boy army trousers and donkey jackets through to the boiler suits and white naval dinner jackets favoured by the punks.

Drummond Street was also where for some reason a lot of southern Indians from Tamil and that part of the world, had gathered and opened restaurants, serving the most extraordinary vegetarian food at the most reasonable price. And sweets. Ambala, wow, what amazing things. In fact I got a job, via a friend of my mum's, who lived above one of the restaurants in Drummond Street, to paint the ceiling of the Ambala sweet factory in Whitechapel. The two of us perched on wooden scaffolding sixty feet up, painting the ceiling of a disused clothes factory. Paint running down our aching arms, the enormous copper pots bubbling below.

Evaporating milk awaiting pistachio, coconut and caramel. Ambala have over three hundred outlets now.

On your left as you carry on down Hampstead Road towards Camden is the Regent's Park Estate, a huge great sprawling sixties affair. All the tower blocks are named after places in the Lake District – Windermere, The Tarns, Rydal Water etc. God knows why; a cruel joke by the architect I can only presume. A lot of my mates from school lived on the estate. We'd often set off for school there across Regent's Park. Backs to the wind, trying in vain to light fags with Swan Vesta matches.

There was a youth club in the middle of the estate, the Cumberland, where many happy evenings were spent playing five-a-side football and giving the Old Bill the runaround. One time when we were all hanging about outside giving the local PC some gyp he grabbed my arm and pressed a front-door key in my hand. 'There, I've got your prints now.' He was gonna try and fit me up for a flat that had been broken into. Fortunately nothing came of it. I think he was probably just getting a small bit of revenge for all the stick he took.

Down the road past the old Craven 'A' cigarette factory is Mornington Crescent. 'They made me a present of Mornington Crescent, they threw it a brick at a time.' The Camden Palace is one of only three surviving variety theatres outside the West End. We played there when it was called the Music Machine and it is the very place where we first decided to call ourselves Madness. It's now called Koko's. I first went there as a young man with Thommo, our sax player. I can't remember what band we were going to see, but I remember the entrance fee was 50p and Thommo, being a man of great ingenuity where saving 50p was concerned, showed me to a more financially agreeable entrance. Via a fire escape at the back of the building.

Once on the roof of the theatre it was just a small matter of jumping through a small hole in the green copper dome that adorned the building. The only problem was that it was pitch-black and impossible to judge the depth. Thommo was quietly confident, as he'd done it before. I dropped a couple of matches down, but could see sweet FA. 'Come on!' he exhorted, starting to worry we'd get caught, and in I went. We reappeared on the VIP balcony, trying to look casual while covered in smuts and pigeon shit. I saw a lot of great punk bands during that period there, The Stranglers, The Adverts, 999 and The Damned, pogo-tastic times.

Just past Camden Palace was Alfred Kemp's imperious second-hand clothes shop, a veritable Aladdin's cave of sartorial treasures. It was a double-fronted emporium with the proud words 'We Fit Anyone' above the door. Up the high street to the Tube station and you're in the very heart of the place. Camden Town started like most of Greater London as a small village on the outskirts of the City proper. It's described in *Pickwick Papers* as a desolate place surrounded by fields and ditches. In fact Dickens lived there for a bit, in Bayham Street, and obviously loved the place, describing it: 'as shabby, dingy, damp and mean a neighbourhood as one would desire not to see'.

The nineteenth-century Regent's Canal, and then the railway extinguished the village as it was, and made it what you see today. Thousands of migrant workmen had flooded into the area, mostly Irish, to dig the Regent's Canal which would run east to west across London.

The Camden Town I first encountered still had a big Irish

community. Pretty much all the pubs were Irish, mostly big old boozers with function rooms out the back and lock-ins. The other half of Camden, going back down to Mornington Crescent, was predominantly Greek Cypriot. Good cheap Guinness and good cheap Greek food. Camden was the perfect breeding ground for an impoverished young chap like me.

Having said that, I don't remember seeing a girl in Camden till 1979. I don't think they'd been invented. But the amount of pubs that could put on live music in their converted function rooms and cellars meant it was almost inevitable that Camden would become a hotbed of live music when punk burst onto the scene.

The Carnarvon, the Dublin, the Tally Ho, the Falcon, the Bull and Gate, and Dingwalls. Pubs that would give you a chance and cared nothing about what racket emanated, so long as there was a modicum of racket coming from the till.

There were a couple of great record shops, Rock On and Honest Jon's, where many happy afternoons were spent flicking through LPs in the pursuit of something special and rare. Sid's the barber's, full of a right bunch of old characters. Tilley's, a restaurant run by George Tilley, whose mum made the most amazing pies.

And Holts the shoe shop. It specialised in all things Dr. Martens and did a nifty line in brothel creepers. Alan Roumana, the owner, had been the drummer in a swing band. He drove an enormous Ford Zephyr and kept his drum kit in the boot, out of habit, just in case the phone went and he was needed at a gig. He was a kind man who, if he knew you were short, would give you a discount or let you have a pair of boots on tick. In fact he told us that a struggling young artist called Elvis Costello had a pair of creepers on the never-never, and never-never went back to pay for them.

He was a funny man, and loved young people, so the shop was

always full of teenagers. We'd often while away an afternoon in there listening to tales of the swing era. Holts became a mecca for alternative types from around the world, and I really think had a huge part to play in the incredible explosion of Camden market. It's still there, as the British Boot Company, serving each new generation of Airwair devotees.

I had seen a suit I really fancied in Alfred Kemp's shop window. Most menswear shops in the High Street had strange window displays, often involving wheelbarrows and cartwheels draped in fabric. But Alfred's was straight to the point. Suits, shirts, coats and jackets hung one above the other on rails all along the windows of its double-fronted exterior. And there, bang in the middle, was what had caught my eye – an aquamarine tonic suit sparkling in the sun like a glass of champagne.

With a week's wages from the butcher's in my pocket, a princely eleven quid, I went inside, the first thing you noticed was the smell, or lack of it. Instead of that noxious mix of sweat and urine (and dare I say it death) that accompanied most second-hand shops, Alfred's was all Windolene and floor polish. The place was light and airy and the clothes were arranged in size and colour. Suits and shirts on one side of the shop, coats and shoes on the other. The whole place was run more like a Savile Row tailor's than a second-hand shop in Camden Town.

The staff wore white shirts, tape measures round their necks and eyes in the back of their heads. You could nick stuff from Oxfam, but not here. You'd never get out of the place alive. Surveying the whole scene from the cash desk by the door was the all-seeing Mr Kemp himself. He could judge the value of a pile of clothes just by looking at them, and tell your measurements correctly at fifty paces. He could also detect the slightest thought of thievery before it had properly formulated in your head. They said every trader in Camden would be roused if you tried to nick one of his suits, but I never saw anyone try.

The clothes were beautifully cleaned and presented, and it was a treasure trove – proper tailored gear from the fifties and sixties, from velvet-collared coats to spats, and a fine collection of suits. But it wasn't cheap.

'How much for the tonic suit in the window?' I enquired.

'Let's have a look for you, son,' said a fella with black greasy hair in a neat side parting. He hooked the suit down with a long pole and squinted at the label. 'Nine quid, son, including alteration.'

What! I only had eleven. That left me two quid for the weekend. But when I held that shimmering two-tone fabric in my hand, I had to have it. It took an hour to have the jacket taken in a smidge, and it fitted like a glove.

The next thing I'm bowling down Tottenham Court Road like Jack the Peanut, and all that scraping fat and mincing pigs' unmentionables had been worth it. Shimmering in the late afternoon sunlight, feeling like a cross between The Four Tops and Johnny Reggae. 'He's a real tasty geezer.' I was on my way to meet Chalky and some of the others at this new club they were calling the Roxy, in Covent Garden.

I'd seen the words, 'The Clash' sprayed in ten-foot letters across the smoked glass of the Capital Radio reception so I was intrigued when I saw them on the cover of the *NME*, they were going on about how all the records these days were made by old farts. Which was sort of true. But it was the picture of them that caught my eye. They looked good, they were young and they had short hair and straight trousers. The picture showed them with their backs to the camera and their hands on the wall like they'd just been nicked.

The rest of the paper was full of old geezers in capes, or middle-aged brickies in glitter and stack-heel boots.

The Roxy was where all the kids were headed to check out this new scene they were calling punk. It was 1977 and I was sixteen years old. As we piled down the dingy stairs covered in homemade posters and into the dark basement, I couldn't believe my eyes. The place was full of kids, kids my age, all wearing gear that wasn't the status quo or indeed worn by Status Quo.

There was a fella in an undertaker's outfit with green hair, a couple in matching boiler suits which had the words 'Fuck' and 'Off' on the back. Kids were dressed in all sorts of weird and wonderful homemade get-ups. Don Letts with his long dreads was in the DJ booth pumping out the bass-heavy *Two Sevens Clash* by Culture. I went to the bar and even the barman had blue hair. I

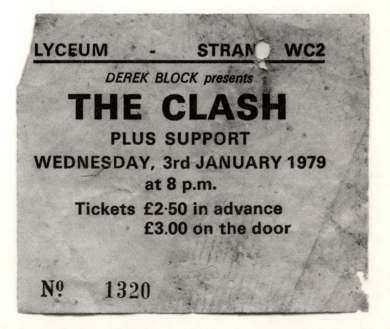

got a pint and suddenly there was what sounded like an explosion. I nearly dropped my beer. It was a band called Eater striking up the first chords of their set. They started leaping about on stage like lunatics. Their average age fourteen. I'd never seen or heard anything like it. The bands I liked (Roxy Music, David Bowie, Cockney Rebel, Alex Harvey, etc.) all had edge, but this was a new dimension. Everyone in the room was jumping up and down. The barman shouted: 'Fuck off, you cunt,' and I turned round thinking he was talking to me. Until I realised everyone was doing it. It was like a coded greeting. Muriel from the Colony would have loved it.

Eater's short frenetic set ended as chaotically as it had begun, with guitars on the floor and the drum kit kicked over. The whole notion that you could be young, really young, was a revelation. Kids doing exactly what they wanted and doing it themselves. Musicians had always seemed on some distant pedestal, but this lot were just lying about on the floor in front of us.

The reggae started to boom again. It was a strange mixture, but as there were hardly any punk recordings yet, dub reggae was filling the void. Exhilarated, me and the others headed out and round the corner for a last pint. But to get there we had to get past a notorious and dangerous disco called the Sundown, where hooligans from various teams would congregate on a Saturday night to kick the fuck out of each other to the strains of Minnie Riperton.

Some of them were gathered on the pavement outside, all flares and long hair, and a couple of them had beards. 'Fuck off, you punk pricks.' They were West Ham, so we did. Out of sight of the Sundown we dived into the relative safety of the Angel round the back of St Giles. By the time we got in some of our new punk mates were in there already. We got chatting about what a laugh it had been, and exciting. The undertaker fella was at the bar showing our small gathering a homemade magazine he was involved in, a fanzine called *Sniffin' Glue*. It was a lot of photocopied pages stapled together, with pictures and articles on all sorts of outrageous-looking new bands.

Chalky and I took our pints and we sat in the corner. We both agreed it had been a great night, but Chalky wasn't too sure about the music. 'I loved the reggae but the other shit was just a bit too mad.' I was in the middle of telling him that that was the point, when the pub door burst open. The place fell silent. 'Oh great, it's the West Ham.' They'd followed us.

I surveyed the scene – to my right the undertaker with the green hair, to my left a bird in a bin bag held together with safety pins, and the couple in the 'Fuck' and 'Off' boiler suits. In the middle, yours truly, resplendent in an aquamarine tonic suit. I tried to look inconspicuous. The fellas in the beards lurched in, wild-eyed. No way out. I wanted to shout: 'Hang on, we're not exactly with this lot, we're football chaps too.' But that was no use now. Tables, chairs, bottles and glasses were flying in all directions.

There was nothing for it so me and Chalky stood up. Someone went to punch me, and I ducked just in time to meet a boot coming in the other direction. It hit me squarely in the nose. I fell forward on the floor and my jacket flipped over my head. Never mind my nose, please let nothing go over my suit. Peeping out from under the jacket all I could see were feet stomping up and down and glasses smashing on the floor. The punks were scattered in all directions. Chalky was disappearing backwards into the Ladies, carefully holding three pints of lager. The West Ham fans, satisfied with their work, and having upheld the right of every democratic British citizen to punch the fuck out of anyone you don't like the look of, marched off back to the genteel civility of the Sundown.

NEW YEAR'S EVE

It was New Year's Eve and I was potless, Mum was out and the gang were all meeting at the Duke of Hamilton in Hampstead. The guvnor there was a decent sort of bloke, and you could always rely on a lively teenage crowd in the cellar bar. He'd also started a happy hour for girls, half-price drinks between six and seven, so it attracted girls, unsurprisingly. Hampstead girls who lived in big houses and who had fridges with food in them.

There was nothing in the flat except a bottle of whisky that Mum had won in a raffle, and a half-finished packet of tablets. I slipped the bottle in my inside pocket and looked at the tablets. They were blue. I'd heard something about 'blues' on a track from The Who's *Quadrophenia* album. There was some line in a song on the album about taking blues because they got you going.

I put the pills in my pocket, took a big slug of the whisky, and headed out. From Camden Road I took the overground to West Hampstead. I had the compartment to myself. I looked at the pills, took one and then another, washing them down with the whisky. I stared out of the window at the backs of broken houses as the train, stopping now and then, clattered west. No-one else got on and the hypnotic clickety-clack was starting to make me feel a bit drowsy. The train slowed and stopped. I came to, opened the door and stepped out, but unfortunately it hadn't quite reached the station. I was running in the air like a cartoon character before I fell into a huge puddle at the side of the track. I pulled myself up, great, my suit trousers were soaked, walked down the line and bunked over the fence.

Up the hill I stopped and knocked at my schoolmate Terry's house, and his mum answered. They were Irish, from Mayo. The old man was sitting on his own in the parlour, flat cap on the back of his head, drinking a bottle of stout and listening to The Dubliners on their mahogany record player. He worked on a building site. He looked at me and pointed at the ceiling. 'He's upstairs.'

When I went up, Terry wasn't in his room. I heard him call from his brother Tommy's room. I went in. Terry was in the wardrobe looking through his brother's stuff. Tommy still had a lot of old skinhead gear, which he'd grown out of, but which we thought was great. Crombie, sheepskin coat, Ben Sherman shirts, brogues, loafers, all really good gear. Terry chucked on his brother's sheep-skin and we had a swig of the whisky. I showed him my pills. He looked at them closely. 'These ain't blues, you fool, have a look.' He peered at the packet. 'They're Valium, 100 mills.' I didn't know what he was on about, but I was feeling great.

'You must be mad,' he said. He popped one of the blue pills out of the packet and rolled it round in his palm. 'Like drinking three pints in one go!' Downstairs the front door slammed, which signalled that his mum and dad were off out to the pub. We went downstairs. Terry grabbed a couple of bottles of Guinness from the kitchen and we retired to the parlour.

Terry's brother also had a great collection of sixties and seven-ties ska and reggae records. Terry put on 'Double Barrel' by Dave and Ansell Collins. 'I am the magnificent . . .' It sounded great on the old mahogany player, the bass was booming. The speaker was on the bottom of the player, so Terry and I ended up lying on our backs, heads under the speaker, dancing with our legs, laughing our heads off. We didn't hear Tommy come in. 'What are youse two pricks up to?' he said, throwing his car coat on the sofa. He had on a skin-tight jumper and big beige flares. He was a big fella generally, and well known locally.

He went out, we got back up to our feet and he came back with a bottle of beer, flopping on to the chair. I proffered the whisky.

'Where you two tosspots off to tonight?'

'Probably going up the Duke in Hampstead.'

'What, they're all weirdos and poofs up there, ain't they?'

'Yeah, and girls.'

'Girls? What? They ain't proper girls. You wanna see girls? You wanna come with me down to Rupert's in Paddington. That's girls, that's girls with make-up and skirts, not dungarees and monkey boots.' He took a swig of my whisky and kicked off his platform shoes. I was feeling very strange.

By the time we got to the Duke it was packed, old farts upstairs cradling jugs of ale, the cellar bar steaming with testosterone-fuelled teenagers. I couldn't believe it when I first went in there, a real eclectic mix of kids into fifties and sixties clobber, Hampstead Teds, Kentish Town yobs, the Aldenham Glamour Boys, and the posh daughters of lefty intellectuals. 'Mull of Kintyre' was playing on the jukebox and a couple were swaying along. When it got to the bagpipe bit I felt strangely moved.

Johnny Hasler, AKA Billy Whiz, had his feet on the table. Wearing Blackburns with a white stripe painted down the back, beaming his wide grin, fag between his teeth, pint in one hand and the other arm of his yellow Lewis leather jacket draped across his girlfriend Kate's shoulder. In the corner Chas Smash, AKA Cathal Smyth, and Si Birdsall, both with cropped hair, immaculate in Prince of Wales and Kid mohair suits respectively. Chas standing, one brogued foot on the bench, talking to Si, who is sitting arms outstretched between their girlfriends, Sarah and Jo, the Brown twins with their long blonde hair. Si sporting a livid side parting, the remnants of a scar left from a Rockers' chain across his nut. Lee 'Kix' Thompson and Barzo, both wearing sheepskin coats, are leaning up at the bar, ensconced in heated conversation with 'Rockin'' Tony Hilton. Thommo in black turtleneck and cream sta-prest, bright green DMs sticking out at the bottom. Barzo wearing a button-down shirt, unbuttoned, and Levi's, clutching his pint with a hand spattered with spray-paint from the previous night's exploits along the Overground line.

They were arguing about music. We were always talking about music, day and night, and apart from sporting the finest quiff since Elvis walked the earth, Tony knew his stuff. He was a big fan of fifties rock 'n' roll as were Barzo and Thommo, but Tony had started going back, right back through the Rockabilly stuff and off into the country, hillbilly ways. Sourcing obscure music was hard, but Tony knew his onions. He didn't just look, he was 'the part'. Chalky was talking football with Arsenal boy, 'Binsy', a Hampstead local, but a local from the council flats.

Chrissy 'Boy' Foreman was chatting to Pat, Paul and John Jones. A fair contingent of the Aldenham boys were gathered in the corner. Occasionally you'd see their feathered haircuts bobbing up and down the stairs, in and out, for a spliff. Everyone swigging on pints of light and bitter, the hand pumps always poured a bit more than a half, so you got slightly more beer for your 30p. Bryan

Ferry's 'Tokyo Joe' was blasting out of the jukebox and Debbie, Thommo's girlfriend, was dancing round the tables with her mate Marion. The pub was packed with the usual mix of hooligans, Teddy Boys, posh Hampstead girls, and the nucleus of what would become Madness.

The place was more than a little lively come closing time and Johnny Hasler told me there was going to be a house party nearby. There often were, held at the homes of those posh daughters of Hampstead intellectuals whose parents, God help them, were away. Excitement spread through the cellar.

I didn't hold my breath. Being a few years younger than the rest of them I was way down the pecking order, and charming as my teenage self may have been, I was no match for 'Rockin'' Tony and the rest, in the dewy eyes of seventeen-year-old Hampstead girls. Even with my chest puffed out as far as it could, I'd often see the heels of the gang disappear through a big polished front door, only to be met by it slamming in my face. Of course it was dog eat dog with the older boys and, in fairness, I'm sure there were only so many yobbos a posh girl wants/needs in her house at any given moment. But, man, these houses were something to behold, big old gaffs with plenty of room to spread out, bedrooms all over the place. Big living rooms with good sound systems, loads of records and plenty of room to dance. And lest we forget, big fridges, with food in them.

I sat in the corner cradling my bottle of whisky, and my head was decidedly wonky. Jenny, a girl I'd seen around, floated into view. I liked her and I'd been to her flat a couple of times, nothing much had happened. It was a nice mansion flat with a communal garden. Her mum was an old hippy who'd get a bit fruity when she'd had a few. But she liked me, which was something, and she was very funny!

'Want a fag?' I certainly did. She handed one over, which I put in my mouth the wrong way round, then fumbled and dropped it.

'You OK?'

'Yeah, yeah, just a bit pissed.' The Valium seemed to have turned my fingers to rubber. Terry was standing on a table singing 'Auld Lang Syne'.

'Sit down you prick, it's only half ten.'

Terry threw his beer in the air. He was one of them people who would suddenly go. Someone pulled him off the table. There were some real hard nuts in the pub, but there was no real malice in the air. Everyone was straight back into the new years jollities.

Jenny went to get a drink and came back with a Bacardi and coke. I was starting to feel a little more human. Well, just drunk, not completely mangled.

'You want to come to the party?' She squeezed in next to me on the bench.

'Yeah, why not?' She smelt great and my senses were definitely returning.

The party was in a big house just down the road and I got in, which was a result because, as I've said, I didn't always.

I headed for the kitchen; the fridge was already surrounded by admirers. I was starving. Mmm, ham, cheese. I made myself a sandwich and headed towards the music which was coming down the stairs. In the living room the lights were low and a few people were dancing. Jenny appeared with two warm cans of Breaker, some trendy new Canadian lager, but I wasn't in a position to care. I took another of the blue things. 'Fancy a dance?'

There was a rock 'n' roll compilation on the turntable and a few Teds were jiving away. I quite liked the old-style rock 'n' roll, especially the Fats Domino stuff, the New Orleansy gear, it had a good roll. I smooched round the room a couple of times with Jenny on slightly wobbly legs before the song ended and we both collapsed onto a vacant sofa. With my arm round her shoulder I was sinking back into the dreamscape. A radio started broadcasting the bells of Big Ben and they sounded like they were being played through water. My head was resting on her shoulder.

'Happy New Year,' she said, and we chinked our warm beer cans. The lights went out and she kissed me. People saying 'Happy New Year' and singing 'Auld Lang Syne' echoed distantly round the room. I felt someone tug at my arm and it felt like they were in another room. The kiss swallowed me up and I was sinking to the centre of the earth. Someone shouted: 'The lights have gone.' Someone else lit a candle and the girl whose house it was started screaming, 'You bastards!' In the melee, someone had turned off the fuse box and had half the record collection away. The lights came back on and everyone had to leave.

When I got outside Terry was asleep on the steps – he hadn't been let in. Jenny said: 'Do you want to come back to mine?'

'Yes I do, but I can't leave him here.'

The girl whose party it was was crying at the top of the steps. Some of her dad's cameras had gone too.

'Just fuck off, the lot of you. I'm calling the police.'

People were streaming past on either side. 'Come on, let's go.' Jenny was pulling my sleeve. I can't leave Terry here. He came to, with a start. 'You snide bastard! Why did you leave me out here? I'm freezing.'

'Come on, Terry, we gotta go.' I tried to pull him up, but my fingers felt like celery. The blue things were working their magic again and the world was fading in and out.

'Stay there then.' Jenny ran down the steps, I followed on rubbery legs. The world faded back in just in time to see Terry throwing a bottle at me. It missed, he lurched towards me, we took a couple of wild swings, albeit slow ones, at each other before we ended up rolling on the ground.

I could hear Jenny shouting in the distance. I was deafened and blinded by blue flashing lights, sirens, sight and sound all jumbled together, swirling like psychedelic dishwater down a giant plughole.

I woke up in Hampstead police station, feeling like death. I was cold, really cold. They let me out and made me sign for all my worldly goods – a three-quarters-finished bottle of whisky with a few diced carrots and chips floating about in it, and 20p. I would have to appear at Highbury Magistrates' Court in the Happy New Year.

When I got home I phoned Jenny. Her mum said she wasn't in.

When the day came, Mum accompanied me to the court. We sat in the waiting room. It was a sunny day and the room was getting hot and stuffy and filling with fag smoke, so someone pulled up the blind to get a window open. Mum lit a fag and stared absent-mindedly out of the window. It looked onto the back of Highbury station.

'That's weird, Graham,' she said. 'Isn't that the stupid name they call you?' I looked out and there, painted on the blackened brick wall was the word 'Suggs' in giant ten-foot white letters. I looked away.

'Nah.'

THE GLAMOUR BOYS

The graffiti was getting even more preposterous. 'Suggs is every-where!' 'Suggs is our leader.' 'Who is Suggs?' Yes, that was a question a lot of people were starting to ask, including a notorious gang from North London called the Aldenham Glamour Boys, whose members included Mr B and Kix – graffiti tags I'd seen round Kentish Town and Hampstead. They were surprised to meet a skinny sixteen-year-old. 'What, you're Suggs? And you think you're our leader?' I most patently was not.

The Aldenhams were two or three years older than me and got their name from the youth club they hung out at, and the fact they were into glam rock like Roxy Music, T-Rex, David Bowie and Mott the Hoople. They were smart and sprayed their boots a variety of bright colours. They looked like a packet of Smarties coming down the road, but you wouldn't say that to their faces. Other gangs from round and about would come down just to pick fights with them.

For local lads they were well travelled. When we still made cars in Britain, train loads of Cortinas would come up from the Ford factory in Dagenham and stop at the signal crossing at Kentish Town West. The Aldenham boys would board the train, climb in the cars, hot-wire the engines, get the heaters and radios going and ride the trains, sometimes all the way to Continental Europe. Until they got caught and deported back home.

Mike Barson, Lee Thompson and Chris Foreman were three of the Aldenham Boys I'd met through John Hasler in the Duke of Hamilton. One night we all went to see the film *American Graffiti* at the South End Green Odeon. It was all diners with waitresses on roller skates, Cadillacs, drive-in movies, good-looking wild-eyed American teenagers all going crazy at the high school hop. The music played as much a part of the story as the dialogue. It was really loud and really good – Fats Domino, Jerry Lee Lewis, Chuck Berry and Little Richard.

I was still singing 'See You Later Alligator' when we all piled out of the pictures. I even surprised myself. This was a vocal talent that up to this point had only been utilised in singing folk ballads such as 'Come On You Blues', 'We'll Never Be Mastered By No Northern Bastards' and of course the timeless classic 'You're Going Home In a Fookin' Ambulance!'

John Hasler was standing at the bottom of the steps with a few of the Aldenham chaps. He was staring up at me.

'D'you wanna be in our band?'

Even though my mum was a good singer and there was always music around the house, I'd never considered singing before. I can't say I had the best voice, but I was a pretty charismatic young chap. And anyway it turned out their previous singer had left, so I got the job. We were the North London Invaders, and we'd rehearse three nights a week (and twice on Saturdays) in a variety of exotic locations such as Mike the keyboard player's bedroom. Mike, Chris and Lee had started to play together. Chas joined them on bass and John Hasler on drums. Their original singer was a fella called Dickron. I'd seen them play at a party at Si Birdsall's, who lived just over the road from the Hope, in his back garden. Although it was very early days, they weren't too bad. I think it may have been that very night that Dickron, who was an out-and-out fifties rock 'n' roll man, was becoming disillusioned with the more eclectic musical direction the others wanted to go in, and decided to leave. Which was most fortuitous for me.

I'd get the 24 bus up to Chris's flat in Kentish Town and call for him. He lived in a mansion block not unlike Cavendish Mansions, called Penshurst, but it had a kitchen and bathroom. He was newly married to a girl called Sue Heggerty, and I knew her brother Tony, one of the Chelsea Boys who lived on the Regent's Park Estate in Camden.

Chris and Sue had a two-year-old son, Matthew, and the flat was in the process of being decorated. Chris was working on the council at the time, which meant he had a bit of time to do some DIY and practise his guitar at home. Working on the council was the cushiest number you could get: everyone was skiving and chipping off early, even the supervisors. I sat with Chris in Matthew's newly-painted bedroom and wrote my first proper song with him, 'In the Middle of the Night', about a knicker thief.

Before we set off for rehearsals we'd have a coffee and Chris would play whatever new record he'd bought. I remember it was where I heard Dr Feelgood for the first time – 'She Does It Right'. It jumped out of the speakers. And for some strange reason I can remember Chris playing 'Here Come the Warm Jets' by Brian Eno. We were always listening to music, but it wasn't always easy to come by. You could spend hours in a record shop trying to find something your mates didn't have.

After coffee me and Chris would head to Mike's house in Crouch End, on the bus. Chris was a very funny bloke and we laughed all the way, always paying half fare with our Dr. Martens on the heater at the front of the top deck, smoking Embassy Regals and being told by the conductor that old chestnut: 'If you're old enough to smoke, you're old enough to pay full fare.' Mike was living in Crouch End at the time and his bedroom was on the first floor. There was an upright piano and a drum kit with a blanket over it to muffle the sound for his long-suffering mum.

We also rehearsed in the basement of a disused dental surgery in Finchley Road, where we rocked out amongst plaster casts of North London gnashers, and in a church hall in Crouch End. Lee, the sax player, used to collect our subs to give the vicar his rent of two pounds a week. One day the vicar knocked on the door and said: 'I'm ever so sorry to interrupt, boys, but it's been over three months now and I was wondering if you might have some money for me?' We all looked at Lee, he looked sheepish and we had to leave.

But, bit by bit, the rehearsing was starting to pay off. We were getting somewhere. Like most young bands we were mostly doing covers. Covers of the music we loved, fifties R & B, Fats Domino, The Coasters and soul, and Motown, Stevie Wonder, Smokey Robinson. Ska and reggae, Prince Buster, The Cats, Toots and the Maytals, Desmond Dekker. Music that no one else seemed to be doing at the time. Music that was relatively easy to play but would really get people going on the dance floor. And we were putting a lot of effort into our image. The way we dressed, the way we walked, bowled down the street, even the way we smoked. And of course the way we danced.

But most of the effort was going into the music. We knew there were better bands around musically, but we felt we were onto something new and different. We were really young – I was seventeen – and there was a real excitement.

The only problem was I had two singing jobs. The band rehearsed on Saturdays, but I still had my vocal duties with the chaps down at Chelsea, where I also felt a real excitement.

As shit as Chelsea were in the mid-seventies, I loved going to the football. It was the highlight of my week. Squashed in the Shed with thousands of other kids like me, singing, chanting and clapping in unison. Like the Slade song at the time you could literally 'feel the noize'. Other teams' fans would sometimes invade the Shed and try and take over, but it was mostly just huge waves of pushing and shoving and running around. After one particularly dull game, I cheered myself up with a copy of the *Melody Maker*. On the bus going home I'd nearly finished reading it when I spotted an advert in the back pages.

'Semi-professional North London band seek professionally minded singer.' Hang on, that's Mike's phone number.

When I got home I phoned him and put on a funny voice. 'Ahem, yes, I was just enquiring about the job of singer in your band. Just out of interest, what happened to the old one?'

'We had to let him go. He had an attitude problem, always down the football,' came Mike's dulcet tones.

'You bastard!'

'What, is that you Suggs? Sorry mate . . . Look, we could do with you back actually. On drums.'

'On drums! What's happened to John?'

'He's auditioning for singer.'

'What, you want me to come back and play drums? Go fuck yourself. I never want anything more to do with your shitty band!'

So there I am a week later in Mike's bedroom playing the drums somewhat erratically, as a succession of Robert Plant lookalikes are rejected one after the other. And to add insult to injury John got the job as singer and I was sacked as drummer.

Three weeks later The Invaders are playing the school dance at William Ellis School in Highgate. I'm standing at the back trying to look nonchalant as the band are going down a storm. All the Camden schoolgirls are down the front shouting and screaming at the band. It's like a scene from *American Graffiti*. Suddenly my commitment to the chaps down at the Shed begins to wane a smidge. And I'm hit by the blinding realisation that I need to be up there, not down here. As luck would have it John (the drummer turned singer) was taking a break from The Invaders to go on holiday in France, and with a couple of gigs imminent it turned out I was the only one who knew all the words, Chris phoned me and I found myself back in the band. We were playing a gig at 'Heavy Petal', our mate's mum's flower shop on Hampstead High Street.

The gig was going great. Admittedly there were more bouquets than fans, but we were storming it among the gladioli. Then a gang of Teddy boys walked in. After a couple of numbers, they were looking deeply unimpressed and started lobbing everything they could at us: roses, daffodils, chrysanthemums, buckets of water, great chunks of oasis (the green foam, not the band) were flying round my head. A Party Five flew past my head, hitting John on his and nearly knocking him out.

Once again I was desperately trying to protect my beloved aquamarine suit. Next thing, they found a box of bulbs, a bombardment of Amaryllis bulbs! Mike's brother Danny, who was singing in local legends Bazooka Joe, jumped out of the audience and grabbed the microphone.

He started singing the opening lines of 'Jailhouse Rock'.

I didn't know what the fuck was going on until I noticed the Teddy boys had dropped the buckets and were happily jiving away at the back of the room.

The next gigs weren't much better, but amongst the mayhem we were getting somewhere musically. People were starting to recognise us, and people knew our name.

Then we found out there was another band called The Invaders, who'd got a record deal. What! After all that, we were gonna have to change our name!

When we turned up to support Sore Throat at the Music Machine in Camden we found out Mike had taken it upon himself to rename the band after the mode of transport we were using at the time: 'Morris and the Minors'. It was all over the posters outside. Well, I can tell you, I wasn't mad on being Morris, and the others weren't too keen on being the Minors neither.

It was decided there and then that we would choose a new name for the band from one of the songs we were playing at the time.

'Shop Around'. Er . . . no.

'Poison Ivy.' Fuck me, no, sounds like a heavy metal band.

'Tears of a Clown.' What do you think?

'One Step Beyond.' Not bad, but a bit novelty.

'Madness,' said Chris.

'Madness' was a Prince Buster cover we were doing. 'Madness'.

'Yeah, not bad,' we all said. Could be.

'Nah,' Chris said. 'It'll never catch on.'

HOPE AND ANCHOR

The Hope stood on a corner of Upper Street and was a hotbed of new music. The walls were covered in photocopied posters, graffiti and, more often than not, sweat. It had been the launch pad for a lot of the good pub rock bands like Dr Feelgood, Chilli Willi and the Red Hot Peppers, Red Beans and Rice and Ian Dury's first band, Kilburn & the High Roads. These were bands that opened the way for punk, bands that proved you didn't have to be some kind of musical prodigy to get on. That energy and attitude were the backbone of the live music scene in London.

The live room, described at the time as spartan and grubby, only held about seventy people. Going back there is a bit like going back to primary school – the place is tiny. But it made for the most exciting place to see a band. You really felt part of what was going on, part of something special, that the band was yours. I'd seen lots of up-and-coming bands, including Eddie and the Hotrods, prior to their hit 'Do Anything You Wanna Do', which I loved. The singer came on stage with the whitest teeth I'd ever seen, turns out he'd Tipp-Exed them. For our younger viewers, that was a white substance you used to blot out mistakes on a typewriter. Well, it was a double whammy for our man: not only were his teeth California bright, but Tipp-Ex got you high, as we discovered at school. Unfortunately halfway through the show it began to peel off, and he spent the next few numbers spitting lumps of white glue into the front row, exposing gnashers of a somewhat darker hue.

Punk was on the horizon and the weird and wonderful were congregating at the Hope and Anchor every Friday night. The place was buzzing with energy and ideas. John Eichler, the guvnor, was an enlightened chap and real music lover. But he was also a big chap and didn't suffer fools lightly. He let our lot in, even though some of us were of dubious age. He took a shine to us, and we weren't really any trouble, although we may have looked it to the untrained eye. John's eye was well trained and we really respected him and his wild pub.

We'd all congregate in the corner and up the stairs round the jukebox. John had increasingly let us put more of our records on it – some old reggae, ska, and fifties R & B and sixties soul. I think that was partly why he took to us, because most of our crowd had good taste in music. Our contributions made the jukebox even more surprising and eclectic. It would veer wildly from The Lurkers to Prince Buster and then the 'Sultans of Swing'. A fella used to get in there on a Friday night selling these things called tombstones. Well, when I say selling, buying him two pints would get you a handful, and you needed a handful to get anything going. I think they were some sort of slimming tablet. But once they did get going they were a cheap night out. At the weekend there would be all-nighters at the Screen on the Green just down the road at the Angel. All-night Clint Eastwood or James Dean movies, back to back, and the tombstones would keep you going. I remember going with a gang from the Hope to see *The Harder They Come* with

Chalky and Si in the Hope

Jimmy Cliff there sitting and dancing in the aisles of the packed, puff-filled cinema. It had one of the best soundtracks of all time.

In the Hope there was a different band on every night, and if they weren't sold out John would let us go down for nothing. We saw all sorts. One night me and Chalky turned up to see The Sinceros, a local band who were just starting to get somewhere. I went to the toilet for a piss and amongst the graffiti-covered walls and, next to the 'Suggs is Everywhere', noticed a fresh 'TOKS' and 'DIXIE', tags I'd been seeing more and more round North London.

The band were good, as always, and afterwards we were having a drink at the bar when I overheard someone shout 'Toks'. I looked round to see a kid about my age and wearing a Harrington jacket and short hair. We got chatting and realised we were both into the same kind of things i.e. football (albeit he was an Arsenal fan), music and clothes. We were both surprised to discover that we were the faces behind the respective monikers we'd seen adorning the walls of North London. Toks laughed. 'What, and you're our leader?' He then took to writing 'But the bar!' after my line 'Suggs is everywhere.' Toks became a really good friend and, like Chalky, ended up working with the band.

There were probably about fifteen in our little gang in the corner of the pub at this point, mostly into retro gear and music, but there was a punk crossover. We liked the punks, the fact they were out of the norm. But at the other end of our spectrum was a respect for fifties rock 'n' roll. It was an odd dynamic, as the hard-core rockers and Teds had taken a real dislike to the punks and their iconoclastic attitude towards Elvis and the like.

You could get stabbed for walking down the street with blue hair, as a mate of mine actually did. But there was rarely any trouble at the Hope. Though I do remember one night when a load of straight goers came up from the Champion down the road to check out the weirdos. Everyone stuck together and me and Toks ended up in Highbury nick for the night.

It was strange that kids whose pubs were only yards apart, and whose musical differences were only a matter of minor increments, could get so wound up. But that's just the way it was. There were all sorts of crossovers and musical mergings going on, and sometimes just leaving your mates and going home alone would be like running the gauntlet. Psychobillies, rockabillies, Teds, punks, skinheads, soul boys, even the mods were coming back and London was a hotbed of youth tribalism. Music was the way we all communicated and it was taken very seriously as a symbol of what you stood for.

John Eichler became a friend too. Our mutual passion for music cemented our relationship with him. He certainly wasn't running the music side of the business to become rich – quite the opposite: he'd often end up subsidising undersold gigs. And I think he appreciated the fact we would all pile downstairs to see anyone and everyone. He was aware that a fledgling band was emerging from our little gang.

We got our first gig at the Hope on the 3rd of May 1979. I remember that date: it was the night Margaret Thatcher got voted in, God help us. We were getting a chance to play in our favourite pub. We were gonna be on the stage we'd spent so long staring at. John Eichler had been following our progress with quiet interest, and when we turned up with a cassette of some stuff we'd been doing in Mike's bedroom, he gave us a break. It was 75p entrance and he guaranteed us forty quid. The gig was like a homecoming, all our pals squashed in that tiny room. With Woody on drums and Bedders on base we had a real rocking rhythm section.

Woody was a good drummer we'd heard tell of around and about. He was a hippy from Camden, but not the sort of hippy who sits around doing nothing. He was the sort of hippy who had motorbike parts all over his flat, and he also had a terrific drum kit and style. Mark 'Bedders' Bedford, a smart good-looking kid from Highbury who was graphic designing for a shop called Blind Alley in Camden and was the best bass player I'd heard at the time. What with that and Chris with his reggae chop glam rock, Lee's unmistakable and raspy sax, Mike's defining keyboards with his fingers flying up and down that Vox Continental, Chas Smash singing and dancing up a storm, everything was starting to connect.

I remember halfway through the show Lee had a raffle for some rare 45s – they were rare, and they were also scratched and knackered. But it all added to the theatre, as Lee has done so many times over the years. Also rumour had it that in the audience to see us that night was a band called Deaf School. We loved Deaf School. They were brilliant and theatrical and had a huge influence on us. Each member of their band had a distinct and a bizarre character. The singer, Enrico Cadillac, looked as if he'd stepped out of a Humphrey Bogart movie. The guitarist was Cliff Hanger (Clive Langer), and their keyboard player, the Reverend Max Ripple, dressed as a vicar who stopped their show halfway through to deliver a sermon on the dangers of celery – something I've carried with me ever since.

Fingers flying across the Vox Continental

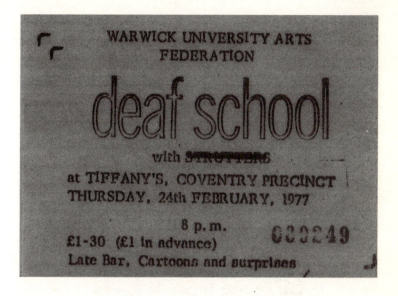

The band member I most had my eye on was the delightful Miss Bette Bright, who dressed as a different Hollywood starlet every night. And to think they were in the audience to see us!

The gig was brilliant, but unfortunately towards the end of the show I put my foot through the monitor in front of me. Cost of repair, the princely sum of forty quid. Our total fee!

But John, being the chap he was, gave us a tenner from his own pocket, on top of our fee, so we could at least join our pals in a celebratory post-gig drink. I thought the gig went great, and I was particularly pleased with my own performance when after the show, backstage, I was sauntering in the direction of the beautiful Miss Bette Bright just in time to overhear her say 'I thought the band were great, but the singer's not all *that* . . .' Well, I may not have had it all, but I had enough 'that' for her to want to go out with me. By this time I was eighteen and things were really starting to happen. I was in a band that was getting somewhere and I had a date lined up with a pop star.

The Hope was like our HQ, and we pretty much knew everyone. One night a strange-looking gang of fellas burst in through the doors of the Hope. All smart suits and Frank Sinatra pork-pie hats. They looked a bit like us, seven of them. They took one look round and filed back out again. What was that? About half an hour later they reappeared, carrying guitar cases and a drum kit. They were a band. They were from Coventry. We were intrigued.

When we heard they were going on, we piled downstairs. The next thing, a fella with really bad teeth shouts, 'All right London, we're The Specials!' Within seconds of the first chords of their opening song 'Gangsters', they're jumping up and down like lunatics. One of them is blowing holes in the ceiling with a starting pistol. They're brilliant!, they're playing ska, and they're from Coventry. I didn't know whether to feel jealous, or vindicated, that we'd been on to something after all.

After their energetic and fantastic turbo-fuelled set, there was real excitement in the air. A very rare thing that I had only experienced once before, in the Roxy. A real feeling something was happening and that we just happened to be right in the middle of it. Upstairs I got chatting to the bloke with the bad teeth. He introduced himself as Jerry Dammers. Coventry was in the middle of nowhere as far as we were concerned. We'd barely been out of London at this point.

They looked like us and had created their own little scene by taking the dormant sounds of sixties and seventies Jamaican music, ska and rocksteady, and making it their own. No one else seemed to have realised what a fertile vein that music was, and how potent it was live. But we were suddenly aware that we were not alone.

The music had always been in the firmament of British youth culture – from the Prince Buster, Laurel Aitken, Derek Morgan, Skatalites days, through to the joyous sounds of Desmond Dekker, Bob and Marcia, Jimmy Cliff, Toots and the Maytals, Dave and Ansell Collins, Dandy, John Holt, culminating with the ubiquitous *Tighten Up* albums and our recent obsession, Linton Kwesi Johnson. It was a musical form that historically had been looked down upon by the British musical intelligentsia. Music that yobbos in Mecca ballrooms danced, and fought, to on a Saturday night.

As far as they were concerned, it had very little real musical merit. Simplistic and repetitive when compared with the complex and indulged world of rock. The music's vigour and subtle infinities of rhythm passed them by. But not us, it was great music to dance to and the attitude, humour and style of them original rude boys sat very well with us, round our way. The style, stance and swagger. If I had a puff I didn't want to just sit round in a circle on the floor of my mate's flat trying to work out what Roger Waters was on about, or marvel at the dexterity of a fifteen-minute-long guitar solo. I wanted to hear one of them hypnotic, melodic, pumping bass lines booming and get on my feet and do some of that old moon stomping.

American R & B and sixties soul were produced in a similar way, lowly paid house bands grooving away like baddies turning out track after track that would liven up a Friday night dance for people who'd been working hard all week and wanted to let off some steam on the dance floor. Sometimes turning out five or six tracks a day with various vocalists coming and going. If the singer didn't make the session the track would immediately be transformed into an instrumental, with one or other of the cats taking a solo, but tracks that never traversed the optimum three-minute line. There was no time for indulgence, it was teamwork.

There's a great documentary about the Funk Brothers, Motown's house band, called *Standing in the Shadows of Motown*, that illustrates this perfectly. A number of mostly jazz players would congregate in the Motown studios. The equipment was set permanently, literally, drum kit nailed to the floor, everything ready to go as soon as you walked in the door. They would play for eight, ten hours a day, creating some of the greatest recordings ever made, incredible tune after incredible tune, and just paid by the hour.

The Skatalites' story is not dissimilar, but more of that later. We were working people and it was an attitude we liked, and aspired to ourselves. Music without ego, music made for and from the people.

Me and Jerry were having a good chat on many collectively held interests, especially where music and fashion were concerned. But after a while it became apparent that Jerry's main preoccupation was finding somewhere to kip for the night. In those days the best chance you had of finding somewhere decent to stay was pulling a bird after a gig. But with those teeth! He ended up kipping on my mum's sofa.

We stayed up late into the night, chatting and drinking beer. He told me it was his idea to get some of the better musicians from local reggae and punk bands and fuse the two. Up-tempo ska was the obvious outcome. I told him about our band and dug out a cassette we'd recently made in Mike's bedroom, and put it on my mum's music centre. It was almost inaudible, and halfway through burst into Lee practising his sax. Jerry didn't seem deeply impressed. But after another beer or two, he told me he had a dream to start his own record label. A British Motown, no less. A stable of like-minded bands that would create the sound of young Britain.

'Don't you think that's a smidge optimistic, Jerry, seeing as you've just played to forty people in a pub basement?'

'It's gonna be called 2 Tone.'

'What, after your teeth, Jerry?'

'Ha Ha, I'm serious,' he said, opening his professional-looking briefcase. An orange and a copy of the *Melody Maker* fell out. 'D'you wanna sign to my label?'

'What with, Jerry? You haven't even got a pen.'

Who could have known we would have our first hit – 'The Prince' – with Jerry's 2 Tone label and take part in the historic 2 Tone tour with The Specials, Selector and later Dexys Midnight Runners, that would roar across the country like wildfire.

SWANKY DAYS!

My first proper date with Bette Bright was to accompany her to the film premiere of the Alternative Miss World. Which is exactly what it was. While the models of the world paraded on Miss World on the box, the artist Andrew Logan had organised an alternative on Clapham Common. I was to meet Anne at the infamous clothes shop Swanky Modes in Camden Town.

The shop was in the middle of a pub that they rented from Truman's. When I say the middle, it occupied a bow window on the corner of Royal College Street and Camden Road, with The Eagle pub running down both sides. The main entrance to the public bar was on Camden Road, and the door to the slightly more expensive saloon bar was on Royal College Street. The shop occupied four floors – the workshop in the basement, shop on the ground floor, living room and kitchen/bathroom on the first and two bedrooms on the top. One of which Anne was renting.

Anne had bought a lot of clothes from Swanky's in her Deaf School days and had got to know the four rather extraordinary girls who ran it. Es, Willy, Judy and Mel, and the Saturday girls, Michelle and Jane. They were all real characters and an enormous

DOOR

amount of fun. Mel was also going out with Clive Langer, who I was just getting to know.

Swanky Modes made some really great gear and, considering they were doing it all themselves, were starting to make a real name for themselves around town. Helmut Newton had done a fantastic shoot of their clobber for the ultra-cool *Nova* magazine. They did a great line in skin-tight lycra dresses, one of which Anne was wearing when she first caught my eye as Bette Bright in Deaf School. These dresses had recently made the headlines when the *Sun* bought a halter-neck version only to photograph the model with the dress back to front.

I was to meet Anne in the public bar of The Eagle. I stood at the bar with a pint of light and bitter, feeling somewhat foolish in a black stetson and ground-length black coat. The theme for this year's Alternative Miss World was country and western. The wiry guvnor, Aiden, didn't bat an eyelid, polishing glasses in his string vest and open white shirt with the sleeves rolled up. He'd seen enough cowboys in his boozer. One time the guitarist from Tom Robinson's band, Danny Kustow, rode his motorbike right up to the bar. Aiden just looked up and asked him what he wanted to drink. But if there was any trouble, the white shirt would fly off and he'd be over the bar in a flash.

The room was lit by two dangling light bulbs, one illuminating the pool table and the other, the bar. The floor was bare, dotted with a few stools filled with regulars watching the pool players. The carpet didn't start until you got halfway down the corridor, past the new-fangled space invaders machine to the saloon.

The fella standing next to me was wearing a Crombie with a Jam badge on the lapel. I liked The Jam and we got chatting. His name was Moorsey, he was an Arsenal fan. His mate Big Tel came in and I knew him, he ran a stall in Berwick Street market although he seemed to spend a fair amount of his time playing cards on a stack of crates.

Next in was Clive Langer and the other swanky girls' boyfriends, Ted, Nick and Melvin. All done up, Butch Cassidy and the Sundance Kids. Drinks were duly ordered. Next thing the saloon doors burst open to reveal five psychedelic Dolly Partons, all yeehaaing and shooting their guns. Resplendent in blonde wigs that would have made Louis XIV blush, white cowboy hats and boots and enormous silver conical bras. One of the regulars dropped his pint. Aiden just laughed; he knew the girls. I was stunned. A stretch limo pulled up and we all piled in and headed up west. When we got to the Leicester Square Odeon it looked like every crazy in town had turned up. Lee Bowery with a molten green candle dripping down his head. Divine, yes the Divine who ate the dog turd in that John Waters' film, in a skin-tight silver sequin dress. There were trannies of every shape and size. It was a scene that would have made the Colony Club clientele seem positively conservative. I'd seen a bit in my eighteen-odd years in the metropolis but this was something else. The film was an absolute hoot and after a round or two of after-show drinks Anne and I danced the night away in a nearby disco.

My time at Swanky Modes was made of very happy days indeed. It was a vibrant and exciting place with all sorts coming and going day and night. The Wag Club was in its pomp and the world seemed to be inhabitated by larger-than-life characters like its owner, Chris Sullivan. I'd only recently left Mum's flat and had been squatting around and about. I was very happy to share the upstairs room with Anne. But I would go home for a bath, as theirs was in the kitchen and it had no door. Sometimes coming back late after a gig and not wanting to wake everyone by ringing the house phone, I'd climb up the drainpipe outside the pub and gain entry via the first-floor window.

One time after a particularly long evening I was up the drainpipe and pulling down the top half of the sash window when I put my size nine DM foot through the bottom pane, only to discover Mel's eight-year-old-son, Ben, had decided to sleep in the living room. The smashing glass sent him running for his life.

There was music on day and night, and I remember some real momentous records blasting out of the upstairs stereo: Donna Summer's 'State of Independence', Blondie's *Parallel Lines*, Talking

Heads' 'Once in a Lifetime', The Jacksons' 'Can You Feel It', and Michael Jackson's 'Off the Wall'. John Lennon's *Double Fantasy*, *Rumours*, 'The Killing Moon', *New Boots and Panties!!* and all the post-punk British stuff.

Clive had made a great solo record with The Boxes, which included Mike Barson's brother Ben. Anne was in the process of making a great solo record as Bette Bright, there was music flying all over the gaff.

There were still a lot of independent record labels around and people were always arriving with hot new biscuits. Parties pretty much every night, with as I say, all sorts knocking about. I remember coming home one night to discover Billy Idol in the kitchen chatting up Anne. He was very shortly chatting down the stairs and out the door. The night went on and as usual we were all dancing about in the living room. It wasn't a big room and was dominated by a 1930s three-piece suite.

Mel suddenly announced that she was sick of the collapsed and uncomfortable sofa, so Clive and I decided to do something about it. We opened the window and heaved it out, watching it explode into a ball of splinters, dust and moths all over the pavement. Mel of course discovered some years later, when somebody was asking her about the two remaining chairs, that with the sofa the suite was worth a small fortune.

Clive and his partner, Alan Winstanley, were starting to become successful producers in their own right. He'd bought himself a black VW Golf, top of the range. I bought myself a white PX 200 Vespa, I remember one night we raced back across the Westway from Nick Lowe's studio in Hammersmith. The VW had a terrific sound system and whenever Clive came back from the studio with a new track I'd sit in the car with him while he played it full blast.

I'll never forget hearing his and Alan's mix of Teardrop Explodes' 'Reward'. The brass sounded like it could take down the walls of Jericho, and I remember thinking it was the best track I'd ever heard. It was a very exciting time, Madness were starting to get somewhere and me and Clive were constantly listening to, or sitting in The Eagle and talking about, music.

> *In Camden Town I'll meet you by the Underground,*
> *In Camden Town we'll walk there as the sun goes down,*
> *In Camden Town.*

FOUR WHEELS

The biggest priority for any band, having acquired a few instruments and learnt roughly how to play them, is transport. Having got to that point via Mike's bedroom, the church hall in Crouch End and the dentist's basement on Finchley Road, we were ready to hit the road, albeit local roads to some local pubs. Lee and Mike both bought ex-GPO Morris Minor vans. Rough and ready, sturdy and a bit eccentric. A bit like the band.

Me, Mike and Lee were working for a gardening company in Finchley at the time, for which the van was perfect. We'd turn up in the morning and get a list of addresses and jobs for the day, load up with mowers, hedge trimmers and tools, and then head straight to the café at Apex Corner for a leisurely breakfast.

In the summer it was the perfect job, Mike driving, me with my feet on the dashboard, no one breathing down our necks, out in the fresh air, and as long as the work was done by the end of the day everybody was happy. We weren't by any means trained gardeners, and the jobs we got were mostly just maintenance. Mowing lawns, cutting hedges, pruning bushes and trees. A lot of the work was for big houses in Hampstead, some huge ones with vast gardens, often second homes with owners who very rarely seemed to be in. The work was sometimes hard but we rarely had too many jobs in one day, and it was mostly simple stuff. Debates between Mike and myself, as we stood in front of an overgrown bed, would sometimes rage long into the afternoon, as we tried to work out what were plants and what were weeds. If in doubt I always went on the assumption, not always correct, that if it had a flower it was a plant.

'Well, it's got flowers, it must be a plant.'

'Yeah, but daisies got flowers and we don't leave them on the lawn.' In the end we'd trust to pot luck and just try and leave the beds looking roughly organised.

One time I was mowing this huge garden, which was more like a field than a lawn, and it obviously hadn't been cut for some time. The grass was ankle-high and dotted in big dog turds – the owners had two Alsatians. It was a hot day and I was somewhat hungover. The smell of liquidised turds through the mower nearly made me puke. I walked off to get my breath back and made the executive decision that for the moment I would mow round the turds, and deal with them later. The grass was long, which meant a lot of to-ing and fro-ing emptying the mower. The whole thing ended up taking about two hours. I was knackered and sweating, but I'd done it.

Basking in the glow of a job well done, and sparking up a well-deserved fag, I leant on the mower and looked up the hill admiringly. A beautifully mown lawn, dotted intermittently with dog turds balanced on tufts of grass. A field of turd flowers, swaying gently in the breeze.

As I say we were no experts but we were mostly pretty consci-entious and enjoyed the job. One morning we turned up, slightly late as always, to be told we'd been promoted to planting. There were too many jobs on and all the trained gardeners were busy. We'd never planted anything in our lives, except our arses in the café.

It wasn't a complicated job, we were told. We just had to plant a row of pine trees at the front of a mansion block in St John's Wood. Pete, the boss, duly explained the process, which consisted of digging a hole, big enough to fit the roots of the tree in, obviously, covering the roots, stamping the earth down, and not forgetting to give them plenty of water.

There were six trees and they were about ten feet tall. We tied them to the roof with some rope, chucked some picks and shovels in the back, and headed for the café. It was a lovely warm day and by the time we got to St John's Wood, it was baking. The commissionaire came out with a little map the owner had drawn him. The trees were to go right along the front of the garden, to give the flats some shelter from the noisy road. Together we paced it out, and one every six yards or so would evenly distribute them right along the front. We untied the trees, got the shovels out and set to digging, but the ground was baked hard and full of rocks, we were getting nowhere. We got out the pickaxe and set to again.

The commissionaire kindly offered us a cup of tea, which we gratefully accepted. Then it was shirts off and back on the chain gang. We spent about an hour and a half picking and shovelling and trying to jam the roots into the hole. No matter how much effort we put in, every time we offered up the roots the hole never seemed quite big enough, so we cracked on again. It was an hour before we got the hole big enough and the roots finally went in. We covered them and stamped the earth down and I was cream-crackered. Jesus Christ, five more to go. I looked at Mike, Mike looked at me, and we broke for an early lunch.

When we came back it became apparent that at this rate we'd be lucky to get the rest planted by nightfall, and we had things to do at nightfall. Big things. We decided to help the process along a touch by trimming a little bit off the roots of the next tree. Just a bit, just enough to hopefully not need to dig such a gigantic hole. We set to with the secateurs, carefully trimming the straggly extremities of the roots. The roots would grow back – there's enough of them. Mike wasn't too sure about the whole process.

Even with the trimmed roots, we only managed to trim half an hour off the digging time. Tree number three had almost all of its roots cut off. Mike wasn't sure, but with number four I took the executive decision and sawed off the entire root ball. I then jammed the trunk down a small hole between two carefully laid bricks. We filled it in and I stood back to admire my work. It looked fine, as good as the others, slightly shorter, but straight as a die.

The new system meant that by half past four we were all done. It looked great, all lovely and watered – a perfectly straight row of trees. We shared a real feeling of achievement. We waved goodbye to the commissionaire and jumped in the van, job done.

Some weeks later I found myself riding past the mansion block on my scooter. I slowed down to see the progress of our handiwork. Our gift to the world, planted with our own hands, our bit for global warming, etc. The first tree was healthy, green and straight, the next two mostly green but slightly wonky and the other three brown and leaning about in all directions. I rode on.

LET'S GO!

Painted the soles of your Dr. Martens white,
Bowling up Hampstead High Street on a Saturday night,
Black bombers, blues and a packet of cigs,
The Saturday nights of them early gigs,

Bazooka Joe, Deaf School and Sha-na-na,
Kilburn & the High Roads, Dr. Feelgood, Daddy's car,
Past proto-punks, hooligans and Teddy boys,
Pumping the funfair, rockin' reggae, fairground noise.

Let's Go!

We flew from Camden Palace like a rocket,
Didn't know where the car was going, but couldn't stop it,
Following the girls in the lovely red Cortina,
Laughing like a cartoon hyena.

You were driving, I was satnav,
Morris 1000 smelt like a portable lav,
The engine smoking, screaming, fifty mile an hour,
Across Blackfriars Bridge and past the Oxo tower.

Let's Go!

Working all week with Mike driving the van,
Filled with old lawnmowers and petrol cans,
By day just a working machine,
But by night our electric, boogie limousine.

Let's Go!

The reason me and Mike were hurrying more than usual to get the tree-planting out the way that afternoon was because there was a big night in store. The band had our regular weekly slot at the Dublin Castle in Camden, the first pub that really gave us a break, but we'd also got a phone call from Rick Rogers, manager of The Specials, asking if we'd like to support them at the Nashville Rooms, the old Three Kings, in Hammersmith.

What an opportunity! I loved what I saw of The Specials at the Hope and Anchor. I'd never seen a band I felt more akin with. How many chances would we get to play with a band who were so up our street?

But we couldn't blow out our gig at the Dublin. We'd been playing our Friday night residency there for a month, and things were really starting to happen. Like-minded souls were turning up from all over London. The thing was really catching on.

Arriving at our mini-Friday night spectaculars we were starting to find queues of smart-looking boys and girls, all dressed the part, snaking round the block. But we couldn't do both gigs. Hammersmith was on the other side of London, miles away. John Hasler, who was now our manager, thought it was too good a chance to miss. 'Fuck it, I'll hold the fort at the Dublin. Youse lot get over to

Hammersmith and show 'em what you're made of. I'll entertain the baying mob till you get back.'

I went back home to get out of my smelly gardening clobber, freshen up and get me gear on. White Ben Sherman, aquamarine tonic suit, Bass Weejun loafers and my beloved grey Crombie with a black velvet collar, spot on.

We all met at Mike's mum's house in Crouch End, there was a real feeling of excitement in the air. Playing on the same bill and ultimately competing with a band like The Specials was new territory for us. We'd been used to running our own little fiefdom down at the Dublin. How would we go down with an audience that had primarily come to see The Specials?

Lee was already there with his yellow Morris 1000 van, loaded up with half of our gear. Mike was swapping the gardening equipment we'd been using that afternoon for the rest of the amps and musical equipment we'd be using that evening.

Vans loaded, it was two in the front and the rest in the back. We drew straws as to who would sit where. Top was shotgun, up front with the driver. Second choice was in the back of Lee's van. Bottom, by some way, the back of Mike's van, which stank of petrol fumes from the recently removed lawnmowers. If you didn't die of asphyxiation, you certainly came out stinking of the stuff. Not the smell a would-be rock star on the pull necessarily wants hanging round him like a cloud. I drew the short straw.

Van doors shut and our little convoy was heading up the Euston Road and onto the Westway, the vans zigzagging in front of each other and parping their horns. The Westway wasn't too bad and we got there in good time. When we walked in the place was buzzing, the whole gaff rammed with kids our age, all dressed to the nines, dancing away to some hot Jamaican biscuits being spun by the DJ.

What a sight, all these kids, on the other side of town, diggin' the scene with gasoline. Well, I was anyway!

All subtly eyeing up each other's threads. Although there's always a certain wariness when a gang of characters come in your pub from the other side of town, there was a very strong feeling of mutual respect and camaraderie. This was our thing, we were part of it. We were doing it ourselves, and the establishment couldn't get a look in. The clothes and the music were hard to come by. There was a lot of effort going into this shit from all concerned. It was a feeling I'd only really witnessed as a kid when punk started, but this time we didn't want to tear our clothes up and leap about. We wanted to look smart and dance. I was one of the players. And it felt unbelievable. Apparently the previous night Johnny Rotten had seen this queue of smart-looking rude boys and rude girls waiting to get in The Nashville and had stopped his car and jumped out. He walked the line staring intently in their faces, shouting at every fifth one, 'Are you for real?' We were.

The gig went in a blur of pumping arms and legs, the odd pork-pie hat floating in a choppy sea of cropped heads bobbing up and down. We went down great. We saw Jerry briefly after, who said he'd really enjoyed it, but there was no time for back-slapping, as we had to get north and sharpish. It was gear away, and all back in the vans in our now sweaty suits, as Mike and Lee raced each other back across the Westway. The old diesel engines screamed as they hit warp factor 65 mph.

When the vans pulled up on the pavement, Chalky and Toks were there to meet us. We all grabbed a bit of gear each and pushed our way through the crowded bar to the function room at the back. It was pandemonium in there. John was on the mike shouting: 'Calm down, the band are on their way!' Every table had three or four people standing on it and beer was flying in all directions. John was soaked, another pint went over him and he'd had enough. He was just about to launch himself into the heaving crowd when he spotted Woody, bass drum over his head, fighting his way to the stage. As soon as Chas's rallying call 'Hey you, don't watch that, watch this . . .' went up, the place went ballistic. Unbeknownst to us a journalist from the *Melody Maker* was there and we got our first-ever review: 'By the third encore half the audience were on the table waving their clenched fists, while the other half were reeling round the glass-strewn floor, jolly pissed.'

Also there was John Curd, a local promoter who had a company called Straight Music and would later book us to play at The Electric Ballroom supporting Echo and the Bunnymen, which was an extraordinary clash of haircuts. He then booked us on the March of the Mods Tour which included Secret Affair, The Lambrettas, The Merton Parkers and a lot of other bods.

We were supposed to go second on the bill but when we turned up at The Lyceum we saw that on the posters we were fourth on the bill. I shall never forget leaning over the balcony to see John striding in the direction of the manager of the March on the Mods Tour, and to see John raise a huge rubber torch and accidentally drop it on his head. The March of the Mods manager fell to his knees and the next thing we were back second on the bill.

And much later John got us a gig supporting The Pretenders at The Lyceum, and that's when we really knew we were getting somewhere beyond the world of our mates. We went down extraordinarily well, and proceeded to do a nutty train across the stage while The Pretenders played their set. We also took it upon ourselves to announce our victorious entry into the wider world of pop music by spray-painting our names up and down the corridor outside our dressing room. We got a phone call from John ordering us to come back the following day and paint it over. We did.

MORE CRAP JOBS

As winter descended it turned out gardening wasn't the fun it seemed in the summer. Indoors work. I got a job with a pal of my mum's painting a big house in Camden for a famous actor. There were six of us on the job, most of whom were proper painters. I, of course, was given the menial tasks. Sanding the skirting board up the stairs, five floors of stairs, it was hot and hard. 'It's all in the preparation' came the constant reply to my exhausted sighing. I went in the kitchen for a glass of water, as it was nearly lunchtime. One of the younger chaps was in there painting. 'Here, come and have a look at this.' He opened the fridge door, and got out a small unmarked bottle. 'D'ya know what this is?'

'Er, no.'

He looked round, shut the door and took off the lid. He put it to his nose and took a big sniff. Jesus, it stank, even from where I was standing. Like the sweatiest socks. He tilted his head back, grinning wildly, and then started laughing. 'Here, go on . . . Have a bang on that. Honest, it won't do you no harm, it's just amyl. Go on.' He stuck the bottle under my nose. I took a small sniff and, Jesus, it went straight to the roof of my cranium. My heart started beating like a drum and I felt like I was flying.

'Great, eh!' He took another long sniff and put the bottle back in the fridge. He was gurning as the boss put his head round the corner. 'Here, what's that pong? Do you ever have a bath, you slags? Come on, let's get a bit of lunch.'

I was still buzzing when we went in the pub. They were all drinking Directors, a strong bitter they called Death. Go on then, I didn't want to seem like a wimp. It took four pints to wash down the giant cheese and onion sandwiches made from huge slices of white bread (that was the extent of gastro pub food in them days). The beer barely touched the sides of these hardy individuals, but I was away with the fairies. I was ready to take on the world. Briefly.

After lunch I didn't get off to the greatest start – I was told to size the toilet under the stairs. I asked for a tape measure, much to the hilarity of all concerned. I was then sent for six-inch holes and tartan paint. Having eventually established 'size' was something you painted on walls, I set to in the tiny toilet. With the door shut and pipes hot it wasn't long before heat, lack of oxygen and the beer had me semi-unconscious. I came to with the door banging repeatedly on my head.

With this experience under my belt, it was with a certain assurance that I accepted Thommo's offer of some work alongside him in his Morris Minor van. He was painting and decorating for the council, the holy grail of work because any job for the council meant all you had to do was turn up on time to get paid at the end of the week. But to be frank, he told me, although the council allowed free time, the money wasn't sensational, and the real money was to be earned out in the free market. On top of that Thommo had ascertained his painting career might have run its course. Plastering was the thing. Plastering could bring in about £200 a week.

'You got some decorating experience, ain't ya?'

'Well, yeah, er, I've half-sized a toilet.'

'Don't worry about that,' he said, 'I'll get us some proper tools. All you gotta do is hold the bucket and don't say nothing, leave that to me. It'll look good if I've got a mate. All pros got a mate, to mix up the plaster.' Plaster, I thought we were painting!

Once again I was sitting in the front of an ex-GPO van, with my feet on the dashboard, but this time it was an unearthly hour and barely light. We had to report on site at 7.30 a.m. Lee swung the van round a muddy driveway to a new-build block of flats in Willesden. I followed instructions and stayed two paces behind him as he strode confidently towards the site office. I waited outside while he went in to get instructions.

'Right, we're gonna start on the second floor. We're expected to do a room a day. Mind, they're only small rooms.'

Mixing the plaster wasn't too hard as it was a simple equation of plaster powder and water. I piled out a decent amount of the pink powder on to the hod and mixed it with the required water. Satisfied with its consistency, I handed it to Thommo. He got going with the trowel but it wasn't looking too good. For every couple of trowelfuls that stuck on the wall, one fell off. After a couple of hours, he said: 'Here, you're gonna have to give us a hand. We're gonna run out of time at this rate.' The site was run like a military operation, and the painters would be on their way as soon as we were supposed to have finished and the plaster dried.

I started on another wall, if Thommo was a bit wasteful with the plaster, at my rate we were in danger of running out altogether. Every now and then I'd get a trowelful to stick, but it wasn't long before I was almost up to my knees in the stuff that hadn't. By the time we got to the ceiling it was getting ridiculous. We were covered in the stuff, and laughing, 'It's impossible,' trying to get a semi-liquid substance to stick upside down on a ceiling. We collapsed in hysterics. 'Fuck this, we'll finish the ceiling in the morning.'

We packed up the tools and surveyed our handiwork. It looked like someone had let off a bomb in a bucket of plaster, it was all over the gaff. If we'd been asked to plaster the floor we'd have got ten out of ten, but unfortunately you couldn't say that about the walls and ceiling.

The following morning we turned up on site at 7.30 a.m. and I waited once again outside the site office, bucket in hand, for Thommo to reappear. He was in there for some time.

I didn't hear from him for a couple of days. 'Here, I've got it. We weren't far off with the plastering, honestly, the site manager was just a knob. But something else has come up.' Thommo, you may have some plastering potential, but I do not.

'Trust me, I'll get hold of some tools, and be round in the morning, same form, let me do the talking, you just look thick and hold the bucket.'

It was a role I was getting used to, and about the only thing I seemed to be any good at. We pulled up at the muddy entrance of site number two, an office renovation.

'What's going on, Thommo?'

'Plasterboard joining, my son. It's like plastering, but easier, same money but ten times easier.' We found our way to our designated room. The job was to invisibly join the gaps in plasterboard that had already been screwed to the walls with plaster and strips of tape. Simple: all we had to do was soak an appropriate length of tape in the plaster mix and fill the gap, vertically. Easy, this can't be too hard. I soaked and Thommo applied the first strip, and attempted to smooth it down with a little roller-shaped implement. It wasn't easy. I had a go, and the thing kept crinkling and wrinkling and would not, whatever we did, stay straight or smooth. We tried flattening it with our hands. Invisibly joined it was not. My days on the building site were numbered.

I decided to take a job at a second-hand car showroom around the corner from our new flat above the carpet shop. There were a few car showrooms down there, as it was a wide street, which meant cars could be displayed on the pavements. My job, or at least that's what they said when I applied, was to clean cars. Hot water and soap suds. Great. The only problem was they'd failed to explain that the cleaning would also involve a process called T-Cutting.

T-Cut was a product that looked like white emulsion. You applied it to the whole car with a rag and then rubbed it off. In rubbing it off it took a small layer of the car's paint with it, thereby bringing up a lovely shine and removing the evidence of any small scratches. Applied with a cloth it rubbed on lovely and waxy. I was about to rub it off with a clean cloth when I was told to leave it for a minute to set. Leave it to set. That sounded ominous. It was because in order for the T-Cut to work its magic and cut through the layer of paint, it turned into a kind of hardened grit. You could only T-Cut a few times before you were down to the bald steel.

I got going with a cloth, trying to rub the stuff off and, fuck me, you needed the forearms of Popeye to remove it. But after what seemed like a gruelling age of hard endeavour I finished the car and it looked sparkling.

'Right, that's ready to go on the forecourt.' The boss, Fred, sat in the driving seat and we pushed it out onto the pavement. Fred was pleased because with a T-Cut and a fiddle with the mileage he could put 300 quid on the price.

We went back inside and my arms felt like jelly. 'Right, great stuff, now then, what about the Rover?' said Fred. At the back of the showroom was a gigantic 3.5 Rover coupé, more tank than car. This may have been the final straw in convincing me that I might not be T-Cut out for manual labour. A career in a band, precarious as that may be, was definitely the way forward.

MAKING MUSIC

The funny thing was that although we were clowning around, we weren't idiots and we were starting to take songwriting seriously, as well as getting somewhere musically. We knew there were better bands than us technically, but we felt we were on to something a bit different and original. When we were making the early records, things like New Romanticism were being taken a lot more seriously than what we were doing. It took a while for people to understand how much effort we were putting in. Some in the more intellectual trendy press saw us as some sort of novelty act.

The songs were a lot more complex than people thought. I remember some quite serious musicians in a band once saying that they tried to do a cover version of 'House of Fun', which does sound deceptively simple until you try and play it. The song has many strange key and chord changes. The strangeness is in no small part due to the fact that when we'd finished recording the song, which at that point was called 'The Chemist Façade' Dave Robinson heard it and announced it didn't have enough of a chorus. We only had about two hours left in the studio so we went in the back room, wrote a new chorus, and recorded it onto a separate piece of tape. Alan the engineer then had to splice it very delicately onto the master tape we'd already finished. If you listen very carefully, a bit like the middle of 'Strawberry Fields Forever', you'll hear a change in tone when it gets to the choruses.

All seven of us wrote. Our drummer was the first person to write a song, and I remember thinking: Well, if he can write a song then I effing well can. Soon we were all at it, odd, as there were so many different combinations. I'd write the words and Chris would write the music, or Mike would write some music and I'd write the words, or Cathal would write words with Chris, or Lee with Mike, there was never one formula.

But no matter how the song started, when it went through the Madness process with the way Lee played his sax, Mike played his piano, the way I sang and the way Cathal harmonised and sang as well, it came out sounding like Madness. It might be reggae, or start with a Motown or soul or pop or even calypso sound, but it would always end up Madness.

The other thing you have to take into account is that Clive Langer and Alan Winstanley, our producers, were very important to the process right from the beginning. We called Clive the eighth member of the band and he produced all our records. Clive went to school with Mike's brother, Ben, a great keyboard player with whom Clive had played in The Boxes. Clive came to see us rehearse and liked what he heard. He was very good at arranging, and he would add those complexities which sounded quite simple but made our songs very much not novelty songs. I remember other people trying to sound like us, and ending up sounding like those commercials you hear on the radio for trade building companies. They all sound a bit like what they think Madness should, but aren't.

There was a lot of depth and richness to the music, An element of Syd Barrett, psychedelia and that British influence, as much as the ska and R & B music and Ian Dury, Ray Davies and all the other more obvious elements to what we did. Although the seven of us had a lot of similarities, like everyone we had different interests and tastes and we were always adding those things to the pot. So the sound got bigger and richer.

Although seen as happy-go-lucky, we'd often write happy words and put them to sad music in minor keys. Or conversely we'd write really sad words to happy chords. I'd never really heard the word, but Neil Tennant used the term 'pathos', which I now know is a mixture of happiness and sadness. That's certainly a huge element of what we tried to achieve, although it was unconscious. And I must say I've been called pathotic a few times since.

For singing and indeed songwriting, my two biggest influences were Ray Davies and Ian Dury. Both of them wrote songs about ordinary working life, made everyday life situations cinematic, and sang in their own vernacular. Unlike most people, who were trying to approximate west coast America. There were a lot of similarities between Ray and Ian. They often wrote songs with lists of everyday objects – Ray Davies's 'The Village Green Appreciation Society' is a great example. And Ian Dury wrote a song called 'England's Glory', again just a list of all the great eccentric things about England.

They were both influenced by music hall. For me as a kid, music hall didn't mean much more than a funny old programme on the BBC called *The Good Old Days*, which seemed primarily to involve blokes with stripey jackets and moustaches and boaters, pushing ladies in big nylon skirts on festooned swings, singing 'Daisy, Daisy,

Give Me Your Answer Do'. Which wasn't much competition for *The Avengers*.

But it was through Ian Dury that I started to learn a bit more about music hall, and the connection with all the people we'd been watching on TV who we liked, Tommy Cooper, Morecambe and Wise and Les Dawson. All those people who'd come from that vaudeville tradition, that black comedy, gallows humour. And also I feel there was a bit of a musical lineage from music hall through the Small Faces, The Kinks, Ian Dury to us. Ribald street music.

Funnily enough I've only met Ray Davies once. He was organising a Meltdown Festival at the South Bank and he asked us if we'd play one night. I was in my dressing room, and they said: 'Ray Davies is next door and he wants to say hello.' I walked in and he had a camera on. The first thing he did was interview me, which was a very surreal experience, as I'm sure I had a lot more questions to ask him than he had to ask me.

Ian Dury and I only met a few times. Although we were both on Stiff Records, as was often the case you rarely came across fellow musicians because they'd either be on the road themselves or making their own album, so your paths didn't cross very often. But I got on well with Ian. He liked us, but I think he thought there was an element of us usurping his mantle, which we kind of were, because we were so influenced by him. Especially by his first band Kilburn & the High Roads, which had pretty much the same line up as us – saxophone, piano and all the rest of it.

It's an amazing feeling hearing your own song being played by the rest of the band for the first time. A mixture of excitement and trepidation. You can never know until it's in full flow how it

My short-lived psychedelic phase

will turn out, and that takes a while until everyone in the band gets the hang of it and works out their own parts. You can have written your best lyric, enthuse it along, sing the best you can, but it's ultimately in the lap of the gods.

Some songs work and some songs don't. That's the great joy and mystery. When you hear a song on the radio you can't always tell if you really like it until you've heard it a couple of times. And yet when you're writing a song, you're creating something from nothing. An instinctive impulse tells you whether you're getting somewhere or not. But it's only when the whole band are playing it that it really comes to life.

With 'Baggy Trousers' it was pretty instant. I'd had the idea after hearing Pink Floyd's 'Another Brick in the Wall' with the line 'Teacher, leave them kids alone.' Roger Waters had obviously had a very different experience at school from me. For all the stupidity I showed at my school I always felt it was more like 'Kids, leave them teachers alone . . .'

I was thinking about these things as I lay on the floor of Lee's flat in the Caledonian Road. We'd been up the Hope and he'd kindly let me kip at his. On the way back we spotted a scooter outside the swimming pool which had been there for some time. Thommo reckoned it was dumped. So we took it upon ourselves to rescue it and wheeled it round to the wasteland at the back of Lee's flats. I've had my karmic comeuppance as a number of my scooters over the years have befallen the same fate.

Lee and Deb had gone to bed and I was lying face-down on the floor in a sleeping bag, pad and pen in hand. I started writing a list of all the things I could remember about my days at Quintin Kynaston school. It wasn't the easiest job at first, as I'd hardly been there for the last few years. But the memories began to trickle in. 'Naughty boys in nasty schools . . .' In a couple of hours I had the bulk of the verses done – all sorts of old nonsense that we used to get up to.

I hoped that at some point, a title and chorus would emerge. And they did. 'Baggy Trousers' just sounded like an unusual title; I couldn't think of anything better. Although when the record came out, some thought I was referring to Dickensian workhouse clothing, it was in fact a reference to them horrible great big trousers that were all the go in the seventies. Great flapping things they mistakenly called Oxford bags. With four-button waistbands and for some peculiar reason pockets down by the knees, the ensemble set off perfectly with a lovely pair of snub-nosed stack-heel shoes.

The chorus was a bit trickier, as I was trying to get across the craziness that occurred at school in the battle against boredom, but balanced with a certain sympathy for the beleaguered teachers.

Oh what fun we had, but did it really turn out bad,
All I learnt at school, was how to bend not break the rules,
And oh what fun we had, but at the time it seemed so bad,
Trying different ways, to make a difference to the days.

By the morning it was done. Lee and Deb had gone to work and I realised I had no money to get home, which is why I'd kipped there in the first place. Thommo had two round biscuit tins on a shelf in the living room. One was full of mint-condition Blue Beat 45s, and the other full of twopence coins. I borrowed 12p, just enough for ten fags and my bus fare home.

I must pay him back one day.

I turned up at rehearsals with my new words. Chris had a bit of a tasty ska riff on the go, and the words just slotted in perfectly. The melody, if you can call it such, materialised spontaneously. Humphrey Ocean, a great painter and old pal of ours, who'd also played bass with Ian Dury's first band, Kilburn & the High Roads, did a fantastic pencil illustration of the group standing outside Chalk Farm station for the cover, and a video was made at a school in Islip Street in Kentish Town. It's the one in which Lee flew over our heads hanging from a crane while the rest of the band performed in the playground staring up at him. And into the bosom of the nation it disappeared, only to reappear some thirty years later.

Yes, who'd have thought that some thirty years on, we'd be rearranging and deconstructing 'Baggy Trousers' for a huge Kronenbourg campaign? I thought they were joking when they first phoned up, asking if we could do it in a sort of ballad style. I think the whole premise of the promotion was things slowing down. Which always struck me as a bit odd, lager isn't a drink I immediately associate with drinking slowly, but anyway, that's not my problem. And as those of you who've heard 'Baggy Trousers' will know, it is an up-tempo and not overly melodic song. When we first started rehearsing and trying to slow it down it seemed like an impossible task.

We got to the point when we started to sound like Tom Waits, then someone, Chris I think, came in with the bright idea that maybe we should do it in the style of a French chanteuse – I'm not sure if Kronenbourg is French or Belgian, but anyway, somewhere on the border there – with accordion, violins and all that. But still we were struggling a bit, and then Woody suggested we did it in a waltz style, and suddenly it all came together. It was a rather fascinating and extraordinary thing, to see this song that we had been playing for thirty years, refilled with life in a completely different and unexpected way.

We were then flown to Prague, and I'm very pleased to be able to talk about this, because it's an example of quite how hard I work for my money, having to sit for three days in a bar in Prague doing nothing except sip cold lager. Believe me, I don't know how I stood it. Well, I certainly don't know how I stood up at the end of it. So there we were with a director who looked like he was twenty-five, thirty years on, taking all the references from the original video: Lee flying, people's hats changing shape, and doing a vague impression of the nutty train as we left the bar.

In fact someone recently sent me a clipping from *Smash Hits* in which a twenty-year-old Suggs tells the journalist: 'There's no way that I'll still be playing that song "Baggy Trousers" when I'm an old man . . . of thirty.'

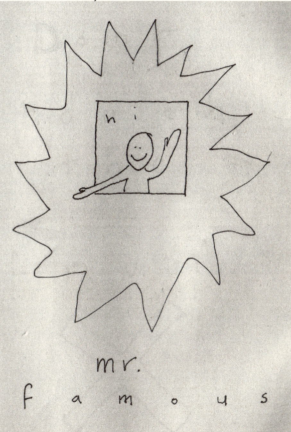

ARLINGTON HOUSE –
ONE BETTER DAY

Arlington House, address no fixed abode, has loomed over the people of Camden Town for over a hundred years. Envisaged and financed in 1905 by Lord Rowton, private secretary to Disraeli, as an antidote to the common lodging houses of the time. Described as the worst public housing ever, before or since. Dozens of lodgers would be crammed into one room, where there would not be enough room to lie down. A rope would be tied from wall to wall, and the men would drape their arms over it and try to sleep standing up. These places were not cheap, but the alternative was the risk of death from exposure, as it still is for the homeless today, on the streets.

In 2005 Madness were invited to play at the hundredth anniversary of the place, which also coincided with its total renovation. It had been transformed, the rooms doubled in size, each with its own washing facilities. And it now even has its own recording studio and radio station. I dunno what old Rowton would have made of that.

The gig was a jolly affair with a lot of locals, and Arlington residents, squashed into the cobbled street at the back, where the market traders still keep their barrows. Afterwards I took a guided tour of the place with Joe McGarry, a one-time resident who'd risen to become the manager of the whole place. A terrific man who could obviously empathise with the chaps staying there, and it was plain from my short visit that the residents loved him.

As Joe took me through the new improved Arlington House, which he was very proud to be involved in, he remembered it as it was when he first arrived as a destitute young man one Christmas in the mid-seventies. He'd walked for miles for the privilege to stay there, as many did. It was raining and he'd been on the streets for months when the 'Big House', as he called it, finally loomed in his direction. He said it was like arriving at a giant ship of safety. Not that it wasn't a tough place. In the cramped space and with an often heady mix of booze and emotional damage, things could get pretty rough. But Joe didn't have a bad word to say about it. As far as he was concerned, Rowton's working-man's hotel saved him.

For me, a budding songwriter with a keen interest in the everyday, Camden Town was a very fertile place to sit and watch the world go by and imagine the former residents' lives. Hanging about in the launderette, in their string vests and suit jackets as they washed their only shirts and trousers. Men sitting on a bench outside the Londis mini-market on Inverness Street, in trilbies and string round their coats, drinking cans. There was a fella they called The Shroud who would march up and down Park Way dressed as an undertaker. Men in sea captain's and army uniforms. Men who'd fallen on hard times, as Joe explained hard times that mainly came from falling out of love and relationships gone wrong. There was also a lady who moved a huge amount of carrier bags filled with rubbish into the doorways at various shops, creating a rather cosy little nest. The volume of which was such that it would take two days to move her on again. It was street theatre of infinitely more richness than the trustafarians juggling and unicycling about the streets today. Mostly the residents of Arlington House were just ordinary men going about their daily lives, who had nowhere else to kip. Arlington House became the inspiration for a number of songs I wrote. Particularly 'One Better Day', imagining a love story about one of the chaps from Arlington falling in love with the lady with the bags. 'She has bags of time.'

Songs come in different guises. Mark had come up with a ter-rific Burt Bacharach-esque chord sequence, and then the lyrics to 'One Better Day' started to come to me when I overheard someone saying on spotting a somewhat dishevelled resident coming out of Arlington House: 'He's seen better days.' It struck me as an odd phrase. 'He's seen better days.' If he had I started to wonder what those 'better days' might have been. I began to build a picture in my mind of a love affair taking place between two homeless people on the streets of Camden Town. Something noble and romantic, and why not? If this chap had already seen 'better days', I wondered whether he may have 'one better day' to come.

Arlington House, address no fixed abode,
An old man in a three-piece suit sits in the road,
He stares across the water, sees right through the lock,
On and up like outstretched hands,
His mumbled words, his fumbled words, mock.

Further down a photo booth, a million plastic bags,
And an old woman filling out a million baggage tags,
But when she gets thrown out, three bags at a time,
She spies the old chap in the road to share her bags with,
She has bags of time.

Surrounded by his past, on a short white line,
He sits while cars pass either side, takes his time,
He's trying to remember one better day,
A while ago when people stopped, to hear him say.

Walking round you sometimes hear the sunshine,
Beating down in time with the rhythm of your shoes,
A feeling of arriving
When you've nothing left to lose.

Now she has walked enough through rainy town,

She rests her back against his, and sits down.
She's trying to remember one better day,
A while ago when people stopped to hear her say.
Walking round you sometimes, hear the sunshine,
Beating down with the rhythm of your shoes,
A feeling of arriving, when you've nothing left to lose.

THIS ARE TOP OF THE POPS!

Jerry Dammers was as good as his word, on my mum's sofa. Starting a record label that would arguably become Britain's answer to Motown. Putting out some of the most vibrant and exciting records of that, and indeed any, period of British popular music. Including our first single, 'The Prince.' Shortly after which, we were asked by The Specials' manager Rick Rogers if we would like to go on tour with them. What! At this point we'd barely been out of London.

On a cold November morning in 1979 we were to meet at the legendary music venue the Roundhouse in Camden, to embark on the 2 Tone tour. There was us, The Specials, Selector and later Dexys. At any one time, twenty-eight deranged musicians squashed onto an old coach. Filled with excitement, I was one of the last to arrive – ironic as I was only living round the corner. There were arms, legs, trumpets and trombones, spliff-puffing faces sticking out of all the small slidy windows. A couple of revs of the clapped-out diesel engine and we were off! Heading up Chalk Farm hill, to the North. We got no further than the Watford Gap.

Someone had taken exception to an exuberant crowd of black and white kids playing football in the car park and larking about in the service station canteen and called the Old Bill. A van load of heavy-handed cops turned up and Lee and Neville were nicked. Two of the band arrested and we'd barely got out of London. It set the tone for the 2 Tone tour. Chaos, anarchy and unbelievable fun. But what I remember most about them gigs was the energy, the venues would literally be rocking. We would often be playing old dance halls with sprung floors. More ballroom bouncing than ballroom dancing. From the stage you could actually see the balconies going up and down within an inch of collapse. Bulbs dangling from the lighting rig as it careered to and fro. Me standing on a bucking speaker stack as the sweat condensed on the ceiling and rained down on us. Unforgettable nights, normally culminating in all the bands and half the audience on stage to sing the finale. 'Madness.' I remember one night in Leeds, there were so many of us on stage the whole thing collapsed. Leaving us in the basement with our heads sticking out just above the stage.

I loved The Specials and when Madness weren't playing I'd follow them around. Yes, and when they were playing it was my thing to climb up the PA and dance on top of the bouncing speakers. In the process garnering a bit of attention for myself on someone else's stage. Something I've not been adverse to over the years!

One time I ended up with them in Montreux, Switzerland. I was standing with Jerry on the banks of the beautiful Lake Geneva, lovely sunny afternoon. Jerry says, 'Here, Suggsy, shall we hire a boat and go out on the lake?' 'Why not.' I says. So we get hold of this small boat with a piddling outboard motor, and there we are, put-putting our way past the yachts and out onto the beautiful Lake Geneva, sun shining, snow-capped mountains in the distance, lovely. When Jerry spots this water-ski jump – he had this thing about James Bond. 'Here, Jerry, hang on, no!' Next thing, I am clinging to the sides of the boat as we hit the jump full throttle . . . we get stuck half way. The propellor is jammed in the wood of the jump. We start jumping up and down trying to free the boat. The propellor falls off and slides into the water. It's three hours before we are rescued. Jerry was a crazed but inspirational character and great fun to be around. He gave us the opportunity to make our first record, and, for the first time tread the hallowed boards that were *Top of the Pops*.

Above Holts shoe shop in Camden were the offices of Rick Rogers, and the London HQ of 2 Tone records. It was in that very office that we waited to hear if we were going to get on *Top of the Pops* for the first time. *TOTP*. Every schoolboy's dream, like playing in the FA Cup Final. In those days *TOTP* was a hugely popular show, watched far and wide. It showed all the up-and-coming bands, and everyone would talk about it the following day at school. Mums would be bemused and absently-mindedly say: 'That's nice, dear', and dads would shout: 'Look at them long-haired layabouts, that's not singing, that's screaming, that is,' grumbling until Pan's People came on. Everybody watched it. A performance on the show would guarantee your record going up the charts.

The charts came out on a Tuesday morning, and it was with much excitement we discovered 'The Prince' was climbing, but that was no guarantee of a slot on *TOTP*. The show went out on Thursday and they announced the line-up on Wednesday after-noon. We all sat in Rick's office waiting for the phone to ring. It did, and things were looking good. Secret Affair, who were higher than us in the chart, couldn't make the show, as they had a gig up north that night. It looked like we were on. But before we had a chance to light our celebratory cigars the phone went again. Secret Affair's record company had hired them a helicopter so they could get to the show.

The next week, 'The Prince' went up the charts again and we did get on, and watching that first performace recently, my girls said, 'Dad, you all look so "little".' Thin, I tell them. It was a truly unforgettable day, but we got into a bit of trouble for messing about and not miming, which began a long love/hate relationship with the all-powerful producer Michael Hurll over our many *TOTP* performances to come. After one performance Mr Hurll, as usual, came rattling down the metal stairs from the gantry like a steam train. He was very red and puffing, and could barely contain himself, uttering the immortal lines. 'You lot are a disgrace, an embarrassment to yourselves, to *Top of the Pops* and to the BBC!' I was surprised he didn't add 'and the Queen'.

It had been a long day, and just getting Madness to *TOTP* was a feat of extraordinary determination. Sonny, the TV plugger from Stiff Records, always arranged for the seven of us to be picked up individually from locations all across London. Sonny knew there was no point in trying to get us to meet at a designated time and place for one pickup. We never would.

It was the dawn-raid approach – nick them while they're still in bed. Which meant waiting about outside our various houses, as various band members took various amounts of time to get themselves together. Inevitably as one got in the minibus another one would disappear, fed up with the hanging about. It was compounded by the fact we had been in trouble with *TOTP* in the past, in fact banned a couple of times for turning up late or messing about. So we got the earliest call time. We had to be at Television

Centre by 10 a.m. For a performance that would not be broadcast till 7 p.m., that was a long day of hanging about, and we would not be allowed to leave.

Bands would give their right arms to appear, but we weren't the right-arm-giving-away kind of people. Although we all loved the show we weren't too keen on being told what to do, and certainly not at this time of the day. Like the old blues musician who had to get up early for a flight once and said: 'Wow, man, I never knew there were two ten o'clocks in one day!'

Part of the fun of the show was knowing that all the performances were mimed, which everybody knew, and looking out for people cocking up (or in Slade's case, playing the drums with blow-up bananas). But the BBC frowned on that. The fun police wanted some colour, but just a faint wash, nothing too vivid and no taking the piss. This was the BBC of old, where young people were to be kept at arm's length or in the *Blue Peter* garden. This was serious, this was live television, albeit pretend live.

There was this theatrical costumier in Camden called Berman's and Nathan's, four huge floors of proper period clobber. They would normally only hire their gear to bona fide theatrical productions – it was not for fancy dress hire and woe betide you if you tried. But for some reason, which I can't remember now, they took a shine to the band. This was great because the gear was the real thing, one time we got our hands on these authentic coppers' uniforms. Can you begin to imagine the fun the seven of us had out on the streets in those. ''Ello, 'ello, 'ello, wot's effing well goin' on 'ere then?' Especially once we found out The Clash were rehearsing near us. We burst into their rehearsal rooms, kicking the doors open and shouting: 'Nobody move, it's the pigs!' We were greeted by the sound of doors slamming and toilets flushing! They didn't speak to us for five years.

A lot of work went in to all that mucking about and over the years we dressed up as bumblebees, birds, ballet dancers, vampires, policemen, traffic wardens, Lawrence of Arabia, charladies, postmen, burglars, spivs, undertakers, soldiers, sailors, businessmen, pilots, air stewardesses, a gospel choir, giant worms, red corpuscles, human rockets, flowers, cats, golfers, gangsters, CID, kamikaze pilots, ghosts, glam rock stars, The Beatles, navvies, bus conductors, cowboys and Indians, chefs, hippies, Russians, schoolboys, chemists, teachers, prisoners, prison warders, flashers, tramps and bag ladies, Hare Krishnas, devils, Fred Astaire AND Ginger Rogers. And on the odd occasion even ourselves.

On this particular occasion Dave Robinson, the head of Stiff Records and the man with a pen behind either earhole and the back of his hand for a diary, had convinced us that it would be a good idea to wear the Lawrence of Arabia gear we'd worn in the video for our performance of 'Night Boat to Cairo'. Sure enough, when we arrived our dressing room was full of pith helmets and khaki army gear. We weren't too sure.

In the dressing room next to ours was Status Quo, so we went in to say hello. They were sitting about smoking extra-long roll-ups, in their white collarless shirts, brushed-denim waistcoats and flared jeans with an ironed crease. Some of us partook, they were really decent fellas. There was a knock at the door, and it was their dresser with their specially chosen stage clothes. She hung them up and took off the dry cleaning covers to reveal . . . white collarless shirts, brushed-denim waistcoats and flared jeans with a crease in them! It was with some hilarity that we re-entered our own dressing room.

We headed up to the BBC bar, normally reserved for BBC employees, but we'd made friends with the jovial Irish commissionaire, and he let us in. That was the upside of getting us to the Beeb so early, as we'd made ourselves honorary members of the subsidised bar.

A couple of rehearsals came and went as the day dragged on, until eventually we got our call to get ready for the show proper. Sonny had found us through much trial and error, because Television Centre was like a maze. The building was circular, and coming out of any door you were never quite sure whether to turn left or right.

Time was now tight, as we were due on set in twenty minutes. For all the messing around we liked Sonny and half appreciated what a stressful job she had, what with us on one side and a particularly prickly BBC producer on the other. We dutifully followed her out of the bar and down the corridor to the lift. The giant doors opened to reveal Hot Gossip, the dance troop that had taken over from Pan's People, and who once a week would interpret a song with a raunchy dance routine.

The lift was big but there were already seven of them in there, but none of us wanted to be left behind, especially with the chance of being squashed up to Cherry from Hot Gossip. We all piled in, and the lift went down, straight into the basement. Sonny reached over and frantically pressed the button again. Nothing. Lee started jumping up and down, and then we all did. Someone screamed 'Stop!' I think it was Sonny. We were stuck in there for quarter of an hour before someone from the technical department rescued us. We now had five minutes to get changed and on set.

Any qualms about looking like *Carry On Up the Khyber* extras had evaporated. Until we bundled, blinking into the stage lights, onto our stage. Opposite, The Specials were about to sing

'A Message to You Rudy', and on the other stage stood Dexys Midnight Runners, cool as you like in their *On the Waterfront* donkey jackets and black bobble hats.

Suddenly I wasn't feeling at my coolest, Status Quo's 'stage clothes' didn't seem quite so hilarious. It came our turn to perform and instead of playing from the spot we'd been designated, so the camera man knew where to find us, Lee leapt off the stage and into the audience, with the rest of the band following, and proceeded to conga round the studio. As Kid Jensen wound up the show, there was the inevitable sound of irate producer feet clanging down the metal stairs.

STOP MESSING ABOUT

We had left 2 Tone and signed to the legendary independent record label Stiff Records. 'If it ain't STIFF it ain't worth a fuck.' Although we'd been fêted by all the major labels, we'd gravitated to a company that cultivated good ideas, rather than palm trees in the lobby.

Stiff had been started by two inspired young chaps called Jake Riviera and Dave Robinson, fiery, determined and full of beans. The label was a home for all sorts of mavericks and eccentrics, and some great artists – Elvis Costello, Wreckless Eric, The Damned, Kirsty MacColl, The Pogues, Nick Lowe, our hero Ian Dury & the Blockheads. Artists the major labels were wary of, and had every right to be, and didn't know quite what to do with. Perfect, it felt like home straight away.

Dave had been interested in signing the band, but hadn't had a chance to get to a gig, so he invited us to play at his wedding. Not sure how pleased his missus was about that, but it was a great night, ending up with Elvis Costello and the rest of the Stiffites joining us in a conga round the dance floor. Dave liked what he saw and a week later we were agreeing a deal in the pub next door to Stiff Records in Westbourne Grove.

Stiff Records relocated from West London to the heart of

Maddyland, Bayham Street in Camden, the very street Charles Dickens lived in and of which he was so enamoured. Dave Robinson had had the vision to imagine how popular music videos were to become – you have to remember when we started making them there were very few places to show them. There was no MTV. *TOTP* would show one once a week. Otherwise there was nothing more than the occasional showing on Saturday morning kids' TV. Dave had an instinct we would get on in the medium. A correct one, because we'd been brought up on a diet of visual comedy: Tommy Cooper, Max Wall, Morecambe and Wise, Benny Hill.

And in his centre of operations in Camden, Dave invested in an old Steenbeck editing machine. It was fascinating when we had finished filming one or other of our ridiculous promos, watching the art of editing when it was still cutting and gluing rolls of film. The videos were very spontaneous. We'd sit around with Dave in a rehearsal room, throwing round ideas of varying preposterousness. Dave drew up a list and worked out which were actually feasible, then we'd go off in a van for a couple of days having the most fun imaginable. I wanted to fly like I was Superman going down Oxford Street, so I found myself hanging off the front of an open-top double-decker bus, with half the band hanging on to my legs and my torso hanging over the top. Superman Suggs.

We dropped a Morris Minor through a ceiling in the 'Driving in My Car' video, which involved Dave sawing through a rope on cue. I remember once Dave bought some footage of an advert he'd seen in France, of a van falling out of an aeroplane and then being parachuted to the ground. We were going to use it for one promo, 'Tomorrow's Just Another Day', I think, but it didn't fit in. Then suddenly we realised the next single was going to be 'Wings of a Dove', so we got this footage of the van falling, then we cut to us in the back of a Bedford van. We just shook the van about a bit and jiggled the camera around. Someone threw in a stuffed vulture and we made it look like we were falling through the air in the back of a van. It was all very DIY, and there were never any expensive effects, just a lot of imagination, and Dave was aware that we were extrovert and interesting blokes but with a short attention span. He had a knack of capturing that, and we never did anything more than twice. Mainly because we'd get bored and run off to do something else.

We had a lot of fun making the video for 'Night Boat to Cairo'. Tommy Cooper's fez appeared, but this time in the context of our version of some cod Egyptian stroke Moroccan place stroke somewhere in the Middle East attire. Not being particularly well travelled at this point, we plumped for somewhere in the middle.

We went to Berman's and Nathan's, whose floors and floors of the most extraordinary clothes from serious dramas included a whole floor of props and costumes from *Lawrence of Arabia*, so we got these very authentic pith helmets and khaki shorts and shirts.

Off we set to a sound studio in West London. Dave had gone to the enormous expense of spreading the floor with what must have been an inch of sand. There were two potted plants and Dave's dog running around, to add a bit of atmosphere. Instead of having back projection, which was what you usually did if you wanted an exotic background of any nature and clarity, we were using the new technology of blue screen. What we didn't realise was is that you need to keep the camera still, so what you see is the pyramids and sphinx all bobbing around to the music. But it added to the anarchic quality of the video.

When we'd finished ten or so videos, we had enough to compile a VHS called *Complete Madness*. Chris would go out and shoot intros to each song, and this particular one was in Clissold Park in the sandpit. Mike, the keyboard player, and Mark, our bass player, were pretending to be buried up to their necks, blowing out ping-pong balls. Of course. What else! Then we're straight into the song, with Lee playing the farting intro on baritone and someone wiggling a pot plant to make it look like it's being blown by the wind.

We also revisited 'The Nutty Train', which had been a symbol of our band for some time, and that iconic image you see on the cover of *One Step Beyond* taken by Cameron McVey. It happened by accident when we were walking down the street one day for a photo session, and they wanted us to be closer together than we were. It was pragmatism because there were a lot of us in the band to squeeze onto an album cover, so we all squashed up. We wanted a bit of motion in the photo, so we were actually walking past the camera, but of course it was tricky for the photographer to get us all in the middle. So we had to stand still but crouched, which made for very painful work on the thighs.

In 'Night Boat to Cairo' and a few of our videos I thought I'd jump off the top of a ladder, another hugely expensive prop. I'd land in the middle of the set and look like I'd just dropped out of space. I can't remember whose idea it was, but in the 'Night Boat' video we have the words on screen, with one of those jumping dots to help you sing along like in old kids' TV programmes. We were always speeding things up and slowing things down, like in a Benny Hill sketch, and on this particular occasion we slowed down the film and the music, then sped it back up, so it made for a very special effect that you can hardly notice.

The video ended with Dave's dog trying to bite people and us all falling about having had a few beers. It sums up the fun and exuberance we had in making the videos. People often ask me if we had as much fun as it looks, and we really did. Seven extroverts all fighting for the limelight, so any excuse to dress up and mess about. The costumes got more and more extreme until Lee turned up as an exploding traffic warden. If you're going to dress up and mess around, then make sure you dress up properly and mess around properly, don't just do it half-heartedly. It made for a sort of enlightening process sometimes. Transcending self-consciousness, if we ever had any.

When we made the video for 'Baggy Trousers' we actually filmed at a school in Islip Street in Kentish Town, close to where we were all hanging around at that time. Lee had had the idea of flying, I can't remember where from. It just so happened there was a building site across the road, and Dave Robinson asked them if we could borrow their crane for half an hour. We literally had a rope hanging from the crane attached to Lee's belt hoop. We swung him around in the air for a bit, and the extraordinary thing is that you can't see the rope in the video. But you can tell from watching it that we're all a bit nervous, looking up in case Lee falls on our heads.

We had this natural instinct for visual comedy. There was only so much time on the screen, and you wouldn't actually get on there unless you did something quite inspired. As soon as we were in a room with a camera it was, and still is, like spontaneous combustion of competition as we all tried to outdo each other. It makes for a very energetic atmosphere. And that's why the fun really does exude from those videos today.

TURNING JAPANESE

In 1983, when we were really at the peak of our success, we were asked by Honda, the Japanese car company, to go to Japan and make some adverts. We'd been to Japan and played there, and got a really good reaction, but I've got to say Japan is one of the most culturally different places I'd ever been to. It takes a bit of getting the hang of. People with white gloves gesture the lift doors open, even though they don't open them manually any more, or they gesture you up the escalator. Cab doors open automatically and because we were doing a commercial we had our every whim looked after. We each had about five people following us around at all times. Everyone being humble and deferential all the time was a bit of a culture shock.

It did get quite alienating. We'd been on the road for quite some time, and one night we all ended up in my or Cathal's room on the seventy-second floor, a vacuumed room that had no windows or doors that opened and in which everything was automatic. The whole room, including the bathroom, was made out of one piece of plastic. I remember looking down on a big park in the middle of Tokyo at eight in the morning and suddenly, on the dot, all these people would pour out of the subway and do an hour's tai chi and then disappear, like ants going down the drain, back into the subway.

Everything did seem so ordered and structured. Even the businessmen in the bar would head off to bed at exactly the same time, all wearing their blue suits. It all started to get very disorientating, and I remember I got a bit freaked out at one point.

And it was odd because making commercials was kind of frowned upon, certainly in England. It certainly wasn't a cool thing for a rock 'n' roll band to do. Obviously now we've had Johnny Rotten advertising butter, Iggy Pop selling car insurance, and some other idiot flogging fish fingers. But back then it was a bit like Bill Murray in *Lost in Translation*, lots of actors and musicians making uncool adverts in Japan and hoping the outside world would never see them and they'd be buried for ever. Of course the internet has messed all that up.

But we ended up having a lot of fun because of the extrovert way we were. Even to this day if you put the seven of us in a room and turn a camera on, I don't know what it is or what you call it, idiocy I suppose, but we're all leaping about and messing around. Like children in a sandpit. You could also call it fun.

I think we were due to make three or four commercials, and they had a few vague ideas about what they wanted us to do, but we didn't know what on earth they were talking about. Some of them were in full traditional kabuki costume and were asking us to do serious and symbolic things that we didn't really understand.

The production involved this huge chain of command. The pecking order was such that the director could only speak directly to the person below him, who could only speak to the person below him, so everything had to go through a chain of two dozen

people before it got to us. And vice versa, so if we wanted to make a suggestion it would take half an hour for that information to get back to the director. There was also the language barrier, which made communication even harder.

We filled up the time just mucking about as we would have done if we were making one of our videos. Whether it was leaping off ladders, or doing the old nutty train, which became a bit of a bane after a while because of the physical nature of it. Or squirting ketchup in people's faces, doing cod kung fu, hitting each other on the head with truncheons or dressing up as a pantomime horse. All the usual old carry-on.

They loved us in Japan and we ended up loving them too. There was this area called Harajuku where everyone dressed in all the phases of pop culture from the 1950s to now. They were all so authentic, so you had your Teddy boys, mods, punks and all the British tribal cultures replicated perfectly on this huge street in downtown Tokyo.

It's funny because although we'd traversed the world any number of times up to this point, the mad and ironic thing about touring with a band is that although you've been round the planet, you've actually seen very little of it. You arrive quite late in a city, play your gig, stay up a bit in the hotel bar, then you wake up quite late and it's time to move on to the next city because of the financial constraints of keeping your crew and equipment in any one place for too long. You have to stay on the move. So ironically, because of those adverts, we ended up knowing more about Japan than half of Europe.

It's been in the periods between working with the band that I've seen more of the world than I did on all those world tours.

TRIGGER
(HEADLINES)
5 KENTISH TOWN ROAD
LONDON NW1
TELEPHONE 01 267 9105

TWINS (ON COACH)

BRADBURY AND HALL
STAPLES AND GOLDING
BYERS AND BAMMERS
ROGERS AND PANTER
DAVIES AND COMPTON
ANDERSON AND BEMBRIDGE
BROWN AND HENDRIKSON
RICO AND DICK CUTHELL
McPHERSON AND THOMPSON
BARSON AND FOREMAN
WOODGATE AND BEDFORD
CARL SMITH AND A.N.OTHER
DUFFIELD AND HASLER

TWINS (OFF COACH)

OSCAR AND CHRIS CHRISTIE
TRUCK DRIVER AND WEBBER
AYRES AND SNELL
HEARTFORD AND ROB
CHALK AND COKINS
EVANS AND GRIFFITHS

SINGLES (ON COACH)

COACH DRIVER
D.JORDEN
S.ENGLISH
P.MURRAY
PAULINE BLACK
J.KALINOWSKI

RICK ROGERS
01 240 5257
(HOME NO)

JOHN T DE VR
01 326 9286
(HOME NO)

Rooming arrangements for
the 2 Tone tour

DATE: SUNDAY 27th. OCTOBER

VENUE: HATFIELD POLYTECHNIC
ADD: HATFIELD
          (MAIN HALL)
TEL:

EQUIPMENT GET IN BY 12.00NOON

SOUND CHECKS: SPECIALS: 4.30-5.30PM
               MADNESS: 5.45-6.45PM
               SELECTER: 7.00-8.00PM

DOORS OPEN: 8.00PM

PLAYING TIMES: SELECTER: 8.45-930PM
                MADNESS: 9.45- 10-30PM
                SPECIALS: 10.45- 11-45PM

VENUE CLOSES AT MIDNIGHT

HOTEL: CREST MOTEL
ADD.   SOUTH MIMMS
       POTTERS BAR
TEL: (0707) 43311

LIQUIDATOR STUDIOS

When our tenure at Stiff Records unfortunately came to an end we signed to Virgin Records. In the process of signing to Virgin we decided we wanted our own record label. It was a bit of vanity really. I think Paul Weller had his own label, obviously 2 Tone had been a great success under Jerry Dammers, and everyone else seemed to be having their own label too.

We didn't really know what we were going to put on it, which was the mad thing, and we also decided to build our own recording studio. There was some sense, we thought, to this because to record an album in those days cost about £30,000, and it cost about £30,000 to build a studio. I may not have got those figures entirely correct, but we thought that if we recorded more than one album in our own studio then it would have paid for itself. And then we could rent it out.

We found this rather charming building on the Caledonian Road and built Liquidator Studios. It went quite well at the beginning. We did some recording there, but then unfortunately Mike left the band and we began wondering why we were going to run a label if we didn't know who we were going to sign. The first person we made a record with was Feargal Sharkey. Cathal wrote a song called

'Listen To Your Father' and it was a hit. But being the young naïve chaps that we were, we hadn't exactly signed Feargal to a contract, so having had a first hit he just left and signed to a big American record label and we were back to square one.

Unfortunately this was all just at the point where technology was starting to move along, and the recording process was becoming simpler and the computer was starting to take over. We didn't realise how quickly the equipment we'd bought would become redundant. Also renting it out as a business proposition required hiring staff and paying wages. We were still hiring a permanent crew, even though the touring was starting to wind down as we all wanted to spend a bit more time with our young families.

We had our own fan club, which had, I think, thirty-odd thousand members, and of course this was when you had to do mail-outs. We were printing our own monthly magazine and *Nutty Boys* comic. It was the old Micawber syndrome of annual outgoing twenty pounds and six pence; annual income twenty pounds; net result misery.

You can't be top of the pops every day of your life, and there always comes a moment when you aren't as hot as you were. If we'd just taken some time off I think we could have put the pieces back together a bit quicker than we did, because by the time Mike left in 1984, the whole thing kind of collapsed. The studio, the record label and the band itself. It was depressing and I certainly didn't know what I was going to do next. It wasn't for another eight years that all seven of us would play again.

HOLLYWOOD

I've had a remarkable string of unsuccessful attempts at acting in movies. The first was while we were recording the album *Mad Not Mad* in 1985. It was a difficult period. We had been really successful for six years, the biggest-selling band of our time. But the schedule was relentless and we were very rarely at home.

Now we were getting tired, really tired, and probably should just have taken some time out. But we had emerged in an era when the record industry was still being run like it was in the sixties. We were expected to make one album a year, release at least three singles, and tour and promote for the rest of the year. There was a feeling that if you took your foot off the gas, even for a second, then the whole thing would run out of steam and disappear into oblivion. We had no idea, as later bands would discover, that it might be advantageous to have a break from each other and the business for a bit, to recharge the batteries. Reignite the inspiration and rediscover why we were making music in the first place.

But here we were in West Side Studios without Mike, one of our founding members, and preoccupied with trying to make an album, our last album as Madness and one that was different from the ones that had gone before. We had been constantly evolving and getting better as musicians. And even if we had wanted to, it would have been impossible to emulate the naïve enthusiasm of *One Step Beyond*, but having said that, the baby went out with the bath water on *Mad Not Mad*. Not to say there weren't some great songs, because there were, but there were also a heap of kitchen sinks and the whole thing had strayed off the track into the land of eighties pomposity.

A veritable army of session players had been assembled. In the middle of this chaotic process Clive and Alan had been asked by an old schoolmate of Clive's, Julien Temple, if they'd like to work on the soundtrack to a movie he was directing, an adaptation of Colin MacInnes's *Absolute Beginners*. It's a novel set in the late fifties about the beat generation, the story of a jazz-loving white kid caught up in the race riots in Notting Hill Gate. Clive and Allan were riding high at this point, having just produced Dexys' 'Come On Eileen', which was number one in America. I'd heard the demo on the sound system of Clive's newfangled VW Golf. The title at the time was 'James, Stan and Me', but it sounded great even then.

One afternoon, while we were putting down another layer of shrieking synths, or something, on *Mad Not Mad*, Clive asked if it would be OK if Julien Temple popped by to talk about the film. He duly arrived and we took a break while he chatted to Clive. After an hour or so Julien came into the recreation area where I was playing pool, and asked if we could go outside and have a chat. Somewhat confused, I agreed.

For some peculiar reason I remember that, after strolling aimlessly, we ended up in a graveyard round the back of Notting Hill. I don't know why, but there you are. After some preamble Julien asked me if I'd ever thought about acting. I told him no, because

I hadn't. Apart from the fact I'd hardly ever seen a decent performance from a pop star turned actor, I always thought it had a touch of the footballer turned pop star. I had a lot of actor friends, people who'd trained and put in the hours in the same way we had to become a half-decent band.

'Well, think about it,' said Julien. 'I think you'd be perfect for the lead part.' The lead part!? 'Look,' he said, 'in your videos you were acting; you weren't just singing the songs.' Which was partly true. But I said no, because to me it just felt too much like a bricklayer thinking he could plumb. But Julien was insistent. 'The character's your age, and look, it's set in the late fifties, you'll be dressed pretty much as you are anyway! Apart from which the story's great. Have a read of the book, think about it, and I'll give you a call next week.'

The recording sessions continued, percussionists, string quartets, backing singers came and went and finally *Mad Not Mad* was complete. Clive had accepted the job of producing the soundtrack to Julien's film and went straight back into the studio. The first exercise in the soundtrack was to record the theme written by David Bowie, 'Absolute Beginners,' which turned out great, and Clive and Mr Bowie became pals.

In fact I ended up staying in David Bowie's house with Clive once, in Gstaad, in the Swiss Alps. He invited us to go skiing with him. We turned up with our respective families in Clive's Range Rover, and there he was beckoning us up the driveway. 'It's David Bowie!' The garage doors swung open automatically, and Clive drove in. There was a huge crunching sound and before we realised the car was too big to fit, we were stuck halfway. Not only that but all our suitcases had been knocked off the roof rack, leaving our underwear blowing about Bowie's drive. Not the coolest start to meeting the coolest man in the world.

He was an absolute gent, I must say, and his son, Joe, was a charming young chap who it turned out was a big Madness fan. But it was hard, sitting opposite his old man throughout the evening, to not keep going, 'Shit! It's David Bowie.' It wasn't the first time I had met the great man. In the early eighties we were to support Bowie at the gigantic Anaheim Stadium in the US of A. Two hundred thousand people, it was by far the biggest audience we had played to. I made the mistake of travelling with Lee. He wanted to pick up a second-hand dinner jacket he'd spotted on Melrose Avenue.

Travelling with Lee more often than not ends up in an adventure of some sort, especially in his more light-fingered days. I don't know if he was trying to pinch it or what, but he was in the shop for ages. He finally re-emerged, leaving us half an hour before we were due on stage. The traffic was terrible and we arrived fifteen minutes late. Our manager of the time, Matthew, was pulling his hair out. David Bowie's enormous production was not going to alter its start time, so our time on stage was quickly evaporating. The rest of the band were on stage and already starting up the first chords of 'One Step Beyond' while I was still getting changed. Dressed, I legged down the tunnel and out onto the enormous stage. The stadium was huge, overwhelming. I felt like an ant.

A feeling I didn't have long to dwell on, as in my haste to get on stage I overshot the edge and started falling, Alice in Wonderland style. Twenty feet onto a scaffold pole, right onto my coccyx! With watering eyes and 'One Step' still blasting away overhead, I clambered back up the scaffolding to the stage above. I crawled up and on to the stage just in time for the song to end. The audience went wild, I think they thought it was a stage act! I could barely move. I was lucky I hadn't broken my back.

Anyway, back in the studio the soundtrack to *Absolute Beginners* was well under way. There were songs being written and recorded by Ray Davies and Paul Weller, and the film was being made by Palace Pictures, a successful English production house. It was gonna be a big deal. I'd completely forgotten about it when the receptionist called to say she had a Julien Temple on the phone. I had read and loved the book, all smoky jazz, Soho and exotic West London characters, but I still didn't feel ready to act. Julien was persistent. 'At the very least come down and meet the rest of the team.'

Palace Pictures had an office in Dean Street in Soho, right next to the French House. It was a lovely spring day and Soho was looking at its best. Mayfair looks like Mayfair whatever time of day or night you happen to be there, the same is true of most of the rest of London, but Soho has distinct patterns, its different micro-seasons changing through the day, and into the night.

My favourite bit is between two and four in the afternoon, in-between lunch and the end of work, before the office workers and tourist drinkers are piling about the streets. Mid-afternoon is a time for theatre actors, writers, directors, painters, club owners, nutters, etc., to while away a few hours in the company of like-minded souls, before the serious business of the night descends. The French is one of the few old-school Soho pubs where you can be guaranteed a decent conversation in the wee small hours of the afternoon.

So, it was with a certain feeling of conviviality that I strode up the stairs to their office on the third floor. It was explained to me that the film would be set in West London, and in and around Soho. It would include many of the things I love: the cosmopolitan nature of the place, the impossible-to-find-twice drinking dens, jazz and rhythm and blues. The whole film was like a prequel to the mod scene that would burst out of London in the sixties. There was clear enthusiasm for the project and my involvement in it, so I left agreeing to take a small screen test to see if: A, I liked it and B, more importantly, I could do it.

Two weeks later I was back in their offices, this time with the lead actress to act out one scene from the script. All the parts had been cast, except for the main character. Things were getting tight as filming was due to be under way in a matter of weeks. They filmed my little audition and I was nervous, but I felt I did OK. The dust had barely settled when it was announced, unbeknownst to me, that I was to meet the choreographer. Whereupon I was whisked to a dance studio near Gower Street. The film had a lot of dance sequences. The meeting, it turned out, was to be a dance audition.

I liked dancing but I certainly hadn't had any formal training. I was nervous and somewhat self-conscious when I entered the mirrored dance studio.

'OK,' said the Japanese choreographer, putting on a Modern Jazz Quartet record and squatting on his haunches. 'Just show me what you can do.' I looked round the room. The producer, director and a few assistants with clipboards were staring at me intently. 'See what I can do.' Right. I felt like I did as a fourteen-year-old when the lights came on at the end of a school disco. I was sweating. Sod it, I thought, in for a penny and all that. I went into a free-form routine, just skipping about and throwing shapes.

I'd been round the room a couple of times and I was starting to run out of ideas, but I kept going, spinning and starjumping. After what seemed an eternity he turned off the music.

'Yeah, yeah, like it. Great, but what I want you to do now is the same, some more leaping, but jump higher, higher, high as you can!' He became quite animated and started twirling and jumping around with his arms in the air. 'Just jump . . . jump! High as you can!' He gesticulated skyward. So I did, jumping and leaping round the room. Like we used to do at primary school, pretending to be wood sprites. 'Higher, higher!' he exhorted. What! I was going as high as I could. 'Come on, higher!' I took one last Valentinoesque leap and landed awkwardly on my big toe. I knew it wasn't good. It was obvious I'd done some damage. But the adrenalin kept me hobbling through a couple more routines and thankfully the session came to an end. He thanked me, the assistants politely applauded, and I limped out of the studio.

I rang Anne.

'How did it go?'

'Mmm, not great.'

'Where are you?'

'In a call box'

'Where?'

'The Middlesex Hospital.' My whole foot was in plaster. I'd broken my big toe. Fate had taken a decisive and sympathetic hand in allaying my fears about acting, and the film rolled on without me.

By the time I was offered a part in *The Tall Guy*, I'd done a few bits of acting in *Press Gang* and *The Final Frame* and found that I enjoyed it. The film was written by Richard Curtis and was to star Jeff Goldblum and Emma Thompson. In fact I'd done a bit with Richard before, because he and Ben Elton had written a TV series for Madness – it seemed like a great idea at the time, that Madness would become the surreal and slightly darker descendants of The Monkees. The plot revolved around the idea that Margaret Thatcher had been discovered to be a Martian and had been returned to her home planet. In a snap election the band had been voted in on the premise that we would give free sweets to kids and beer to adults.

Not a bad manifesto, eh? I was to play the Prime Minister and the rest of the band the Cabinet. It was very funny, and in fact recently I found some scripts and discovered that a few of the sketches went on to crop up in later episodes of *The Young Ones*, which we'd already appeared in. 'You hum it, I'll smash your face in.' And, bizarrely, some beer commercial.

Unfortunately the BBC, in their great wisdom, decided it would be fine to film the pilot in a café in Camden. Not exactly the House of Commons. It was great fun to film and it turned out well, but the Good Fair Café was a rather difficult location to try and engender the majesty of Parliament. Funny as it was, it was deemed by the

BBC as too expensive to replicate Westminster for a funny old band from Camden Town.

The script for *The Tall Guy* duly arrived. It was to be directed by Mel Smith and was about a comedian living in Camden Town. I was excited and when I found my part, it read: 'Suggs sings "It Must Be Love" and is duly blown up!' It was to become a theme.

My next brush with Hollywood came some years later. I got a call asking whether I would like to write the theme tune for a Hollywood blockbuster starring Sean Connery, Ralph Fiennes and Uma Thurman. What! This was an out-of-the-box winner. Getting a song into a film like that would virtually guarantee me a worldwide hit. A whole new career opened up in front of me – writing music for films.

I came up with a lovely up-tempo ska number with a dynamic brass section called 'I Am A Man'. I wrote my Grammy acceptance speech and booked myself in to have all my teeth capped. In the cinema I was surprised not to hear my song played over the opening sequence. As the final credits rolled in the now empty cinema I did hear it. Albeit for ten seconds. Until it was drowned out by the cleaner, hoovering round my feet.

Still, *The Avengers* garnered a whole plethora of nominations and one major award . . . at the 19th Golden Raspberries – it picked up the trophy for Worst Remake or Sequel, and nominations for: Worst Picture; Worst Director; Worst Actor (Ralph Fiennes); Worst Actress (Uma Thurman); Worst Screen Couple (Ralph Fiennes and Uma Thurman); Worst Supporting Actor (Sean Connery); Worst Screenplay. In the end, never mind the big hit, I was just happy to come out of it unmentioned.

I was just about to give up on Hollywood when finally the perfect job came along. My agent rang.

'Do you fancy doing some acting? Starring in *The Edge of Love*, a romantic movie set in the Blitz with Sienna Miller and Keira Knightley?'

Any reticence about acting evaporated. 'What? Do I? Course I do.'

'I'll send you the script and you can have a read before you say yes.'

'Yes, I'll have a read of the script. Just tell them yes.'

They wanted me to play Al Bowlly, the legendary forties crooner. I'd get to act and sing with the delightful Misses Miller and Knightley. This was it. This is the big one. Forget *The Tall Guy*. Forget *The Avengers*. This is the real deal. Maybe there'd even be a scene where the gorgeous Miss Miller succumbs to the irresistible charms of the suave, well-dressed lounge singer. Maybe they both do! Picture the scene. The focus softens as all three move to the boudoir . . .

Well, you can imagine the eagerness with which I ploughed through the script trying to find my, er, bit . . . Ah! Here it is:

'Al Bowlly steps on stage at the Café de Paris and sings "Hang Out The Stars In . . ." A bomb drops through the roof killing everyone.'

REDIFFUSION

I kind of fell into TV completely by chance. I was in the process of making this solo record and I got a call asking me to host a music show for a newfangled broadcaster. Who could have known how big satellite broadcasting was going to become? At the time there were two fierce rivals, Sky TV and British Satellite Broadcasting. Sky TV, as we all know, is now a household name. Well, you can guess which one I was on the phone to. But BSB, as it was known, had a secret weapon in the technological race to dominate the airwaves. Yes! The Squarial! Who can forget it? Who wouldn't want a piece of that space-age bling on their roofs? Well, as it turned out, not many.

The show was really good fun. It mainly showed videos, but I also had guests on. I remember sometimes I'd get some young bands that I knew so little about that I'd actually swap chairs and make them interview me. But one night I did have Anthony Wilson, George Best and Mark E. Smith on, and we all just took the crew down the pub. I was in the managing director's office when the first three weeks' audience viewing figures came in. Four.

Literally four people watching it at any given moment. I once left my chair empty for ten minutes to see if anyone noticed.

Nobody did. But knowing that no one was watching did give me the advantage of being able to learn how to become a television presenter, and a certain freedom which I took hold of.

By that time I had been called up by Channel 5 – someone there had seen the programme, God knows how. 'We need somebody to guide us through the intricacies of later Victorian steam engine restoration, someone who's going to appeal to the front-room engineer and geek.' I know, the singer of Madness! It seemed a strange casting choice, going from a TV music show to hosting a programme which involved me standing in a field, wielding a giant rusty spanner, enthusing about the restoration of a broken-down combine harvester. I couldn't even put up a shelf!

But perversely I started to enjoy it. I met some very interesting characters, went to a lot of interesting places, but it was sad to see the demise of so much of the great British days of engineering. The last spring-makers, the last boiler-makers, indeed the last manufacturers of hovercrafts.

My next TV job – talk about the sublime to the ridiculous, or vice versa – was a Saturday night show called *Night Fever*, which was basically a karaoke show where the audience was divided between the boys and the girls. And blimey, even that simple device had everyone screaming like lunatics.

There were two teams of five 'celebrities', again boys versus girls, soap-opera actors, pop stars, people from various TV shows, and the idea was that you would see people singing who you wouldn't imagine could sing, and some who couldn't. There was a competition, in which I awarded points according to a fairly spurious system, helped along by the Pop Monkey, the unforgettable Pop Monkey. Every week we'd have a band of some sort or another, but sometimes it was a bit of a struggle.

I remember one time we got The Three Tops, another time we managed to get one Weathergirl, as the other one had got stuck in a shopping trolley. She'd been pushed in one down the corridor by the producer and couldn't get out again. We also had the last surviving Drifter.

But who could forget Bernie Clifton? Yes, Bernie turned up one time, you know, the fella riding the out-of-control ostrich, with his pretend legs flying around. Well, Bernie turned up to the studio in a car on his own. The producer said, "'Ere, Bernie, where's the ostrich?' Bernie said, 'Oh, that? The ostrich? I've moved on, that's my old act, I don't do that any more, I'm more stand-up, these days.' The producer said, 'Bernie, I booked you and an ostrich. No ostrich, no fucking fee.' Well, Bernie looked up, defiant for a second, before saying, 'All right, I'll go and get him out of the boot.'

It was an enormous amount of fun, *Night Fever*, and we ended up on a beach in Malaga. Wave your Magalufers! The only slight technical hitch was that, as it was a karaoke show, people had to be able to read the words to be able to sing along, but LED screens don't function very successfully in broad sunlight, so we ended up having a karaoke show in which people just made the words up as they went along. This wasn't too much of a problem as the show was recorded at midday, just as 2,000 kids were tipping out onto the beach from an all night rave-up.

The great tragedy was, the last thing we heard was that the next series was going to be shot in Costa Rica, on the beach, between the rum and the cigar factories. As is the way with these things, Channel 5 was taken over by a new director, and he had other ideas, and the show was dropped. But they were great days, happy, ridiculous days.

THINGS THAT GO BANG IN THE NIGHT

I met The Farm through an old pal of mine from Liverpool called Kevin, in the twilight of the Liquidator Studios, and at a point in my life when I really didn't know what I was going to do next. And in walked this gang of Scousers wearing these tweed jackets and deerstalker hats and a variety of trainers very rarely seen in this country that had been 'acquired' in various trips around Europe with Liverpool Football Club. I liked them immediately; their swagger and style reminded me a bit of ourselves when we were younger, and they had some great songs.

They were good lads; they were a laugh. I helped them record a song called 'Hearts and Minds' which John Peel cottoned on to. And they also produced a football fanzine called *The End*, which was hilarious, it was a kind of precursor to *Viz*. An amazing sense of humour, ahead of its time, extracting ruthless fun from the pretentions of what was going to become the Premier League. Great cartoons and great writing.

I kept in touch with them over the years and then they came into a bit of money in Liverpool and started an independent record label called Produce. They remembered some work I'd done with

My idea for a 'Shit Joke' series. Unfortunately *The End* had already come to an end at this point

them previously, and with the demise of my own band I was very happy to give them a bit of advice.

The idea of being in a studio with a band, and working on their music, seemed to be a bit of light relief from the intensity of the last few years. So I helped them produce the album *Spartacus*, which included the big hit 'All Together Now'. Things were going really well for the band. They had another hit with 'Groovy Train', which, along with their first success 'Stepping Stone', made it three hits in a row as well as a number one album.

The success culminated in their being offered a tour of America with Big Audio Dynamite. The tour was to start with a five-night residency at a big club in New York. I went there with the editor of

Loaded, James Brown, just at the time that all that laddish stuff was becoming popular. Having been anathema for years football was becoming vaguely trendy. Up to that point you'd be embarrassed to mention you were a football fan in certain circles. At dinner parties, people would drop their knives and forks, fall backwards off their chairs.

The first night The Farm were going down great. I was standing at the back of the hall and the gig was going brilliantly. There was ecstasy . . . in the air. Let's just say we were all having a bit too much fun, when the headline act, BAD, came on, I found myself dancing on the mixing desk in my socks making what I thought were crucial adjustments to the sound. I was just trying to get a bit more out of the bottom end when I lost my footing and the faders shot to max. There was an almighty bang and we were plunged into silence, which obviously no one was particularly pleased about. All this while Kevin, who was the co-manager of The Farm, stood beside me, lobbing the contents of the complimentary backstage fruit basket at the headline act. The following night when we turned up, we were rather flattered to find photographs of ourselves pinned to the stage door, and I thought, Aye aye, no need for backstage passes, here, Kev, in we go! But we were somewhat shocked to be manhandled out of the entrance to the club by two bouncers, and told that we weren't welcome. We'd been banned from our own gig. The writing was on the wall. It was at that precise moment that I realised I might not really be cut out for management.

We had a bit of a night of it, drowned our sorrows, let's put it that way. Next morning Kevin announced, as we sat red-eyed in someone or other's room, that he remembered we had an appointment to go and see an executive from a big American record label who'd suddenly shown a bit of interest in the band. I said, 'Look, I'm just done in, I can't go, you'll have to go on your own'.

Kevin disappeared for an hour and a half and came back looking quite dishevelled, with a hat on the side of his head. I said, 'How did it go?' He said, 'Yeah, I think it went brilliantly . . . but sort of twenty minutes into the conversation the record company executive turned into a giant clucking chicken, and I couldn't understand what he was saying, and the worst bit of it is, he offered The Farm a deal, but I can't remember if he offered us $100,000 or $1 million.'

I sat up. 'Kevin, even in my current state I know there's a huge amount of difference between 100,000 and a million.' He said, 'Well, what do you think I should do? Do you think I should ring him up?' I said, 'Of course not. What do you think'll happen if you ring up and go was that a 100,000 or was that a million?!!' To their great fortune it turned out it was a million, but at that point I'd already decided that my managing days were over. I really needed to get back into making music again, up there amongst the flying fruit.

Which I did with the help of Mike Barson and the legendary producers Sly and Robbie. I had a big hit at this time with the Simon and Garfunkel song 'Cecilia' and on *Top of the Pops* I was introduced by the guest presenter, the world champion boxer Chris Eubank, who looked nervously into the autocue before uttering the immortal lines, 'It'th the thenthational Thuggth, at number thixth, with "Thethilia"!'

CELERY

It was the 1997 FA Cup Final and we were off to Wembley up against Middlesbrough to try and win the cup that had not graced the trophy cabinet at Stamford Bridge for thirty years. Barbara Charone, the legendary press officer at WEA, was a huge Chelsea fan and had suggested I record a song for it. This was part of a long tradition of Cup Final singles in this country, 90 per cent of them shite. They usually involved an embarrassed-looking team, bedecked in some hideous identical suits, tunelessly shouting some terrible song that sounded like it had been written five minutes before they'd entered the *Top of the Pops* recording studio.

But a song had landed on Barbara's desk called 'Blue Day', written by a chap called Mike Canaris. Barbara wasn't easily impressed, but she was excited as I sat in her office and put the CD on. I was surprised. It really was good and the first line was spot on: 'The only place to be every other Saturday, is strolling down the Fulham Road, meet your mates, have a drink, have a moan and start to think, will there ever be a blue tomorrow . . .'

Having a moan is exactly what we'd been doing for the last twenty-odd years and this wasn't the sort of line you'd get in the average bowl of clichés that made up most football songs. 'We've waited so long but we'll wait for ever . . . and when we make it, it will be together . . .' Yeah, very good, and it had a huge rousing chorus. The song ended and we both sat there smiling.

Heading for the studio I was still nervous, as the last Cup Final song, 'Blue Is the Colour', from the 1970 squad, was an exception to the rule. It was a good song with a good melody and had stood the test of time. Unlike most novelty songs it was still popular, and played at every home game as the team came out. It had almost religious connotations, as it was a reminder of our ancient, glorious past. But here we were on the cusp of glory and finally on our way to Wembley after all these years.

Mike had the arrangement all ready to go and we recorded my vocal quite quickly. The song suited my voice and the track was sounding good. We then took the tapes to a big studio in West London for the icing on the cake, which was getting the team themselves to holler along with the chorus. The team bus turned up and a really great bunch of characters piled out: Vialli, Zola, Dennis Wise, Mark Hughes, etc. Legends all.

There was a real feeling of fun and camaraderie in the room. The Italians were a bit bemused at first, as there was no tradition of this kind of carry-on in Italy, where it all tended to be about being cool. But Dennis soon got everyone going. Vialli played the piano and Wisey was reading out the lyrics and giving English lessons to some of the less confident English speakers, lessons that up to this point had mostly involved swearing. The day went well and we were all jolly satisfied with the result. We made a video clowning about down at their training ground, and if you look very closely there's one scene of me nutmegging Mark Hughes. Which I have done quite a number of times! The record came out, was well received,

SUGGS
AND THE
CHELSEA TEAM

BLUE DAY
Get The Cup Final Song Here!

and it started to move up the charts. It became a hit and reached number 22.

The night before the final I put 300 quid and my ticket in a jacket and hid it in the airing cupboard, I don't know why but it was just paranoia, I guess, that it would get lost or robbed. I woke up early the following morning, grabbed the jacket and its precious cargo, and headed out. The sun was shining, and at the end of the road a milk float went past, covered in Chelsea flags and parping its weedy electric horn. Life could not have been better.

I was off to meet some pals at Vauxhall vegetable market, where the bus had been booked to meet us and take us to the hallowed turf of Wembley. The Lays were three brothers, John, Steve and Alfie, all lifelong Blues fans. Alfie was a very funny and generous man with a great family. His dad was called Alfie and his son, Alfie Junior, went to the same school as my daughters.

As my cab headed south more and more blue and white began to adorn the streets, with flags, bunting and scarves hanging out of hooting car windows. The cab pulled into the market and I was greeted by a sight that could have come straight out of *South Pacific*. The Lays and all their mates were standing about in Hawaiian shirts, with flower garlands, on a small desert island made from two tons of sand that Alf had had delivered that morning. On the shoreline, a twenty-piece calypso band was playing 'Blue Is The Colour' on steel drums. A huge barbecue was smoking away and all and sundry were happily sipping exotic-looking cocktails. What a sight for sore eyes!

It was eight thirty in the morning. The Lays worked by night, as that's when the market did its business, so this was the end of a hard day's work. This was evening for the boys. The open-top bus duly arrived and we piled on, merry as the month of May. We were waved off by wives and girlfriends like soldiers going to war. Which is sort of how it felt. Two years earlier we'd got to the Cup Final after a wait of twenty-seven years, only to be humiliated 4–0 by Manchester United.

But this time it was all going to be different; this time we would return from the war victorious with silver treasure. The bus was loaded up and because there wasn't supposed to be any booze on board, it was filled with innocuous-looking plastic containers of fruit juice. The driver asked if he could have a sip. 'That's nice,' he said. 'I'll have another of them.' Alfie thought best not, and someone tried to find him a bottle of water.

I took my place on the top deck. Foghorns blared and the old diesel engine roared into life, but as the bus ground into first gear and lurched forward there was a shriek from below. Someone had fallen off the back of the top deck! We all rushed up the back and looked down, and fortunately the fella had landed in the sand. So, to the sympathetic cry of 'Grab his ticket and let's get going', we headed west.

There can be no finer feeling than riding the top deck of an open-top bus to a Cup Final. Even the hardest faces have to crack a smile. Kids up the front were as happy as dogs. The tinfoil FA Cup was aloft, ribbons blowing in the wind. Every kid worth his salt has dreamt of being the captain of the cup-winning side, waving that century-old trophy at the hordes of beaming fans below on a victory parade up the high street.

Every other pub we passed had a huge gathering of fans outside, all waving and cheering, even though they'd have given their right arms to have seen any one of us fall off and get our ticket. But we were the chosen ones, the ones to represent our club at Wembley, the twelfth man. And the people on the street knew that, and were empowering us on their behalf as they screamed and shouted outside their various pubs, to cheer the Blue boys on to victory.

The traffic crawled but that was all part of the fun. Waving and singing at the crowds walking alongside as the famous twin towers peeped over the horizon. The bus pulled up in a car park as near as it could to Wembley, and we all hopped off into the chaotic throng. But unbeknownst to the rest of us, in the confusion big Paul (a strawberry wholesaler) and his son had got off the bus straight into a minor altercation with some Middlesbrough fans, and had been carted off!

The atmosphere around the stadium was pure joy, with people I hadn't seen for years passing left, right and centre. The Old Bill was searching people for celery, that dangerous and offensive weapon. The only offensive thing about the celery was the song it alluded to:

> *Celery. Celery.*
> *If she don't come,*
> *Then tickle her bum,*
> *With a stick of celery.*

This song, which had lain dormant for twenty-seven years, reappeared spontaneously like a great natural wonder. The celery was being confiscated at the behest of the TV bods, who didn't want any of that ribald old nonsense coming out of their broadcast on a Saturday afternoon, thank you very much.

I got split from the others, as my seat was in another part of the ground. On my way I bumped into some chaps I'd seen at the Bridge before. People you'd only see at football and whose names you often don't even know. They were headed for the Wembley hotel for a glass of champagne, which sounded jolly civilised, so I tagged along.

The hotel bar was rowdy, with a big group of touts at one end, flashing their ill-gotten gains. Cup Final day was a big payday. Everyone was shouting and the place was packed. I went to the toilet and when I came back out the bar in front of me had cleared.

A bottle flew past my nose, shit, and then another in the opposite direction. A fight had ensued, involving rival touts, who were now at opposite ends of the bar lobbing bottles at each other.

I stepped back into the toilet only to be nearly knocked over by the rugby player Brian Moore bursting through the door. I then spent one of the more bizarre ten minutes of my life locked in a toilet cubicle with an international rugby player. Still, if you wanted someone on your side in a situation like this I couldn't think of any better. We stood in silence until the noise outside subsided, before we peeked round the corner to see if the coast was clear. It was. Brian and I shook hands and went our separate ways.

The conviviality of the bar returned as if nothing had happened. I couldn't see my mates, so I bought one of the few bottles of wine that hadn't been thrown across the bar, and headed for my seat.

I snuck the bottle into my pocket, slipped past the celery police and found my spot. I had a good view. There was a young fella to my left who'd had a nice few, and on my right a young girl with her dad. Behind me was an old bird who was shrieking right in my ear: 'Come on, you Blues!' It was still ten minutes to kick-off. The game started and the girl next to me stood on her seat and kept lookout while I took a swig from my bottle.

Ninety minutes and two goals later, and there we are, it was over, we'd won. We'd won the FA Cup! I stood on my seat to get a better look at the team running down the pitch in a long line, arm in arm, and diving on the turf in front of the goal. When suddenly 'The only place to be every other Saturday . . .' the first line of 'Blue Day', burst out of the Tannoy system. I couldn't believe my ears, and things had now gone way beyond surreal. I looked round and the place was going ballistic.

The little girl next to me was too young to know who I was,

but the old bird behind me wasn't. She leapt on my back and shouted, 'You helped us to win this!' My seat collapsed and we both tumbled forward. They proceeded to play 'Blue Day' and 'Blue Is the Colour', back to back, three times in a row. Until there was no one in the ground but Chelsea. I can't really describe the feeling but I had now, in some small way, played a part in something which had played such a big part in my life, Chelsea Football Club.

We all got back on the bus, piled upstairs and headed back into town. The pub on the Fulham Road went bananas when we walked in. Chelsea had won the war and we were the living, breathing representation from the front line, witnesses to prove that it had really happened. Short of the team coming through the doors with the cup themselves, it couldn't have been more joyous. We stood on the bar, careful to avoid the ceiling fan at one end, and we sang songs long into the night. At closing time me and Alf sat on the steps of the pub, and there was nothing more to say. I was tired, it had been a long day, but it was one of them days you just didn't want to end. Alf was completely knackered and drained too.

A couple of weeks later I got a call from Alf and we got chatting about what a great day it had been. The Lays don't do things by halves. Then Alf said that unfortunately Big Paul and his son were being done for affray, and he wondered if there was any way I could see myself writing Paul a character reference. Of course, no problem.

I set about writing what a straight, hard-working chap Paul was, and how long I'd known him, etc. Which was all true. I finished it off with a résumé of my career in the entertainment business, and explained that I was not writing this lightly, given the importance of reputation within the industry.

I didn't see Alf till the start of the following season. We were standing outside Finch's on the Fulham Road, chatting and moaning as usual. 'Oh, by the way, how did Big Paul's case go?' I asked.

'Not too good.'

'What, did he not get my character reference?'

'Oh yeah, halfway through the case the prosecuting barrister pulled it out and said: "Ah yes, Graham McPherson, aka Suggs. I remember this gentleman's band. Madness, wasn't it? Yes, they played at my college when I was studying for the bar, and their fans smashed the place up!"' Hmmm.

TELLY HOST SUGGS GOES NUTS

Partying at London rock hangout the St. Moritz Club, Cobalt says: "We fell out because we were seeing too much of each other."

★ EIGHTIES chart-topper Suggs shocked thousands of viewers by wrecking a telly studio as his late night show was scrapped.

The 30-year-old Madness veteran, who now manages Liverpool rave band The Farm, went on the emotional rampage at the end of Suggs on Saturday, his show on BSkyB.

Suggs, whose million-selling band styled themselves The Nutty Boys, ripped through the backdrop and ran around kicking over furniture.

And while the presenter — real name Graham McPherson — ran

wild and performed his Nutty dance. Even cameramen joined in.

But last night Palace Music Channel, which managed the show, denied that Suggs was drunk.

"He just decided to get rid of the set," said a spokesman.

"Everybody was having a bit of a party because it was the end of the show."

The show was axed as telly bosses pulled the plug on The Power Station.

WILDMAN: Suggs

SPLASH REPORTERS: Julia Kuttner and Alix Sharkey

SKA

I first heard 'One Step Beyond' with Chalky in a pool hall in Tottenham Court Road. It sounded like it had come from outer space via a smoky club in downtown Kingston. Smooth and smoky, but busting with character, it was the B-side of Prince Buster's legendary 'Al Capone', which ironically would inform The Specials' first single 'Gangsters'. The music had always been an integral part of British culture, and ska/rocksteady/reggae tracks would show up regularly amongst the other pop hits like 'My Boy Lollipop', and Prince Buster and The Skatalites in the sixties, and in the seventies the likes of Desmond Dekker, Jimmy Cliff, The Upsetters, Dave and Ansell Collins and Johnny Nash. Althea and Donna, 'Conscious Man', were often one-hit wonders from the Trojan label or ones that had made it onto the radio in Britain from established Jamaican artists. And of course Bob Marley, who with Lee Perry was pushing the boundaries. Marley's appearance on *The Old Grey Whistle Test*, with his budding dreads and Peter Tosh in his bug-eye glasses, performing 'Concrete Jungle', was the talk of the playground in my school days.

I started collecting relatively obscure Blue Beat records in the mid seventies. There was a great stall in Berwick Street market which had a good selection of Jazz, R&B and Blue Beat singles (at 10p a pop). At first I bought a couple out of curiosity. Of course, had I been around a few years earlier I would've been able to walk into Soho's mod clubs like the Scene or the Flamingo, not more than a few yards away, and heard this kind of music every night!

Anyway, by the time I was about seventeen my collection of Blue Beat and old reggae singles had grown to a couple of hundred, and a fair proportion of these 45s were by Prince Buster, including one called 'Madness'. I really liked the song, and I remember I had it for some peculiar reason when I went into the punk clothes shop, Boy, in the King's Road, and I was explaining to the owner that we were starting a band.

He said: 'What sort of music are you going to play?' so I said: 'This kind of music.' And he put the single on – it had a lot of brass, and a kind of swing, although it was ska. He said: 'Jesus, this sounds like the Glenn Miller Orchestra,' which it did compared with the thrashing punk that was coming out of his record collection.

I finally got the chance to go to Jamaica in the early nineties, to present a documentary for Radio Four called *The Story of Ska*. I was very excited because the music had always seemed mysterious and unattainable to me. It was researched and commissioned by Sarah-Jane Griffiths and I was about to go on an amazing, once in a lifetime, adventure. Prince Buster, Count Matchuki, Duke Reid, Clint Eastwood – these were names inspired by Wild West films and gangster movies, and here was the chance to unravel some of those mysteries. Everyone wants to go somewhere exotic when they're a kid, escape from the humdrum to Hollywood or the hippy trail, but for me and my mates it was Orange Street in Kingston Town, home of Jamaican music.

In the last forty years Jamaica has produced more records per head of population than any other country in the world. And for such a small island it has had a massive impact on music around the world. Including a small corner of North London. We got our name Madness from a Prince Buster song. 'One Step Beyond', the title track from our first album, was a cover of another of his tracks. And our first hit, on 2 Tone records, was a homage to the man himself: 'The Prince', which includes the line 'Even if I kept on running, I'd never get to Orange Street.'

Well, I did get there. I found myself standing in Orange Street, the music street, right outside Prince Buster's record shack. But my twenty-year wait had been in vain. The signs were still there, but the shop was shut, as were most of the other record emporiums in the street. It was all just clothes and wholesale food stores. In the sixties and seventies, the street would have been booming with music. Competing sound-system owners had their own shops to sell the records that they were making themselves, the tunes they had tried and tested, and were kicking up a storm at their own dances.

Finally made it to Orange Street. Unfortunately Prince Buster had already vacated it

The sound systems were basically giant mobile discos. Prince Buster had his 'Voice of the People' system, and there was Vincent Edwards' 'King Edwards' Giant', Duke Reid's 'Trojan Sound' and, most famous of all, Sir Coxsone Dodd's 'Downbeat System'.

Duke Reid was the pioneer. A fearless ex-policeman, who notoriously never shied away from trouble on hot Saturday nights in downtown Kingston, he was a renowned crack shot, something that would stand him in good stead when rivalries between the competing sound systems got violent. In the mid-fifties it was normal for shop and bar owners to have a bit of music playing to attract customers. Duke took it a stage further, rigging up a speaker outside his liquor shop attached to a 78 rpm record player inside. The Duke had a winning combination: booze, and by now a good collection of American R & B records. He decided to take this heady mix out on the road to the evening dancers.

He found the biggest speakers he could find and loaded them into the back of his slow, but hardy 'Trojan van'. Which ironically was made in Croydon! As the van approached excited fans would holler: 'Here comes the Trojan!' The 'Trojan Sound System' was born. The sound systems would compete, playing obscure records that would really get the crowd going in order to 'flop' or 'kill' their rivals. Or simply just blast them out with a bigger and louder system. Bass speakers would be put in old fridges to make them boom, speakers would be hung in the trees to broadcast the sound as far as possible. The competition was fierce. Better, louder music meant more customers, more customers meant more money.

Prince Buster was originally employed by The Duke as a bit of muscle, as the Prince was an accomplished boxer. He then went on to work for Sir Coxsone before starting his own 'Voice of the People System' in 1960. No one was more 'from the people, for the people' than Buster, born and bred in the ghetto. He took pride in his impoverished roots.

Clement Seymour Dodd, like a lot of young Jamaican men of the day, had been taking seasonal work in the USA cutting cane, and supplemented his meagre cane-cutting wages by bringing back a huge pile of the latest R & B 78s. And in 1954 Clement Dodd launched his own sound, 'Sir Coxsone the Downbeat'.

I turned up at Coxsone's Studio One complex, known as the Jamaican Motown, just as the heat of the day was rising. It was an intimidating-looking place surrounded by a huge barbed-wire fence. Our presence was noted by a fella at the gates and we were told he would inform Sir Coxsone of our presence. Half an hour later, with us standing in the baking heat of the day, we were informed that the interview could not take place. Coxsone was worried, we were told by an American attorney who looked like Cab Calloway, that we were in some way involved with an American label that Coxsone was in litigation with. We made assurances that we were from the BBC in England, and following confirmation from a couple of experts that our accents were indeed British, oh, and 200 American dollars in cash, an audience was granted.

Who exactly invented ska music is still a matter of some debate. That Coxsone Dodd was there, or thereabouts, is in no doubt. We sat in his office and it was dark, the only light coming through a crack in the office door. He poured me a glass of rum with a splash of fresh lime, and put his feet on a desk that was piled with twelve-inch records, with that unmistakable Studio One label. He took a big draw.

'Coxsone, what do you remember of the early days of ska music?'

He exhaled, and a huge plume of blue smoke whirled in the beam of sunlight coming through the door. 'The sound system days was the great days, it started from the playing of American music. Then came along the rock and roll, but the rock and roll wasn't steady. It had too much rock in it, y'know, and not enough roll,' he said with a laugh.

'So we decided to record songs within the feel of what we would dance to, and it came over good. Well, after being in the business for a number of years, until somewhere around 1959 we came up with a very strong danceable beat. To really get the riff going strong, the band are playing and I'm saying yeah, keep the ska going strong, ska-ska-ska, yeah, that's it!' Ernest Ranglin, the great Jamaican jazz guitarist, who also played with the Wailers amongst many others, said the word 'ska' came from the 'Skat! Skat!' sound of the chopped guitar on those early recordings.

'It was real fun because that night in the local bar, all the guys in there were already going, yes, ska, ska, ska-groovy. With the sound system, at that time, that was the only means of promoting the local recorded stuff. The radio station was still playing Patti and Pete's "Doggie in the Window" and stuff like that. They didn't want to know about our stuff. Until when the music broke in Europe, then they realise that they are sitting on a monster.'

'How many people might turn up at your sound system in those times?'

'Maybe about five, six hundred at a small dance, but when we have a big party it would be a lot you know, thousands. What made it so interesting and for you as a sound system owner, we were treated like the Prime Minister at that time. As a matter of fact when I went away to seek American records to play locally, I think I was the first person who ever had a motorcade to meet me at the airport. Me standing in the back of the open-top car, hands in the air. Timely playing music and the occasional gunshot, and the people on that side as we drove past would realise there was going to be a big, big dance that night and the attendance would boom!'

Chris Blackwell was a young man living in Jamaica at the time, and would go on to be one of the greatest promoters of the music through his Island Records.

'I first remember the checking sound systems from about the late fifties, so I'm sure they were running from before that. It was really a street world, it wasn't a world where some white Jamaican would be hanging out. So I was a bit of an oddity there.'

I asked him whether he could remember the atmosphere of those early dances.

'Yes, it was not unlike they are today. If you drive through a town and there's a sound system dance the whole street is alive, the whole town is alive. But of course in the early days the excitement was electric, as this was the first time the people had heard Jamaican music amplified. These records were Jamaica. Ska in Jamaica. Remember that this is probably the only music that emerged from a studio. Most music emerges from clubs or coffee bars, but this music all rose out of the studio. The reason, I think, was because people didn't have money for instruments, so the musicians that would play on all these records were all jazz musicians and some of them were really great jazz musicians, like Ernest Ranglin, Don Drummond, Roland Alphonso.

'I would go to New York to buy the latest tracks from New Orleans, people like Smiley Lewis, Fats Domino, music with a shuffle that went down well with a Jamaican audience, music that already had some of that off beat that Jamaican artists would eventually accentuate and turn into ska. I would come back and scratch the label off so no one knew what the track was to find another copy and sell it to the sound systems. The ska sound was onomatopoeic, it was literally the sound of the guitar and the right hand of the piano emphasising that off beat, ska, ska, ska. Coxsone was the first I really remember getting that groove. I was trying to make records that sounded like the Americans, clean and smooth, Coxsone was making records for the market that he knew. Really raw and exciting, that really jumped off the turntable.'

Trumpeter Johnny 'Dizzy' Moore is one of the few surviving members of the original Skatalites, the central band of the era. They formed in 1964 and recorded a staggering 200 songs in under a year. An old Alpha boy who was still working with Coxsone Dodd, he remembered all too clearly those tight and pressurised recording sessions.

'In those times musicians used to keep playing eight, nine hours a day. Maybe more, you know. Sometimes in the studio all day, sometimes all day and all night. We'd come in in the morning and learn up the tunes and when we come to the studio it was easy in a sense, everyone came with a line ready, everyone that came in knew what they had to do. And just round one mike, so no mistakes. If one make a mistake then we all have to go over the stuff again. One song could probably take fifteen, twenty minutes, thirty minutes the most, 'cause like we didn't have time to waste.'

Johnny was a product of the Alpha School for Wayward Boys. As were most of the leading lights of The Skatalites. The school is a series of white low-slung buildings on the outskirts of Kingston, run by Sister Ignatius. At eighty years old she is the only nun in the world with her own sound system! She was there at the very firmament of what we now think of as Jamaican music.

Legend has it that although the school had its fair share of real tearaways, boys with musical ability would be inclined to get into trouble, in order to get themselves sent to Alpha, where the boys' military band would give you access to otherwise unattainable musical instruments. Sister Ignatius talked about the Skatalite generation with a real twinkle in her eye.

'Lester Stirling, Don Drummond, Tommy McCook, Johnny Moore, all great musicians. I was into jazz,' she said. 'Bebop, I liked Satchmo, Charlie Parker, I think they called him the Bird. I played the boys the records and they loved them. By day they would have to play the military stuff, but by night I would hear strange noises coming from underneath the dormitories as they tried to remember the jazz stuff.'

She described the trombonist Don Drummond as the best on the island when he was at school, but also 'a little bit off his head'. She went on: 'But as they say, great artists are sometimes a "little off".' After a glittering career playing on countless iconic records, Don tragically went completely 'off', and ended up imprisoned in an asylum, having murdered his wife.

Sparrow, the current band leader, kindly got some ancient-looking instruments down off the wall – Tommy McCook and Roland Alphonso's saxes, and Don Drummond's dusty trombone. Instruments that had been returned to the school after the deaths of their owners, as a mark of respect for the chance the Alpha school had given them. They'd become a great source of inspiration for the current crop. Boys who were showing the most effort would sometimes be allowed to get their hands on these hallowed instruments and blow themselves a part of history.

Astonishingly, The Skatalites were only around for less than a year before internal wrangling amongst a highly volatile group of musicians pulled them apart. Their jazz tutorage from Sister Ignatius had stood them in good stead to turn out some extraordinary arrangements of some classic tunes. 'Guns of Navarone', one of my favourites, still bursts with energy and excitement.

'Yes, I like music,' Sister Ignatius was saying as I left. 'If I tell you what I like, you'll think me strange. "One scotch, one bourbon, one beer".' She laughed. She was anything but strange, she was a marvel. Unfortunately now passed on.

Oliver Foot was my guide for my tour of Jamaica, a member of the Foot family, whose grandad had been the last British High Commissioner of the island. When the country achieved independence he apparently took it upon himself to open the colonial coffers and distribute what was left in them amongst the community. The Foot family are held in high regard. Oliver was a tall rangy chap who'd led a colourful existence, culminating in the formulation of Orbis, the flying eye hospital that travels to remote corners of the world curing eye disease.

Oliver picked us up from the airport and took us to his coffee farm high up in the Blue Mountains. The view was extraordinary, a bit like the Preseli mountains of my youth but covered in dense vegetation. His history meant he knew pretty much everyone, and everyone knew him, and we could go almost anywhere we chose. Like Trench Town, a once affluent neighbourhood which had declined over the years into a bullet-riddled ghetto. Home in its time to Jimmy Cliff, Peter Tosh, and of course the man who made it a household name, Robert Nesta Marley. Oliver also took us to downtown Kingston, an area I certainly would have felt a bit nervous of exploring on my own. He bowled about with no security, happy as can be. A man whose impermeable good humour preceeded him. A man who loved the island and gave off vibes of ferocious positivity.

ALPHA BOYS' SCHOOL
COMPREHENSIVE HIGH
26 SOUTH CAMP ROAD
P.O. BOX 8072 C.S.O.
KINGSTON, JAMAICA, W.I.

Donald Drummond

Founding Member of Skatalites Band
Admitted 10.12.43
Left 31.10.50
Placed in Band 1945 - Trombone - Showed great promise
Grade 5 - Good Scholar
Spent a short time in the Tailoring Department and
Tile Factory.
In School Donald was very neat and clean, soft spoken
and well mannered. He was some-what withdrawn. He did
not show much interest in sports as his whole mind
was on his music.
After leaving School Donald played with Eric Deans
Band and toured some of the Caribbean Islands, he
also played with Gaynair's Band at the Glass Buckett
Club and Sonny Bradshaw's Big Band before joining
with the Skatalites.

@@@@@@@@@@@@@@@@@

Tommy McCook

Founding Member of Skatalites Band
Admitted 21.10.39
Left 20.10.44

Placed in Band somewhere in the early 40's and was at
thatearly age exceptional on the Saxophone.
Grade 5 - Good Scholar - but too involved in his
Music.
Liked games - especially Cricket.
Was very neat in appearance and a little gentleman.
After leaving School he joined Eric Dean's Band which
at that time was one of Jamaica's best.. A stint in
Nassau, then back to Jamaica where he became a Founding
Member of the Skatalites.
Even though the Group was outstanding they did not last
long - and folded in 1965.
In 1985 Tommy left for the States where he linked up
with the original Skatalites and did a lot of Touring
until ill health prevented. May 1998 at age 71 Tommy
died.

@@@@@@@@@@@@@@@@@@@

Sister Ignatius puts me in the picture

'Hey Oliver', 'Hey Mr Foot', the people called and waved from either side of the street as the two of us strolled up the main drag past the bustling bars and shops. Shops piled high with all sorts of exotic-looking fruit and veg. Reggae music curled out of every other doorway and there was a crowd of old fellas sitting under the awning of the Good Times rum shack, shouting and playing dominoes, banging them down on a small metal table, whilst kids munched on giant mangoes and mopeds zigzagged in and out of the traffic.

The only white face I passed all afternoon, apart from Oliver's, was my own reflected in a shop window. Man, the place was alive, truly alive. Oliver was stopping here and there checking, sniffing and buying an assortment of fruit and vegetation, chatting away and slipping easily in and out of thick patois. He'd soon filled two carrier bags. Satisfied with his haul, he invited me to join him for dinner.

We drove down to the sea and along the most beatific beach, small fishing boats were hauling in their nets, and an occasional Rasta would appear seemingly heading nowhere. Oliver explained that there were a number of Rasta communities along this beach, and you could survive just drifting about, as there was always food in the trees and fish in the sea. When I was a kid, if you wandered off in the English countryside you'd be lucky to get a cooking apple or a raw potato, but here it was mangoes, bananas, pineapples, coconuts and all sorts of other weird and wonderful stuff dangling just above your head.

Oliver pulled the car over under a huge banyan tree, standing just off the road on its own and in the middle of nowhere. 'Here we are,' he said, looping his lanky legs out of the car. I got out. It was late afternoon and the sun hung heavy in the sky. I looked around and there was nothing but miles of deserted beach, in either direction.

'Here we are where, Oliver?' It seemed a long way to come for a picnic. 'Oliver?' I looked round but he'd disappeared. 'Oliver?'

'Up here.' I looked up, and sure enough there were his long legs dangling from the nearest branch. 'Hang on a mo.' Just then an enormous basket appeared through the tree's thick canopy above his head. He guided it down, chucked his two carrier bags in and gave the rope it was hanging on a tug, whereupon it started to gently levitate back up the tree, magically disappearing to whence it had come. He jumped down and brushed his trousers. 'Right, should be ready in about an hour.'

He ran down the beach and jumped in the sea fully clothed. I followed him in, we splashed about for a bit in the waves, and strolled up the coast to a small beach-side shack, drying as we went. Oliver ordered two fresh coconuts, the owner proceeded to chop off their tops with a machete, like they were boiled eggs, and added a drop of rum to their milky interior. We sat on two upturned oil drums and drank our very superior pina coladas, the giant red sun frozen mid-sky. Reggae music blasted from one wall of the bar, which turned out to be an enormous stack of speakers. We strolled through the shallows and soon we were back at the foot of the giant banyan tree. Oliver looked up and whistled, and he was answered by a double whistle before proceeding to climb up some small steps carved in the trunk. I followed.

When we arrived at the first big branch a rope ladder uncoiled itself through the foliage and snapped, dangling at our feet. Oliver gave it a couple of firm tugs and started to climb. I followed. We climbed up and up, past branch after branch, until the rope ended and we transferred to a wooden ladder fixed to the trunk.

Remarkably small huts, not unlike garden sheds, started to appear, perched among giant knobbly branches. Some with doors open and people inside, one with a chap sitting outside on a stool nailed to the branch.

A Rasta in a hammock lazily waved and blew a plume of smoke from his nostrils. We must have been climbing for twenty minutes through what looked like a small medieval village with people washing in bowls, cats prowling about, and even a goat tethered on a piece of string. We eventually came to a clearing near the top of the tree where the top five or six branches converged to make a big flattish hollow in which sat a long table with a small kitchen attached to one end and bench seats down either side, which stuck out into thin air.

We were literally on top of the world, with the church spires of Kingston and the endless Blue Mountains behind us and the vast ocean in front, sparkling in the late-afternoon sun like gold. 'Fuck me,' I breathlessly managed to splutter. Oliver laughed. A Rasta lady appeared from behind a huge steaming pot and motioned for us to sit. Oliver sat and started to shuffle out to where the bench and table stuck out beyond the tree into thin air.

Jesus. I looked down for the first time all afternoon and realised my feet were dangling about 200 feet from the ground. The lady banged a pot lid and a stream of Rastas clambered up the ladder to join us at the table. The lady cook sat opposite us as a young girl started dishing up food at the other end of the table. She was smoking a huge spliff and good-naturedly chatting to Oliver, who took a puff himself. I couldn't understand a word they were saying. I live in London so I've heard patois before, but this was a different language entirely.

Oliver passed me the spliff and a big cloud of sensi rolled up my nose and down my throat. Another big puff and I could feel my whole body uncoiling from the inside out. And then a miracle occurred. I suddenly heard someone say, 'Where ya from?'

'I'm from London.'

'Whereabout in London, me have relation there?'

Shit. The spliff was acting like the babel fish from *The Hitchhiker's Guide to the Galaxy*. I could suddenly understand everything she was saying. She started quoting bits of the Bible, and I found myself remembering biblical snatches from the far-off days of Sunday school in Wales. We got talking about the nature of things and it was all making perfect sense!

A beautiful-looking plate of steamed vegetables and plantain broke the spell. It arrived with a beaker of fresh pineapple juice and was the most delicious meal I have ever tasted. A warm breeze rustled through the leaves and the huge red sun dropped into the sea. An open-back truck full of kids in white shirts and bow ties, singing gospel songs, drove up the windy road below us, headed for a different kind of church.

RADIO-RENTAL

Amongst the many other things I was doing after the band split in the 1980s, I got asked if I'd like to DJ on XFM. I remember my daughter Viva saying 'Dad! You, a DJ? What do you know about music?' My first show blasted onto the airwaves with three minutes of silence as I tried to work out which fader to push. I carried on for a few months, and good fun it was too, filled with a right bunch of characters, but they wanted me to be there five days a week, live, and that was getting a bit onerous. To be perfectly honest I was no expert on Indie rock, so I was finding it a bit hard to enthuse about some of the stuff I was playing.

But through doing that I got a call from Virgin Radio, asking me if I'd like to host a show there. A Friday night show, like a big party. So I started doing that and it was really good fun, and it became the most popular show on the station. It was supposed to set off your Friday night, so there were lots of big party tunes, Motown songs and just stuff to get you going. Basically I'd just sit there with a few cans of beer, getting merrier as the evening went on. Only out of pure selflessness – to be at one with my listener. Obviously.

I remember one particular evening when my wife, Anne, said

she nearly crashed the car. One of the links between two of the songs I was playing was just me opening a can of beer. She said, 'You actually get paid for that?'

Then Virgin asked me if I'd do five live shows a week, during the day. I said, 'Look, I really can't. I tried doing that at XFM and it just got too much.' I was still trying to write music and be involved in other things. They said, 'Tell you what we'll do. You can pre-record three of the shows, and do the other two live.'

It all went well, but it was quite difficult I must say, trying to pre-record a live show not knowing what was going to happen on the day of the broadcast. I couldn't mention the weather, anything in the news, or anything relevant to anything. So I just had completely abstract conversations about electric cars and people's favourite biscuits. This reached surreal highs.

One day I had to meet my cousin off the train from Wales for his stag do with a load of his mates. I was late and I jumped into a cab. The cab driver looked up in horror and he said: 'Hey, Suggsy, I love your show and I listen to it every day, but you're cutting it a bit fine, mate.' Before I had the chance to say anything he'd flown off in completely the wrong direction for Paddington.

The radio was blaring and he said: 'You're on in five minutes. Don't worry, I'll get you there.' I didn't have the heart to tell him it was actually a pre-recorded show. So we screeched to a halt outside Virgin Radio in Golden Square and he said: 'Run, Suggsy, run. Forget the money, just run.' So I ran, rather half-heartedly, into reception, and hid behind the desk until he'd disappeared round the corner. Now I was trying to work out how the fuck I was going to get to Paddington in five minutes.

Funnily enough, I did make it to meet up with my cousin and his six mates, and we went dog racing that night. We were all doing very badly and then I saw Jimmy White, the snooker player, arrive. He was sitting on the table next to us counting out huge wads of cash. So I said, 'Jimmy, come on. What's the SP?' He obviously had the golden touch that night, so I gathered all the money we had left between us, put it on the last dog of the last race, and we all won. A lot of money.

We carried on into the light fantastic in the West End, which culminated in someone's room in Hazlitt's Hotel down in Dean Street. At about 6.30 a.m., as the sun was coming up, I thought I'd go out and get a coffee as everyone else was sort of crashed out all over the room. I went down to the Bar Italia and there were a couple of firemen and a cab driver there, and I suddenly remembered that my family had gone down to Whitstable and I'd said I'd go down and meet them.

So with £400 still in my pocket I said to the cab driver, 'How much to drive me to Whitstable?' He said, 'A hundred quid,' I said, 'Great.' I grabbed a croissant and a cup of coffee and off I bounced in the back of a very old black cab all the way down to Whitstable.

LIVERPOOL AWAY

Halfway through my Virgin Radio show one morning Dave, the head of PR, burst in.

'Oh yes, my son.'

'Oh yes, my son what, Dave?'

'Wanna go to the second leg of the Champion's League semi-finals?'

'Yeah, course I do.' Dave had managed to get four tickets for the return leg at Anfield.

'That sounds great, Dave, but where are the seats? I don't fancy being in the Kop.'

'No, no, I double-checked. Neutral seats, middle of the ground. Oh yes, and not only that but the full executive first-class treatment. Hotel, the works.'

Great.

On the morning of the game me, my producer Mark, Dave and the boss, Paul, set off from Euston in high spirits. It was an early train.

'Why are we going so early, out of interest, Dave?'

'Well, that's the only problem we've got. All the hotels are jumping with people wanting rooms, so the only way I could get us some rooms was on the proviso that we would check in by 4 p.m. If we don't they'll have to let our rooms go. People are going up the walls for somewhere to stay. Still, it'll give us a chance to settle in and have a few drinks and a wander.'

The train was trundling along and we were availing ourselves of all that first class had to offer, whilst poring over possible team selection and formations. When we got to the Runcorn Bridge the train slowed and stopped, and after twenty minutes Paul got up to find the guard and see what was going on. He came back looking worried because someone had lobbed a brick at the train window.

'We're gonna have to get off at Runcorn and change.'

The train limped into the station and we all hopped off. The next train wasn't until 3.30. 'Shit, we won't make it in time to secure our rooms, they'll give them away,' said Dave.

'Oh great, a night on a bench in Liverpool.'

The full first-class executive treatment! Paul frantically got on the blower to the hotel, and after a chat he told us that they were gonna have to let our rooms go. We were sitting in a dejected line on the platform bench, sipping lukewarm cans of Tennant's, when Paul's phone went.

'What? Are you sure? Really? The hotel have had to let our rooms go, but they have a sister hotel just outside town in the Wirral and they can let us have some rooms there. They also have a courtesy car which will take us to and from the game.'

Hoorah. We raised our cans and eventually climbed aboard the 3.30. At Lime Street we jumped in a cab and headed for the Wirral. Things were really looking up when, three-quarters of an hour later, we were pulling up at a rather grand-looking country house. The owner was there to meet us. He assured us there would be no trouble

ABOVE: Dave Robinson, the boss of Stiff, directing the 'Tomorrow's Just Another Day' video. Thommo, obviously, dressed as an elf.

ABOVE: Chalky, Rob, Toks, Me, Lee and Woody. The hugely unsuccessful Madness five-a-side team.

OPPOSITE: 'I'm home, dear.'

RIGHT: Woody.

BELOW: Hanging out making the 'One Better Day' video.

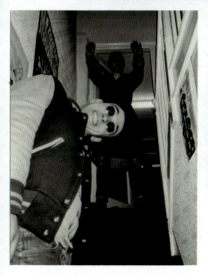

ABOVE: In-flight entertainment.

LEFT: Toks and Chalky in the offices of Liquidator Studios.

ABOVE: Camden
Mews, Scarlett
about to be born.
The lovely Karmann
Ghia, whose days
were numbered.

RIGHT: At home
with the McPs.

OPPOSITE: Getting
married. Anne
ordered snow.

LEFT: 'I've been riding on my bike'.

BELOW: Madstock – an earthquake had erupted.

ABOVE: On top of the Palace.

LEFT: Closing the Olympics.

BELOW: Me and Mamba watching the football.

getting to the ground in time, and the driver would be outside and ready to go whenever we fancied. Perfect.

I went to my well-appointed room, dumped my bag and headed down to the bar. The bar had double doors leading out onto beautiful manicured lawns and garden, so I sat on the veranda and the barman brought me a vodka and tonic. Twenty minutes went by and the others still hadn't appeared. I phoned Paul's room and he said: 'Come up, we're having a bottle of champers.' When I walked into Paul's room it was like walking into the Liverpool club shop. There were Liverpool shirts of every size and colour draped over the furniture and hanging off the wardrobe. Paul was wearing a 1998 away top and looking at himself in the mirror.

'What d'you reckon?' he said, doing a twirl.

'Er . . . great,' I replied.

'What do you fancy?' he said, waving his hand in the direction of some stuff hanging off the chair. 'Have what you want.'

'What? What do I fancy, what?'

'What you gonna wear? We're all going to look the part. Aren't we, Dave? Gotta look the part.'

Dave looked sheepish, and Mark was holding a glass of champagne and staring out the window. I went back down to the bar, and nearly spat out my drink when Mark came round the corner wearing a home Liverpool top and a white sleeveless hoody. A hoody. Followed by Dave and Paul in their Liverpool tops.

'Hang on, Dave, did you say we had neutral seats? You do realise I am a relatively well-known supporter of Chelsea, what with "Blue Day" an' all?'

'Yeah, here, have a look for yourself,' and sure enough the seat numbers were in the middle of the ground, well away from both partisan ends.

The manager came in to say the car was ready and that we should think about making moves shortly. The three stooges traipsed out, Mark pulling his hood up. I finished my drink and followed them out to the courtyard. When I got there Paul and Mark were draped over the bonnet of a huge metallic-pink Bentley, having their picture taken by Dave.

'What's going on? What you doing? Careful you don't scratch that. That's gotta be two hundred grand's worth,' I said.

'What d'you mean? It's ours.'

'All right Parker, where's Lady Penelope, and more to the point where's our car?'

'That's what I'm saying. This is our car. And look, here is fookin' Parker.' A chauffeur in full regalia stepped out. I looked round the courtyard and there weren't any other cars in sight.

'You've got to be joking,' I said. Dave looked blank. 'D'you think I am going to a highly volatile football match, in Liverpool, in a metallic-pink Bentley, with you three?'

Mark and Paul slid off the bonnet and the three of them stood looking at each other, baffled but resplendent in their brand-new football tops and hoodies.

I went inside to find the manager, thinking, I'll walk if I have to.

'Do you by any chance have another car? You know anything, and preferably something that doesn't scream "I AM A PRAT!" Perhaps something a smidge less tasteless, like a lime-green Lamborghini or a turquoise Ferrari?'

The manager looked as blank as the others.

'Surely you've got just an ordinary car.'

'I'm sorry, sir, but our other cars have all gone already. It's the only car we have available.' He looked deflated. 'We saved it for you. We thought it might go some way to making up for your inconvenience.' He waved at it. 'It's the finest in our fleet.' I didn't doubt it, but wasn't surprised that no other guests took it to a football match.

'Yeah, sure it's a lovely car ... if I was going to Heaven in Charing Cross Road, but I'm not going to a gay disco, I'm going to Anfield. Do you have a number for a cab?' I asked.

'I'm afraid there won't be any free now till after the game.'

I was on the back seat, slumped as low as I could go, as we entered the outskirts of Liverpool, the cathedral spire and the top floors of hotels my only clue as to where we were. I phoned my mate Kevin, manager of The Farm, to see if he was about and explained my predicament. He was meeting his mates in a pub near the ground that he thought we would probably pass. The car slowed as we approached the ground. A kid pressed his nose against the window. 'Here, look at these knobheads,' he said.

A small crowd of scallies were soon gathered at every window. I pulled my jacket over my head. 'Here, isn't that that fella from that band? What is it, Bad Manners? He's Chelsea, ain' 'e? Here, yer big twat.' Someone started banging on the window. My compadres puffed out their chests trying to show their club colours more clearly. Fuck this, I thought, so I pushed the door open and dived out through the legs surrounding the car.

We were nearly at the ground and it looked like what I thought was the pub Kevin said he was going to be in was just over the road. I disappeared into the throng and headed that way. It was like a sauna inside, literally steaming, packed with a crowd of people singing and dancing round the bar. A fella put his face right in mine and asked: 'You that Madness fella?' He had froth at the corner of his mouth and a bubble coming out of one nostril. 'Kev's over there,' he said, pointing behind him but still looking at me.

Thank God. Kev waved me over and I found my way to the relative safety of a corner of the pub he and some of The Farm boys had made their own. I got a pint and looked out of the window and there in the middle of the ambling crowd was the pink Bentley crawling along. Drinks were drinked up and it was time to head for the stadium. Roy, The Farm's drummer, very kindly said he would help me find the section where my seat was. As we ambled along he asked to see my ticket.

'You in the Chelsea end?'

'Er no, I don't think so. It's in a neutral part of the ground.'

'Neutral? There's no such thing here, mate. This is Anfield. Let's have a look.' I showed him my ticket.

'Oh, you're in the Centenary Stand.'

'What, is that bad?'

'No, it shouldn't be too bad, but it certainly ain't neutral.'

It started as soon as I got in the queue – good-naturedly at first. 'Here, Chelsea boy, what you doin' here?' But the comments started growing in venom once I was inside and heading for my seat. By the time I got to my seat, small sections of the crowd were starting to pipe up behind me. 'Yer dirty cockney bastard, yer dirty cockney bastard.'

Paul, Mark and Dave were already in situ. 'Great seats, eh?' said Dave, enthralled. What an atmosphere! I felt a gob of spit land on the back of my head. 'Yeah, great.' In fairness the atmosphere was deafening. There was a huge contingent of Chelsea to our right but the other three sides of the ground were drowning them out. The game went off like a packet of crackers, and there was no love lost between the two sides. Most of the crowd were now into the game, but a small crowd behind me weren't gonna let it go. 'Who's the wanker on his own, who's the wanker on his own?' Dave perceptibly shifted towards Mark. Another round of 'You dirty cockney bastard', and one more gob in the hair and I'd had it. And sure enough it came – I even heard the bloke behind me snarling it up his nostrils before it plopped on the top of my head.

'Great seats, yeah, great. Thanks,' I said, but Dave was oblivious and engrossed in the game. I got up and headed back up the stairs, past a phalanx of hands making the international gesture of farewell. The wanking sign.

I found a steward inside and asked him if there was any chance he could fling me in with the Chelsea. I knew it was a long shot as Anfield was an all-seater stadium and the days of moving around a ground were long gone. But maybe, just maybe, someone hadn't turned up, left already or been thrown out.

'Let's have a look at your ticket, mate.' I gave it to him, wiping gob from my hair with my sleeve.

'Sorry, mate, no chance, it's rammed in there. And anyway this is a ticket for the Centenary Stand.'

'I know that. All right, fuck it, maybe I'll hang about and go back at half-time, see if it's calmed down.'

'Sorry, mate, can't give you your ticket back now. There's no re-entry.'

'But I haven't left the ground yet.'

He shook his head and pocketed it. By now there were more stewards gathering and a copper poked his nose in. 'You causin' trouble, cockney? Anyway, you shouldn't be in the Liverpool end.'

I stormed off trying to find an exit but there wasn't one, and there were still bands of urchins scouring the streets trying to find a way in. The whole place was tubbed up. I tried doors, emergency exits, nothing was open. Finally I asked a fella manning one of the turnstiles.

'Sorry, lad, they only open one way.'

'What? Let me out. I swear I'll kick one of the doors out!' He relented and let me out.

On the street it was like a scene from *28 Days Later*, that zombie movie where they all move really fast. 'Got any spares, Mister, let's have yer ticket, Mister.' Much as I wanted to tell them to get lost, I wasn't about to open my gob and reveal where I was from. The streets round Anfield are narrow and winding. I forged on past the urchins and turned the corner just in time to see, of all things, the pink Bentley pulling away. 'Oi! Hang on,' I shouted. I certainly had no qualms about getting in the horrible thing now. 'Oi! Wait!' Too late; it disappeared up the road and round the corner.

My heart sank but I resolved to just get as far away from the ground as quickly as possible, and with no idea where I was headed I just started walking. It could have been ten minutes, could have been an hour, I didn't know, but just tried to keep going in a straight line. By some miracle I hit a ring road with signs in all directions, one of which was the Wirral. A cab came past, so finally things were starting to look up. I hailed it and jumped in. The driver knew the hotel and said it was a fair distance, but I thought at least I could have a bit of dinner and watch the second half.

We were not too far off when I had the idea to ring the hotel. Of course, I should have guessed, the hotel's four stars did not include Sky effing TV. As we flew along the dual carriageway through the suburbs, a council estate loomed into view and I spotted a pub with a big Sky TV banner outside. 'Hang on, driver, here, mate, d'you know what that pub's like?'

'No idea, son, I expect it'll sell beer, and by the looks of it it has Sky TV.'

'Very amusing. Could you just drop me here?'

'We're still a good five mile from your hotel, son.' I got out, and the cab pulled away. I really was in the middle of nowhere, but at least I could watch the rest of the game. I should have known that a pub built into a block of flats does not get much passing trade. They're very much local pubs, for local people.

Inside the place was packed, and I walked through the door just in time to see Liverpool score on a huge screen. The place erupted with beer and beer glasses flying in all directions. No neutrals in here then, either. I pretended to do up my laces and backed out the door. Now what was I gonna do? There was nothing but motorway in either direction, so for want of a better idea I headed in the direction the cab had been taking me. I walked for about twenty minutes without passing another soul or car. Everyone was watching the game, except me!

I was approaching a huge roundabout when my phone went. It was Anne, so I explained the situation, and there was a pause before she said, 'I told you, you should have watched it on the box.' I trudged on and phoned the hotel.

'Is the Bentley back?'

'Where are you?'

'Just past the so and so pub.'

'Well, go back there, and we'll come and get you.' I don't think so.

Eventually the pink Bentley appeared round the corner and went round the roundabout a couple of times before the driver spotted me lying in the middle of it.

I'd had a couple of cold drinks by the time the others came back to the hotel. My sense of humour bypass wasn't helped by the sight of the three of them swaying through the door of the hotel bar, grinning like idiots and waving scarves of the victorious Liverpool above their heads.

MADSTOCK

In 1992 we decided to invent our own festival. Cathal was working for Go! Discs, and having worked with a lot of great bands like the La's, he also saw a lot of bands he realised weren't as good as we were and started to get a bit frustrated by seeing what they had and we didn't. After much enthusiasm and many phone calls, people joining in and unjoining, we did finally get back together. Eight years since the band had last played together. There'd been a growing sense that we'd never properly said goodbye to our fans.

After much umming and ahhing about doing a farewell tour, we fell into conversation with Vince Power the promoter who organised the big Irish festival, the Fleadh, in Finsbury Park, on our doorstep. It was his suggestion that we might want to try doing our supposedly farewell concert on that very site. He could keep up the fencing and the staging so it wouldn't cost that much. The only problem was that it held 35,000 people, and were we in a position to sell that out? Well, as it turned out we did, plus another day, so 70,000 people turned up for 'Madstock' on the weekend of 8 and 9 August.

We had got a bill of great bands like Ian Dury & the

Blockheads, Morrissey, Flowered Up and Gallon Drunk. Mid-afternoon, about four hours before we were due to go on stage, Vince came in to say that the cheque for our deposit had disappeared. Various stories did the rounds, one that it had been left on the roof of a taxi, which seemed fairly far-fetched. Another that it had been stolen. It was suggested at the behest of our management that the quite considerable sum of money we'd been guaranteed would have to be collected in cash from all the beer tents and hot dog vans. Which it duly was. Two stuffed mailbags appeared in our dressing room about an hour before we were supposed to go on stage.

I remember walking up the stairs to the stage feeling like I was leading the England football team out to a World Cup Final. We were all very nervous. Spontaneously we all just lined up across the front of the stage and the audience went completely crazy, the gig was one of the most memorable we've ever done – we were suddenly exposed to all that we had achieved. The park went ballistic. People going mental – the crowd further than the eye could see, across the whole park, jumping up and down in unison. The whole of Finsbury Park felt like the sprung dance floor of those early 2 Tone gigs. It was beyond words!

Even causing an earthquake, as this extract from *The Times* explains . . .

On 8 August the police phoned the British Geological Survey, saying people had reported an earthquake in North London. People were frightened. Tower blocks were evacuated because they thought they were going to collapse. An earth tremor registered at 5 on the Richter scale. Seismologist Alice Walker told the BBC:

When I told the police that I thought the cause of the earthquake was a Madness concert in Finsbury Park, they were sceptical. [I bet that's not the word they used.] When the same effects were felt at exactly the same time the following night they had to believe me.

I remember leaving the venue seeing people literally emotionally and physically exhausted, lying on the pavement outside. It was a truly monumental moment in the history of Madness. Our compilation album *Divine Madness* was number one in the charts. Mike agreed to return, minus the balaclava. And we were a band again.

An earthquake had indeed erupted.

ATHENS

In the last ten years we have been asked to play more and more festivals. In the olden days when we started out there were only about four festivals in Britain that I can think of, and even fewer in Europe. I can only really remember playing Glastonbury in the eighties, and no other. Reading was for heavy metal and the Isle of Wight was for serious 'rock'. The facilities were shit and you had to bring your own food. I can't honestly say I would have chosen to go to these things anyway. But boy have things changed. There are now festivals for every taste, from book reading to body piercing, folk to flower arranging. Big ones, little ones, urban ones, festivals up mountains, on the beach, in peoples' back gardens. All with toilets, showers and food from around the world.

In the last ten years we have played: Bestival, Camp Bestival, Port Eliot, Leeds, Reading, The V festivals, T in the Park, Henley, our own Madstock, Rockness, The Hull festival (in the car park of the Co-Op), Kew Gardens. The whole thing has exploded, which is great for us as we are, even though I say so myself, a great live band. I think almost in direct proportion to the downturn in record sales there has been an upturn in the desire to see the real thing. You cannae download the live experience, Jimmy.

We've played all over Europe. Way back when, I can only remember playing Pink Pop and the Festival of Fools in Holland, I think that was about it. But now we have played festivals in Spain – we were the first non-electronic band to play at Sonar – Germany and Montreux jazz festivals. Belgium. Italy. The Weenie Roast and Coachella in California. Viva Latino in Mexico city (to 80,000 screaming kids – we felt like a boy band for the first time). Buena series. All round Australia with Elbow, The Kaiser Chiefs and Snow Patrol. And even more recently in Eastern Europe, Moldovia, Croatia, Serbia, Czech Republic, Poland, a few times in Russia and the Communist one in France, Rock en Seine.

Rock En Seine is the biggest festival in France. It was the usual old carry-on. Our compartment packed with our wives, girlfriends, uncles, aunts, kids, mates, the mates of our kids' mates, people I'd never met in my life. I remember thinking: They never show this much interest when we're playing in Hull.

The usual mayhem: someone's daughter's boyfriend (it could have been mine) is being frogmarched from first class; the trombone player's nicked a couple of miniature bottles of Chardonnay from the drinks trolley (even though they're complimentary); two of the band are vociferously sorting out their differences and one of them's shouting 'Whose side are you on?' in my ear.

And as we all piled off the train at the Gare du Nord, in a cascade of shouting and laughter, it was obvious to anyone that we'd all had a good time: bodies, bags and broken bottles tipped onto the platform.

Looking down the train I see Noel Gallagher, getting out of his first-class compartment, on his own, a newspaper under his arm. A veritable Oasis of calm.

And for a second, I almost wished I was him.

When we get to the festival we're told Oasis, the headliners, don't want us to play the main stage before them. We've been relegated to a smaller one. We didn't know why. We didn't know if it was them or their management. They just didn't want it.

We were pissed off, but we'd never blown out a gig before and we weren't about to now. All the crowd who wanted to see us on the main stage were crushed into a field half the size. People were hanging out of trees, trampolining on top of the beer tents, and crowding on the roofs of the hot-dog vans. It went berserk.

After the gig we're backstage relaxing in our smoking jackets when there's a clang that sounds like the first chord to 'A Hard Day's Night' coming from the Oasis dressing room. Liam had smashed Noel's guitar and there'd been a fight.

We're relaxing and having a post-gig drink or three when the promoter flies in through the door.

'*Sacré bleu!* Oasis 'ave gone home! Zey 'ave gone 'ome! Zey're not playing. Zey're not ever playing. Zey've fucking split up! Pleeeeze will you go and play instead of zem on ze main stage?'

Our hardened roadies are nervous and aren't sure it's a good idea. 'Listen, there's a massive crowd screaming and throwing bottles at the stage – you'll get lynched.'

'Come on, chaps. Let's do it.' After a little negotiating, including pretending to get in a cab, I throw on a pink suit and we head for the stage.

'Alright, let's not mention Oasis. Let's have some dignity, yeah, and respect. Don't take the piss.'

We walk out on stage, doing the Liam walk.

'All right Pariiiiiiisssssss! Let's fookin' have itttt'

It turns out to be one of the best gigs of our lives.

And as the band strike up 'One Step Beyond' I look down at the stage. And there, between my feet, is a strip of tape with the word 'Liam' written on it.

But the most unforgettable of all our festival experiences, for all the wrong reasons, was the Exit festival in Athens.

Anne, my wife, was in Italy staying with an old pal of ours who'd moved to Salento, the southern most tip of the heel. She'd flown over there to sort out some problems with a house we'd just bought, an old farmhouse in the middle of nowhere. Difficult to get to as there were no direct flights, but a most beautiful unspoilt part of the world with a stunning coastline. The first time we went we flew to Rome and caught the night-train down there – the most amazing trip. Like Cornwall, with a bit more sun. Laid back, lovely people, and terrific food.

Salento is only a hop and a skip from Greece. Anne was planning to come with Toby, an old friend who was helping me write my one man show, and his girlfriend to meet me and the girls in Athens, whereupon we'd all go off to the festival together. It was Toby who suggested it might be more practical and fun to take the boat to Greece. There were overnight ferries every day from Brindisi, the big shipping port, gateway to the Orient. The boat would take about ten hours to get to Patras on the Greek mainland via Corfu.

Me and the band flew out from Heathrow with a big contingent of family and friends, as is often the case when we're playing somewhere nice. There were my two daughters, Scarlett and Viva, and their pal Tansy, two of Debs' brothers and an assortment of waifs and strays. We were all at the venue by the time Anne and Toby rolled up, windswept and interesting after their all-night ferry trip from Italy. Their hair standing on end. Toby'd been involved in a documentary about the sinking of the *Estonia* and thought it might be prudent if they all slept on the deck, where it was windy but warm. Anne was laughing. Just before they left the boat Toby got in a row with a Berlusconiesque character who was complaining about all the bloody foreigners. Toby was asking him what he thought about all the Italian emigrés to America, etc., to little or no avail. Shouting and gesticulating Toby left the boat in Patras, only to be greeted by a Greek cab driver saying exactly the same shit. Anne said, 'Toby, leave it'. It's a long drive to Athens.

It was about sundown when we hit the stage; we were supporting the Beastie Boys in the old Olympic basketball stadium. There were about 50,000 in the crowd and the gig went great. Apart from Woody falling off his drum stool during 'Wings of a Dove'. Actually that was the very last time he had a drink, and he hasn't touched a drop since.

Our dressing room was crowded by the time we came off stage and discussions were taking place as to who wanted to stay and see the Beastie Boys, and who wanted to go back to the hotel straight-away. A big contingent decided they would rather go back now. The bus would then come back later to get the rest of us. Me and Cathal from the band, Anne, Scarlett, Viva and Tansy, Debs' brothers Darren and Mike, and Hugh and Jim from the management decided we'd stay. We loaded up with drinks from the dressing room and headed out into the arena. It was a beautiful balmy evening. The Beasties were rockin', all done up like the FBI in trilbies and raincoats and giving it some. They kicked off with '(You Gotta) Fight for Your Right (To Party!)' and the place went ballistic.

After a few numbers a bunch of us headed back to re-stock, but once in the dressing room we ended up staying and chatting. As time went on more people started to drift back and the talk was just turning to heading to the hotel when the window right next to my head imploded. Then the next one. What the fuck! Then the one opposite; glass flying in all directions. Our dressing room was like a corridor, with windows down either side. I instinctively grabbed Anne and headed for a big steel filing cabinet in the corner. I opened the door to inexplicably discover two Japanese girls in there already. Double what the fuck! One by one, every single window came in. It was like a horror movie. I looked side-ways out of the window nearest me, street-side, to see hundreds of kids drifting silently down the road on mopeds, their engines cut, wearing full face-helmets. Dropping the bikes to the ground they were systematically smashing the place to pieces, with baseball bats and axes. On the other side somebody shouted that the Beastie Boys had left the stage, and the crowd was screaming and running in all directions. Through the broken window nearest the door Toby was passing towels and water out. The guy guarding our dressing room had been attacked and was lying on the floor in a pool of blood. It was carnage.

For the first time I looked round the room, everyone was staring at each other in shock and complete disbelief. Everyone except Scarlett and Viva. It was like time stood still. They were still out there somewhere in the crowd. Smoke started to drift in. We gotta get out, they're starting to torch the gaff. Anne rang the girls and tried to explain through the pandemonium that everything was fine and that they shouldn't come back to the dressing room. What we didn't know was that they could see the anarchists breaking through on the other side, chopping their way through the fence that protected the bar area with machetes and heading for the dressing rooms. They weren't leaving their parents, they were headed straight in our direction.

A fire bomb could have come through the window at any moment; we were sitting ducks. Hugh and Jim had taken their lives in their hands and gone to take a look outside. After a few seconds they came running back in. Hugh was of the opinion, given the short time he'd been out there, that what appeared to be indiscriminate violence was in fact being very specifically directed at the venue, and the people associated with it.

By now half the stadium was ablaze. We took off anything that connected us to the gig, passes, etc. I looked around the room – plastic chairs, tables. There was nothing of any use. Debs' brothers clinked two empty wine bottles together and said, unforgettably, 'We were born together, we'll die together!' And with that, we went for it.

The first door we passed was the band Underworld's dressing room. A Coke machine lay on its side, and next to it, one of Underworld. There was blood coming out of his head, a steward was shouting, 'Leave him, he's been shot!' But his bandmates weren't having that, and we helped them drag him to his feet. He had in fact been hit on the head by a brick. He was in a bad way, but he wasn't dead. The end of the corridor spilled out into the main entrance. To the right the venue, to our left the road. It was full of people screaming and running this way and that. We turned left. Outside the door we were surrounded by a phalanx of crash-helmeted, baseball bat wielding anarchists.

It felt like we were in the middle of one of those coups you read about, where everyone is slaughtered. The mood was out of control. But it was too late now, we ducked and ran through them. Hugh's theory seemed to be correct, they were leaving us alone. We spilled out in the road, into a throng of people desperately trying to get away and formed a small circle against the tide. All we knew is that we were on the wrong side of the stadium and we had no idea where to go. The orange light of fire was filling the night sky.

The girls! Anne and I looked at each other, unsure as to what we'd said to them during our brief garbled conversation on the phone. A patrol car with its lights flashing came down the road, thank God! As it approached, a Greek copper jumped out, took one look at what was going on, grabbed a traffic cone and jumped back in! The car about-turned, wheel-skidded, and shot back up the road. Great!

A minibus came towards us from the opposite direction, Jim jumped in the way, Hugh pulled the door open it was empty, the driver looked petrified. 'Jump in!' There was no way Anne was going without the girls. I was still of a mind to tell them to get out of the stadium any way they could. 'Just go, we'll wait.' Then, really like some miracle, Scarlett, Viva and Tansy appeared out of the crowd running towards us. Hugs and tears all round before we realised we better make the most of our newly commandeered van. Our rightly terrified driver was trying to drive away, but our entrance was blocked by a fella who'd squeezed in front of us, struggling to get two wheely bags in the van. 'You can get them out of the way!' We all piled in, followed by the man with the suitcases who dragged them on his lap as the van took off. Turned out he was the Beastie Boys' bag man (accountant.) The cases were filled with the merchandise cash. Wide-eyed he clung on for dear life as we shot up the road.

Back at the hotel everyone was amazed and horrified to hear what had happened. Our agent bought drinks all round and suggested it may have been a rival promoter or a disagreement amongst rival security firms. We huddled round the telly in the bar waiting for the news to come on. It did and there was no news of the riot. We asked the barman to put on the local news. 'This is the local news.' What! We explained what had happened to us. He carried on polishing glasses. 'They burnt down a bank earlier. It's happening all the time, the whole place is going crazy.' Little did we know what was to come for Greece.

We couldn't wait to get out of the place the following morning. I joined Anne on the ferry for the return trip back to southern Italy and the relative tranquility of our house.

BASSO SALENTO

Salento is the area, and it's a simple and beautiful part of the world, the perfect antidote to the hectic hustle and bustle of my beloved Londinium. It's a place of abundance, the climate perfect for growing just about anything. One of the many joys has been planting sapling fruit trees or, more to the point, watching Anne do so, and seeing them bear fruit only a matter of a few years later. A miracle that never ceases to amaze me. We have a small vineyard, a vegetable patch and a consumptive cat called Mister Mange. The house has its own well. If we got a couple of goats, we wouldn't need to go to the shops at all.

The food is completely seasonal. If it's artichoke season we eat artichokes. Courgette season, courgettes, etc. The vegetables are home-grown, fresh and delicious. The local wine is home-made, varies from village to village, and comes in unmarked containers. One of my favourite beach-side restaurants is in Porto Badisco. A very simple family-run affair with plastic tables and cutlery. But the food is excellent. Once in the early days, during a most agreeable lunch, I asked for the name of the fabulous rosé we were drinking. The owner looked at me quizzically, scratched his head and said, 'It is wine, *signore*.' Everybody makes their own.

We go to Porto Badisco to swim, and when they're in season, sample the local delicacy of sea urchins. *Ricci di mare*, literally hedgehogs of the sea. They look like small black hedgehogs rolled into a ball. Two girls man a marble table on the street, carefully snipping the spiky creatures in half so's to get at the delicious orange roe within, and laying them out on plastic trays. You scoop out the roe with brightly coloured plastic ice-cream spoons, or bits of torn bread. The flavour is delicate, somewhere between oyster and fish paste. It tastes like condensed sea. A bit like oysters, *ricci* are an acquired taste, I found later in life. The ritual of eating them is a big part of the pleasure.

Ricci are only available for a few months of the year, and when they are people come from far and wide to eat them with almost religious fervour. Like oysters, they're supposed to have aphrodisiac properties. When a full tray is delivered to a table of *ragazzi* there will be a spontaneous round of applause. Fishing and diving for *ricci* play a big part in the lives of the peninsula-inhabiting Salentinis. In fact I went diving once for *ricci* with Gigi, the local vet. We had a wondrous afternoon, drifting along the coast in his little fishing boat. A gentle day of snorkelling in the clear waters just off the most beautiful beaches.

Gigi promised to bring some *ricci* round when we invited him for lunch one Sunday afternoon in July. As is so often the case in this part of the world, disparate people started dropping by. There were eventually about twenty of us crowded round the table in the back garden, including my brother- and sister-in-law, Keith and Alanah, and my two nephews, Jerome and Jacob. The local bar owner, several artists and musicians, a priest, and even the colonel of the Guardia di Finanza, the Italian version of Customs and Excise, in full uniform. The courtyard was starting to look like another scene from *The Godfather*. Gigi the vet turned up with a few fishermen pals and a huge tray of the promised *ricci*, and was duly applauded. The priest blessed the proceedings, including Scarlett and Viva for bringing said proceedings to the table. Great food was scoffed, oceans of wine were quaffed, and a great afternoon was had by all.

During coffee and limoncello, a particularly delicious and potent liqueur, Gigi suggested I might want to go fishing with his pals the next morning who at this point were having an intense and animated row about the correct way to peel an orange. Why not? The limoncello flowed, songs were sung and dances were danced while Jacob and Jerome abseiled down the side of the house using knotted sheets. I couldn't have been happier.

Scarlett and Viva and pals decided they would go in search of music and dance of a slightly less *rustico* variety, and were off to the bright lights of the nearest town, the holiday village of Torre dell'Orso. Chelsea were also playing in the Champions League that night, so me, Keith and Jerome said we'd accompany the girls into town to see if we could find a bar that was showing the football. Keith drove us, as he'd eschewed the limoncello and wisely stuck to coffee.

After the match Keith made an executive decision that Jerome could go and hang out with the girls. He was only fourteen but it was one of them irresistible holiday moments. Keith drove back to the house and I accompanied Jerome up the moonlit road in the direction of the pounding disco beat of the beach party to see where the girls were.

When we got there the outdoor disco was in full swing. The girls were leaping about on the dancefloor and were pleased to see Jerome. Don't worry, they said, we'll keep an eye on him. I had one more drink, left the girls to it and headed for home. Look after him they did, with swigs from their lemonade bottle filled with vodka, which had him throwing up in the bushes, and again when he got home.

When the turbulence subsided Keith asked him what he had learned from the experience. 'I should have thrown up earlier,' he replied. Ah, the joys of youth.

Having left the girls, the walk back to the house was only a mile or so, but I wasn't progressing terrifically well. It had been a long day/night. I passed an ice-cream parlour and caught sight of a man with a big red face and his hair stuck to his forehead, staring at me. What you looking at? I thought.

It was a mirror. I staggered on but seemed to be going backwards. In desperation, I called Keith to see if he would come and get me in the car. Praise the Lord he did, but when my head hit the pillow it was 3.30 a.m.

I was just slipping into unconsciousness when I heard a distorted car radio playing Abba outside our bedroom window. Headlights swept across the ceiling. 'What?' A car horn beeped.

'Who the hell is that?' I sat up.

'It's the fishermen,' Anne mumbled.

'What fishermen?'

'The fishermen you said you'd go fishing with.' Anne turned over.

'Oh, bollocks.' It was starting to come back to me. I looked at the clock: it said 4.30. I flopped back down.

'Oh, no, I can't go fishing now.'

'Then why did you say you'd go?' Anne said through the pillow.

'Because I was drunk?' The car beeped again. 'Bollocks.'

I clambered out of bed, threw on a T-shirt, shorts and a pair of flip-flops, said goodbye to Anne and headed out into the dim light. Cesare, Gigi's mate, was leaning against a white jeep. 'You ready?' What a question! I don't think I've ever felt less ready for anything in my life. 'Yeah,' I mumbled. I clambered into the jeep. Anne shouted through the bedroom window, 'When you gonna be back?' I looked at Cesare. 'We should be back by seven,' he said. 'I'll be back in about three hours,' I shouted back. 'See you later.' As we drove down the coast road towards the harbour, the sun was just starting to peep over the horizon I started to look on the positives. C'mon Suggsy boy, a few hours poodling up and down the coast. Fresh air and swimming, this'll do you good.

I don't know what I was expecting when we reached the harbour – a small dinghy, a sailing boat? But we walked past some of those, and the bigger boats and the yachts, until we came to the great rusting hull of an industrial fishing trawler, engines throbbing. I looked up to see giant nets and a crew of men in rubber boots. Oh yes, this was it. I followed Cesare up the slippery ramp and the first thing that hit me was the smell. *Gesù Cristo*, I don't think there is a smell on earth to compare with that of burning diesel and rotting fish. My guts nearly went. My head was throbbing and my mouth was dry as a chip. The four-man crew were sitting on the nets happily chewing on dry biscuits and sipping red wine.

Er, was there perhaps any water? It seemed not. I was handed a luke-warm bottle of red wine. I shook my head, it was replaced by a bottle of luminous green pop. The engine throttled up and we pulled out of the harbor, the first rays of dawn breaking along the horizon. I held on tight to a stanchion and was managing quite well as we bobbed out and into a relatively calm sea. I was most assuredly green about the gills, but I was coping, just. Then we stopped. Now the boat wasn't just bobbing up and down, but rolling from side to side as well. The whole boat had turned into a giant seafaring waltzer.

I was starting to feel very peculiar indeed, with the sun now well in the sky and beating down. I felt faint. 'Come on Suggs, pull yourself together,' I heard myself saying out loud. 'You're British, for God's sake. A direct descendant of an island race that ruled the high seas for hundreds of years.' The bile was rising. I took a swig of the luminous pop and hummed 'Rule Britannia' through my nose. A huge net was lowered into the sea and thank God we seemed to be moving forward again.

After a couple of hours' trawling the ocean bed, the winch was cranked into reverse and the net slowly hauled out of the water. The engine smoked and the winch screamed as the bulging net burst through the surface of the water. It was jam-packed with flapping fish of every shape and size, but as the crew turned the winch to land the catch, the overloaded thing broke. The net burst open and the whole silvery catch rained down, splashing back into the sea from whence it came. Engine smoke drifted across the deck and the crew fell silent. After much shouting and gesticulating, Cesare turned and looked at me. Hang on, was I the Jonah, in my weakened, near-sunstroked daze?

I began to imagine they were gonna throw me overboard as some sort of sacrifice to Poseidon. Cesare came towards me, stopped, and proffered a bottle of red wine. It was even warmer. Great, just what I need, mulled wine. But I was so thirsty I took a swig. It nearly came flying straight back out again. The sun was now high in the sky, the boat had no cover, I was really feeling it. We were right out in the middle of the Adriatic, I could see the coastline of Albania quite clearly in front of us.

Er, Cesare, aren't we supposed to be back at seven? 'We are,' he said, somewhat distractedly. I looked at my watch, it was midday. Yes, he said, we will be back by seven, seven this evening. My knees buckled. I only thought we'd be out for a few hours. I had no suntan lotion, no hat, my phone wasn't working and no water. I took another swig of the warm wine. I had been hanging on for grim death and now had another seven hours of this hell to look forward to. I seriously contemplated throwing myself in and swimming back, but the coast of Italy on our right had all but disappeared. The crew were in no mind for compromise. They'd lost a big catch and were determined to make up for it. The net was dropped and the boat ploughed on.

On the horizon another boat appeared, the first I'd seen all day, and it was heading our way fast. It was the Guardia di Finanza. They spent a lot of time patrolling the waters between Italy and Albania, on the lookout for drug and human trafficking. Within seconds their well-armed speedboat was roaring alongside. I was unceremoniously ushered below deck, where I was told to sit quietly on a stool, in the engine room, till further notice. The door closed, leaving me in the deafening, boiling hot, smoky dark. Well, my Italian wasn't up to much, and I didn't have my passport. Bollocks! Maybe I would be mistaken for an Albanian refugee, who'd been drifting out at sea for days. It was certainly how I was beginning to feel, and look. I really didn't fancy spending a couple of months in a southern Italian prison.

So I sat still in the engine room, breathing through the sleeve of my T-shirt. After a while I saw the silhouettes of feet shuffling past the door. They hovered for a second, and then they went. After what seemed an age the door finally opened and the blinding sun burst in. I scrambled out, gasping into the fresh air. I couldn't give a bollocks if I was being arrested or not. A southern Italian prison cell would have been heaven compared to that.

Cesare was standing there. With my broken Italian, I couldn't understand what he was saying, but boy was I glad to be back on deck, hot and stinky as it may have been. As I once again hung onto my stanchion, the will to live had almost evaporated. The boat zigzagging across the sea, the net being let out and winched in time and time again.

We finally pulled into the harbour as the sun was on the wane, having caught very little. 'Seven o'clock,' said Cesare, pointing proudly at his watch, pleased with what he saw as an unusual piece of Italian punctuality. How I managed the long hours till 7 p.m. I am not sure. With my last ounce of strength I crawled ashore, weakly thanking all concerned, and climbed unsteadily onto my feet. Back, at last, on dry land.

All that time at sea had left me with what felt like legs made of rubber. 'Hang on,' said Cesare, as I began to wobble off down the quayside. He disappeared into his lock-up and reappeared with a big polystyrene box. 'A present,' he said. 'As we caught nothing today, it's a little something from yesterday's catch.' It was all I could do to turn around. I thanked him again and set off home, pitching and rolling like the fishing boat, as I struggled not to drop the slippery box of fish.

I was pulverised, dehydrated, sunburnt as I veered up the drive to the house. I was in such a state of delirium that I began to imagine that the lid of the box was moving. I stumbled on, the front door almost in touching distance. Hang on, the lid *was* moving, a tentacle was making its way from under the lid and round my left wrist. Then another, then another. The lid came off to reveal six or seven live octopus, all making a break for it. By the time I got to the front door one of them had got right up my arm and had a tentacle wrapped round my face. Anne unsurprisingly looked shocked. Jesus! She'd been really worried as I hadn't phoned. I didn't have the energy to explain. Nor did I have the energy to deal with half a dozen frisky cephalopods.

At this point I was perfectly happy to accept that the octopuses had won. Anne began prising them off with the handle of a wooden spoon and flinging them back into the box. She got them all in and sat on the lid. What are we gonna do with these, then? I couldn't speak. What we are going to do with them, I couldn't care less. I didn't have the strength, never mind the inclination, to kill the things. It would all be over in a matter of minutes, and I'd be the one on the barbecue.

Anne didn't fancy it either. We'd only witnessed the preparation of live octopus once before, on holiday in Greece. It basically involved grabbing them by the tentacles and bashing their heads on the rocks. Maybe we should let them go and put them back in the sea. No, we couldn't waste the things; they were a very highly valued luxury in this part of the world. It would be a terrible insult to the chaps that bought them. Hmm. Anne rang our next-door neighbour. She was round in a trice and very happy to take them off our hands/face. The car pulled away and I flopped in a chair. I still couldn't speak.

The vaguely familiar sounds of a beeping car horn and distorted radio were coming up our drive. Seconds later Gigi and Cesare were standing on our threshold. They clapped their hands together, rubbing them vigorously. 'Right, where are those delicious octopus?'

THE BARBIE BIKE

I've always loved cycling. I think it started in my early teens when me and my mates decided we'd cycle from the courtyard of Cavendish Mansions to Salisbury Plain. I don't know why; I think I'd seen it on a map at school. Maybe it was something to do with the army range. And well I remember strapping my transistor radio to the handlebars with an octopus clip. It was a warm summer's morn and we were off to the tinny strains of Cockney Rebel's 'Judy Teen'. Unfortunately the batteries ran out at St John's Wood and so did my legs. But fortunate in the end really, as we had no tents, food or money.

The bicycle is the ultimate leveller. No matter what your worth, on a bike everyone is equal and you don't need no gas. There are not many better feelings than weaving side to side down a country hill, imagining you're on a motorbike, or many more challenging things than puffing up the one that inevitably follows.

Clive Langer, Madness's producer, is a keen cyclist too, and I've been on a few trips with him, from the early days of the London-to-Brighton, through the 180 miles of the Bath-to-London. Trips round Brittany where terrific lunches would be followed by bouts of enthusiastic competitive cycling which would wilt in the late-afternoon heat, to the point that on one occasion we pulled up at our destination in the back of a local farmer's tractor.

It is a fantastic feeling pulling off in the morning into the unknown, pedalling past the countryside at a pace that allows you to take it all in. The sights and smells of the great outdoors. Finding yourself really in the middle of nowhere, surrounded by fields of sunflowers and corn. Stopping in a one-horse village for a coffee and restorative shnoofter. Up hill and down dale, free as a bird, waving at the occasional passer-by and stopping for a well-earned lunch at a small auberge, where the wine is already open and on the table.

Clive says that, apart from making music, it's one of the only times he really feels alive, feels life's purpose. Most of my friends cycle, and in fact the whole band did at one point. I remember the big pile of bikes outside our rehearsal room off the Cally Road, or setting off in a big pack from North London to Clive's studio in Notting Hill Gate. Up round the back of the Regent's Park Estate, along the private road that runs along the front of the magical Nash terraces, and up through the park.

We've cycled from London to Brighton, Bath to London. Clive and I even did a ten-day charity ride in Thailand with about thirty other people, which was great. Beautiful people, great food, truly spectacular scenery, hills, rivers, and a 400-foot golden Buddha. We arrived in Chang Mai for the moon festival where thousands of those sky lanterns were released, and an equal number of candles were set on the river. It was a most memorable trip, marred only by the fact that the party on the road was broken down into pretty much three camps, going at their own tempo, with a lorry bringing up the rear with all our bags. It was also there for those who needed a break from the saddle, or who felt like giving up.

The first group were the super fit, iron men, triathletes and the like; the second a mixed bag of pretty fit people; then came a group of the less fit who poodled along chatting. Then a couple of old grannies with bikes with baskets on the front. Then me, with the chugging engine of the truck of death breathing down my neck, day in and day out. I remember one particular afternoon crawling up a steep hill, one of them where you don't look up, you just focus on the white line and try not to fall off, given that you are in the lowest gear possible and barely moving. Helmet on the side of my head, each painful pedal filled with the mantra. 'I'm not giving up, I am not giving up', the growling truck of death licking at my heels. The sun was beating mercilessly, my tongue was hanging out and my head felt like it was about to explode, when Clive drifted backwards into my sweat-blurred view.

He'd dropped back to see how I was, which was nice. We rode together for a bit before he said, 'How are you?' I wanted to say 'Fuck off', but all that came out was, 'Ffffff . . . ine'. He rode alongside me for a little while before picking up the pace, which wasn't difficult, seeing as I was being overtaken by ants. He shot off again, with a terrifically encouraging, 'You look terrible.' The last thing I saw was the back of Clive's head, before my attention was once again focused on the white line. 'One, two, musn't give up . . .' Pedal, pedal. Rumble of lorry engine. 'Three, four, musn't give up.' Pedal, pedal.

Needless to say Clive was in one of the fitter groups and had prepared properly and I spent most of the trip looking at the back of his head. My training for the Thailand trip consisted of running up and down the beach on arrival, twice, and having a couple of well-earned cold beers the night before we set off. Ah, but the pain, ultimately so rewarding, darlings, the overwhelming feeling of achievement as you're waved on past the drinks stop that everyone else has had a nice break at, and already left. The thrill of pulling up at some delightful hilltop restaurant for lunch, just as everyone else is pulling away with bananas in their gobs. And who could possibly forget the joy of arriving at the hotel so late, that some of the party are already up doing stretching exercises for the following days ride.

With my Thai experience in mind, I set about preparing myself with a little more than my usual rigour for a trip Clive and I had been planning for some time. A week-long cycle from my house in Salento round the southernmost tip of Italy.

It was decided that we would go in September, when the weather would be a little cooler and the roads would be quieter. The party was, Clive, Sam (my next-door neighbour) and my cousin Hector. We all met at some god-unearthly hour at Stansted, but it meant that we were at the house in time for lunch: I toasted up a bit of bruschetta, rubbed it with garlic, on went the tomatoes, Parmesan, basil and olive oil. A glass of red wine and we were flying.

Humanity restored, Sam was keen to have a look at the bikes. Earlier in the year I'd spoken to Ricardo, one of my Italian neighbours about our forthcoming trip; he'd laughed at the idea that we would pay to hire bikes. He told me he would borrow some on our behalf and leave them in the shed behind the house. I hadn't stipulated what kind of bikes – racing, road or mountain – so we weren't sure what we were going to get, maybe a mixture. Well, you can say that again.

The first bike Sam appeared with out of the shed was an old iron-framed post office job, covered in cobwebs with a basket on the front. The next one was more promising, a proper racing bike, but the only problem was that, on closer inspection, the seat was jammed right down on the frame, at its lowest position. Next came a kid's mountain bike with tyres like a tractor's, which were flat. Lastly, the *pièce de résistance*, a pink girl's bike resplendent in Barbie livery.

'That can't be it surely?' Sam went back in. 'Well, unless one of you fancies riding this?' He came back out pushing an old lawn-mower. Looking at the state of the bikes, that didn't seem like such a preposterous idea. I phoned Ricardo, who seemed vaguely put out at the suggestion these bikes might not be perfect for a seven-day cycle trip. 'That black bike was my grandad's, he rode that every day of his life. And the pink one, that's brand-new. I bought that for my niece. It cost forty euros!' More to the point, the bicycle hire shop was closed for the winter, as does pretty much everything else in Salento. My fellow riders looked on expectantly. I put the phone down.

It was only when we were pumping the tractor tyres on the mountain bike the following morning that we discovered the only bike that looked vaguely fit for purpose actually had a square back wheel. I wasn't sure we'd make one day's cycling, never mind a week, but in the spirit of the great British explorers of yore off we set. It only seemed fair to draw lots to see who got what bike, and then swap them round every day.

It was a beautiful sunny morning, and I can't say we weren't laughing as we headed off down the coast, looking like a troupe Billy Smart would have been proud of. I'd got the racer, which was a lovely smooth roller, but the saddle position meant my knees were up round my chin, Hector had the mountain bike, which was going up and down at the back like a clown's car. Sam had Il Postino with the three gears and his kit in the basket. Clive was top boy, in full Lycra, riding the Barbie machine.

First stop was Dentoni's, the best coffee bar and ice-cream parlour in the whole of Salento, probably the world, in my reckoning. People come for miles to eat Signor Dentoni's cakes and ice cream, and drink his coffee. He has thirty different flavours of ice cream displayed in an enormous cabinet, with the main ingredient displayed on the top. The *barrista*, Maxi, can make coffee in fifty-two different ways, one for every week of the year. He has a mirror above the coffee machine, so without even turning round he will have your coffee of choice on the go as you arrive at the counter.

But the killer, the reason Dentoni's knocks all its competitors into a cocked snoop, are the *cornetti*; miraculously light croissants filled with hot custard. In the summer it gets so busy they employ a raffle-ticket system in which you wait for your number to come up on an LED screen. A ripple of approval as CCTV coverage turns to the white-clad bakers in the basement, filling the dumb waiter with another load of steaming *cornetti*. One summer Signor Dentoni took me down to see the kitchen. At the height of the season he employs forty people, churning, baking and piping. Willy Wonka's for adults.

We drank our coffee, slurped our *cornetti* and hit the road. *Easy Rider* eat your heart out. The first bit of road was long and straight and headed right off along the clifftop. We were aiming for Porto Badisco, which doesn't actually have a disco, but has one of my favourite restaurants, the one that serves *ricci*, when in season. It's run by a fisherman and his family and is only open in the summer.

On the way to Porto Badisco we passed Ricardo's summer business, his campsite, and swung in to say hello. It was midday and Ricardo was swinging in his hammock, the back of his hand draped over his eyes and a glass of wine dangling at his side. Over the summer period, he always complains of being '*molto stanco*', basically knackered, from all the work he has to do at the campsite. Which, whenever I visit, seems to consist of chatting up birds, drinking, riding his horses and pretending to play his mechanical karaoke piano whilst singing at the top of his voice late into the night. Wafting his fingers over the self-playing keyboard he croons romantic Italian ballads to a bevy of attentive northern Italian ladies who come to the site every year. He once quite seriously asked me to form a band with him.

Ricardo looked up and leapt down from his hammock in his lurid orange kaftan and black Prada socks, his black eyes flashing. I'd had a number of run-ins with him over the years, but I liked him. A row to Ricardo was like water off a duck's back. He'd worked hard since he was a kid, and like so many southern Italians, ended up having to go abroad for work. He'd been from Austria to Libya, labouring and roadbuilding, and now in his sixties had created his own little fiefdom down by the sea.

'Ow ar u, *amico?*' He strode towards me, arms aloft. He was about five foot eight and had the physique of a middleweight boxer. He looked after himself, rode his horses every day and taught the tango by night. But it was the bedroom tango that brought the chunky northern Italian women back every year.

'You, Sax,' as he called me, 'are the maestro of the musical *spettacolo*,' he once explained, 'I am the master of the mattress spectacular, ha ha ha!' He then went on in grisly detail to list all the functions he required of the different women in his life, making parallels with his horses. Some were for racing, some for jumping, some for a slow trot and some just to talk to and pat. Not sure who was right for dressage.

Most of my Italian friends were horrified by him, understandably. To them he was a dreadful old cliché of all that was wrong with the world's perception of the Italian male. He made Berlusconi seem positively enlightened. He was of course a huge fan, and Berlusconi could do no wrong.

His schlong stowed back in its sarong, Ricardo led us to a big trestle table in the pinewood. Paolo, his trusted second in command, was already firing up the barbecue, and before we had a chance to say anything our places were being set and three bottles of *vino locale* were opened on our table. Salads arrived, roast fish arrived, more *vinos collapsos* arrived, coffee and grappa arrived, and then Ricardo appeared through the trees, riding a huge white stallion and blowing a trumpet. Followed by a gaggle of giggling Japanese girls blowing plastic trumpets.

We were more than slightly wobbly when we got back on our bikes, and it was executively decided that we would be slightly less adventurous in our day's travels than we had anticipated that morning. We'd stop at the spa town of Santa Cesarea Terme, about an hour's further cycle. We flew past Porto Badisco, and a girl with black spiky hair cutting sea urchins on the roadside from a big ceramic sink, in the late-afternoon sunshine. It was glorious, with the sparkling blue Adriatic on our left, and ahead the ribbon-like coastline heading down the misty peninsula.

It was all downhill and we were flying, full of *joie de vivre* and *vino locale*. My cousin Hector at the front, legs sticking out, going up and down riding the mountain bike like a road drill. Somewhere at the back of my somewhat befuddled mind a voice was reminding me that what goes up, etc., and vice versa. It was steep and we really were going some when we passed a group of serious-looking cyclists, on some serious-looking bikes, puffing up the other side of the road. We waved but they didn't wave back, and then I remembered what we were riding. We must have looked like escapees from the local asylum.

Santa Cesarea is built on a huge steaming lake of volcanic mud, and has two or three extraordinary Moroccan-style hotels which have mined down through their basements and into the stuff. Old people chuck themselves into the sulphurous pong in order to cure themselves of arthritic ailments, which apparently it does. We found a reasonable hotel, had some dinner and played cards in the lobby with a lot of old people and the smell of the devil.

The group were up with a steely determination the following morning to make up the time we'd lost the previous day. I was relieved to exchange the racing bike, with the saddle like a wooden razor blade, for the relative comfort of the mountain bike. Relieved, that was, until we hit the first hill out of town, and what had taken us twenty minutes to freewheel down the previous afternoon was gonna take us a good couple of hours to cycle up. It was the order of the holiday, the temptation to cycle down to some beautiful bay for a dip in the sea tempered by the fact we'd have to effing well come back up again.

We stopped at a small clifftop village for lunch, *panini* and a beer, no time for anything grander. The owner asked us where we were cycling to, having seen our clobber, and was impressed when I explained our trip. Well, impressed until he came outside to wave us off. There were four stray dogs asleep under the tree our crazy collection of machines was resting on. Clive was first off on the racer, Sam next on the Barbie machine, Hector on the post office job and me at the rear, waving behind me at the bar owner and bobbing up and down on my square back wheel.

As we pulled away one of the dogs woke and began to bark.

The others joined in and they started to chase us. They were the usual funny old mixture of mongrels you often see sitting about in Salento villages. One of them was three-legged and was snapping at my wonky back wheel. The faster I went the faster he went too. I couldn't shake him off. As we reached the outskirts of town all but the three-legged mutt had given up the chase and slunk back to the shade of their tree. I'd overtaken Clive on a long straight road and swung to the left, so Clive flew past and the three-legged one went with him. The sight of Clive on the low-slung racing bike, lashing out with one leg as he disappeared off down the dusty road with a three-legged dog snapping at his back wheel, is one I shall never forget.

We eventually made it to Leuca, the furthermost tip and land's end, which is a pretty uneventful out-of-season seaside resort, and headed back up the coast for Gallipoli. Gallipoli is like a mini-Venice, a jewel set in the extraordinarily blue Mediterranean sea, an island that you reach by a small causeway. We pulled up our bikes at an old bar, which turned out to be the local fishermen's club. It was dark inside but the welcome was friendly for the *ciclisti inglese*. We had a much needed cold beer and made enquiries as to where we might stay. I don't know if it was the state of us or the bikes, but they took pity on us to the point that one of the fishermen suggested we could stay in his house. I explained that that was very kind but we were just looking for a small hotel. One was duly found, we had a shower and headed out.

The sun was setting and we found a lovely restaurant overlooking the sea. After a delicious dinner of grilled *orate* (sea bream), we headed off to a bar where there was music. When we arrived people were playing guitars and tambourines in the traditional pizzicato style. After a couple of hours (and drinks) I announced

I was a bit of a singer myself, and joined in on a couple of numbers, accompanying myself on the spoons. I then tried to explain Clive's role as the producer of all Madness's records, plus ones by Dexys Midnight Runners and Elvis Costello, and that he could also play the guitar. He was duly handed one, and I think that in the confusion of my pidgin Italian our hosts thought I was saying he was Elvis Costello. He has the same glasses and is a jolly good songwriter himself, but he's nay Elvis.

They were already starting to look suspicious as he began to strum, and I realised that in the thirty-odd years I've known Clive, we'd never learnt a song we could play together. He didn't know how to play the music to any Madness songs and I couldn't remember the words to any of his. We had a manful go at 'Shipbuilding', in which Clive was struggling to remember his own tune. Ironically, Elvis Costello had written the words, and I couldn't remember more than half a dozen of them. After three goes, and a really shit attempt at 'My Girl,' we were asked to leave, they obviously thought we were taking the piss. It was with some embarrassment that we left the bar with our tails between our legs and shuffled off back to our hotel. Fifty-odd hit records between the pair of us.

The countryside and the days flew past, but on the last day we were still a bit behind schedule, and were cutting it a bit fine in order to get back to the house before nightfall, when we hit the beautiful medieval town of Galatina for lunch. It was decided once again that we would go for the sandwich option and get back on the road. It was a biggish town but there were no obvious signs of life, until we spotted a shopkeeper pulling down the shutters on his clothes shop. I asked him if there was a bar or somewhere we could get a bit of lunch. '*Si, si,* follow me,' he said.

We came to what looked like any other of the small houses we'd already passed, just in time to meet four rather jolly businessmen stumbling out of the door. He ushered us inside. There were two rooms, a kitchen on our right and a dining room on the left with one table on which was perched a giant television. Ubiquitous in all Italian restaurants is a giant blaring TV, only this one was broadcasting nothing more than green fuzz. A fat man in an apron stumbled out of the kitchen, and having established that we were English cyclists started giving us all big hugs. He showed us to the table and the four of us were seated around three sides of the sizzling and glaring green TV.

I think he'd come to the unlikely conclusion we'd cycled all the way from England and proceeded to feed us as if we had. We had our backs to the kitchen and a stumbling and clattering began before the first dishes appeared over our shoulders. Deep-fried cheese and a selection of salamis. More clattering and clanging before deep-fried aubergine and Parma ham. It was slightly disconcerting being blasted by the green light and white noise, and never being quite sure what exotic plates were going to appear over our heads next. And appear they did, *pasta pomodoro*, grilled fish, grilled vegetables, horse stew, it was endless, and I genuinely felt I was going to explode. Then the cheese board arrived.

The wine was flowing and Clive was getting right into it. Ice cream and cakes followed and Sam, who'd had to step outside for a break from the sensory overload, reappeared in time for coffee and grappa. I can't say it wasn't a relief to stand and get away from the hissing green-eyed gogglebox, but standing was proving a smidge difficult. We'd certainly had a bit more than the planned sandwich.

We paid our genial host, who was still trying to ply us with more grappa, and staggered out into the sunlight. We were just heading round the corner for our bikes, when the owner called after us. Sam was almost running away at this point. The owner puffed down the hill and presented us each with a bottle of wine, as if we needed it, for our journey.

But it was with a certain gaiety that we cycled out of town through the deserted streets and into the countryside. A gaiety that lasted precisely one hour before we hit the long straight road home and dehydration, accumulated tiredness and extremely sore arses kicked in. We were strung down the road at quarter-mile intervals by the time we got to the house. The sun was going down and we were knackered.

The following morning, sharing cappuccinos and custard croissants, the pain was forgotten and we were all just laughing and reminiscing happily about our adventures. The crazy bikes, the hills, overcoming the distance itself, and throughout all the trials and tribulations we'd got along really well. A feeling of elation and achievement abounded. At the airport bar, enjoying a cold beer, we were still laughing and joking at our ridiculous adventures and enthusiastically started discussing doing something similar the following year. My cousin Hector looked at us all one by one, put down his beer, and said, 'No.'

THE BACK OF CLIVE'S HEAD

Yeah, I've spent a fair amount of time looking at the back of Clive Langer's head. Cycling apart, as he's been the producer of our records for over thirty years, I hate to think quite what percentage of that time was spent lying on a sofa at the back of some recording studio or other, staring at the back of Clive's head. Weird really to think of it, over all those years, I've probably spent more time looking at the back of his head than the front. His black hair slowly turning from black to grey down the decades as he sat huddled over various mixing desks listening to a playback or recording of one of the hundreds of tracks we've recorded together.

The first time I spent any time looking at the back of his head was in a tiny little eight-track studio in Stoke Newington called Pathway. Clive had managed to get the attention of Rob Dickins, who at the time was the head of Warner Brothers publishing. Rob had championed Deaf School in his days as a record company executive and was an old friend of Clive's.

The only recordings we'd made up to this point were some

dodgy old tapes recorded in the various rehearsal rooms we'd been in. Invariably they cut out halfway through, where Lee had re-recorded sax parts he was practising over them.

We managed to save up 200 quid to record some proper demos. Clive duly booked two days at Pathway – he thought this would be just enough time to record three songs. It was decided that we would have a go at 'The Prince', 'My Girl' and 'Madness'. On the day we piled all our gear, and ourselves, into Mike's trusty ex-GPO Morris 1000 van with 'That Nutty Sound' spray-painted on the back door, and set off for our first day in a proper recording studio. Woody was gonna meet us there on his motorbike, but unfortunately got completely lost and didn't turn up.

We lost the first day's recording, which was not the most auspicious start to our professional career and meant we'd lost our hard earned savings. But Clive managed to draw on Rob's enthusiasm to borrow some cash and extend our recording time. Pathway studios had an anonymous-looking door in a small street round the back of Stoke Newington. Poor old Woody had ridden past it a couple of times as he buzzed round and round North London till he ran out of petrol. (Ah, the days before mobiles and satnav, the kids today don't know what they're missing.)

The studio was tiny, with a slightly out-of-tune upright piano. (An upright that would turn up thirty years later, when we recorded 'The Liberty of Norton Folgate'.) Elvis Costello had recorded 'Watching the Detectives', a song we all liked the sound of, in Pathway. But his band were only a four-piece. There was barely enough room for us lot to fit in the tiny live room.

It was an eight-track studio, which meant exactly that: you could record eight different things. By the eighties studios had forty-eight and even seventy-two tracks. The possibilities could become endless, and often did, as we would later discover.

But with Pathway's limited technology the only thing we could add once the basic tracks were recorded was for Chris to overdub a loud twang! through an echo machine during the piano solo of 'The Prince'. The atmosphere was great and the tracks were sounding good. With a couple of hours to spare at the end of the second day, it was just a matter of mixing them down. Which basically involved three of us, the maximum you could fit in the control room, pushing faders up and down as the songs went onto the two-inch tape, until we all felt the right balance of instruments and vocals had been achieved. Which at about midnight we all did.

We then took it in turns to sit in the control room and listen to the tracks on the BIG speakers. All studios tend to have at least three sets of speakers, one really small one, to hear how your songs might sound on the radio, medium ones that you might have at home, and fuckin' BIG ones you normally saved till the end of the session to hear what your songs might sound like in a club or disco.

We all agreed they sounded great, even if we said so ourselves. We then spent an hour or two recording the mixes onto cassettes, one at a time, so we could all take the songs away with us. Happy days! Really, joyful and innocent times. A feeling I still think you get today if you listen to those recordings. Which I certainly did at the time, over and over again, on my mum's music centre at home.

Rob Dickins liked the tracks and offered us a publishing deal and we were off. The possibility that none of us were going to have to work for the council or polish cars any more was getting to be a reality that was coming our way across the horizon.

It's pretty remarkable that in those two days, and with our very first experience of being in a studio, the three songs recorded would all become such important milestones in our musical career, and are still firm favourites some thirty-odd years on.

'Madness'. Although never a single, the song that gave us our name, our unofficial national anthem, still sending the crowds wild to this day, as our perennial first encore. 'The Prince'. Our first single, and a big hit on 2 Tone. And Mike Barson's 'My Girl'. A song that would alert the world to the fact that as much as we loved the music, we were more than just a ska band.

The next time I was to be taking in the back of Clive's head was when we went into TW studios in Fulham. Dave liked what Clive had done in Pathway, but suggested it might be good if he teamed up with a thrusting young engineer he knew called Alan Winstanley. Alan had worked with the Stranglers and on 'Knock on Wood' by Amy Stewart, an odd combination I'll give you, but it sounded good to us. Alan and Clive became a great team and went on to make pretty much all of Madness's records together, as well as an amazing array of fantastic records for Dexys Midnight Runners, Teardrop Explodes, Elvis Costello, Catatonia, Bush, Morrissey, David Bowie and Mick Jagger.

Dave booked us in to TW on Alan's recommendation for ten days. A whole ten days, and twenty-four tracks. But these were songs that we'd been playing live for nearly two years, so we knew them inside out.

When we arrived at TW, we discovered that the band that had just left were The Specials, having just finished their debut album with Elvis Costello at the helm. The first thing we noticed when we got in there, apart from the faint whiff of Rico's extra-long cigarettes, were some short lengths of tape lying about the floor next to the two-inch mastering machine. While Woody was setting up his drum kit, Alan put them on. They were only thirty seconds or so, obviously bits of music that had been edited out of the final mixes. We were intrigued. We loved The Specials, and I genuinely thought they were one of the best bands I'd ever seen live. But it couldn't be denied that there was a healthy competition between us.

With a bit of a fiddle Alan managed to get the two ends of the first bit of tape round the spindles of the tape machine and we waited with bated breath. What on earth would their record sound like? How much production would Elvis have added, given all the extra tracks you could use in this studio, to their electrifying live sound? Strings, brass ensemble, gospel choir? Alan pressed Play and we waited, the tape spun and then, clang! That's all we heard. Literally, the tape was so short it just flew off after one alarmingly loud snare beat.

The recording went swimmingly and we did add strings to one of our tracks, 'Night Boat to Cairo'. 'Night Boat To Cairo' was a strange song. As was often the case, I was climbing the stairs to Mike's bedroom in his house in Crouch End and I could hear some music drifting out that he'd been writing before we arrived for rehearsal. On this particular occasion it was a rather strange Egyptian-sounding thing, an instrumental with no words. 'Do you have any idea what it's called, Mike?' I asked. He said, 'Yes, I'm gonna call it "Night Boat To Cairo".'

Then I went off and wrote two verses, I think, with the full intention of expanding them into a chorus and middle eights and all the rest of it. But it never happened. So the whole song ended up as this peculiar mix of one minute of instrumental at the beginning, two verses in the middle and one minute of instrumental on the outro. With a fake ending.

Amusingly, Clive had asked the arranger, David Bedford, to score an 'Egyptian' string part, but over the phone David had misheard him and arranged a 'Gypsy' string part. But still it sounded great, as did the rest of the record.

The ten days were up and we all felt we'd done a good job. Dave came down the studio to hear a playback of the whole thing through the BIG speakers. Dave was pleased, pencil behind his ear, beaming, but in the words of Columbo, 'Just one more thing . . .' He'd become obsessed with a short piece of music we had played at his wedding. A bit of old nonsense really, a strange one-minute instrumental we used as our entrance music. We'd been starting the set with the theme from *Hawaii Five-0* but had got a bit bored of it so had replaced it with an instrumental Prince Buster B-side. Dave was convinced the short piece should be the first single from our debut album, but the recording was finished. We'd run out of studio time, and anyway there wasn't enough in it to make a three-minute single.

But while we were down the pub Dave snuck back into the studio and extended the length of the song by repeating the end section and gluing the two pieces of tape together. He put the whole thing through a harmoniser to smudge away the join.

With Chas Smash's now infamous clarion call 'Hey you, don't watch that, watch this . . .' 'One Step Beyond' did become a big hit, and the title track of our iconic first album.

One day Mike was messing about on the piano with an old Labi Siffre song and Dave comes in and says, 'You've got to record that.' It was a great tune but we didn't feel it was right for us – a bit too sentimental. It must be love? Nothing more, nothing less? Love is the best? Who's going to go for that? But Dave was convinced to the point that he said if 'It Must Be Love' didn't get in the Top 5 then he would give us his record company. 'It Must Be Love' got to No. 2 so we never did get to own Stiff Records.

Back from Bath, 180 miles I'll have you know

ME AND MY GIRLS

In 1981 things carried on getting better. 'It Must Be Love' was flying up the charts and it, indeed, must be love, cos Bette Bright said 'I do' to me. It was a beautiful wedding in St Luke's Church in Kentish town. A beautiful white wedding. We'd had two foot of snow the night before. The day didn't get off to the perfect start. In the morning I was round at my mum's going through the day's events with my best man, Chalky. Everything was looking great, the rings hadn't been lost, the flowers were sorted, cars sorted, seating plan arranged, no teeth lost during the stag do, which in itself was a miracle as the evening had kicked off with a lemonade bottle of Pocheen brought over from Ireland by Cathal.

We checked and double checked: all present and correct. The only thing left was for us to get dressed. Well, I must say, we were looking terrific in grey top hats and tails. A real couple of swells. Perfect. These yobbos don't scrub up too bad. Until I went to put my shoes on and realised they had holes in them! I'd just come back from a three-month tour and all that skipping about on stage had worn them through. What to do? I couldn't go home as Anne was there preparing with her maids of honour, and I was in no way allowed to see the dress before the event. The alternative was the pair of blue Converse I'd arrived in. I think not. 'Hang about', said Chalky, 'isn't the shoe shop Holts on the way to the church?' Brilliant.

So off we set to Camden. When we got in the shop my feet were nearly frozen, slushing through that snow with holes in my shoes. Alan was there to greet us and before we got too far into reminiscing about the early days of the band and how that Elvis Costello bloke still owed him 30 bob for them creepers, I explained my predicament. The shop was a veritable mecca of alternative footware, but amongst the brothel creepers, DMs and monkey boots he did stock black brogues. Just the job. 'What size are you, nine isn't it?' 'Yes, Alan, spot on.'

He disappeared behind the piles of shoe boxes stacked to the ceiling, but after five minutes he reappeared empty handed. Scratching his chin. 'Hmm, we haven't got any of them in a nine.' He looked around the shop, there had to be something else. Yeah what, pink pointed brothel creepers, nine hole DMs. I'm getting married, not going to a Sex Pistols concert.

I was starting to panic. 'What a about a pair of loafers', he said, 'they're smart'.

'Hmmm, a grey mohair dress suit and oxblood loafers, I don't think so, Alan.'

We stood in silence, the only other shop for miles was Dunne & Co., the old man's gaff. Great, a pair of beige carpet slippers and a trilby would give the in-laws something to think about. Probably more than what they were going to think about giving their lovely daughter away to a spotty herbert kneeling at the altar exposing holes in his shoes.

Time was running out, I was doomed. Maybe you could feign a sudden conversion to Islam as you enter the church and take your shoes off, ha ha. Chalky suddenly piped up, 'I've got it, at no point in the service does the best man have to kneel down. You'll have to borrow my shoes.' They were well worn and a size too small but the soles were intact. So with the help of a shoe horn and three strong men, on they went, and off we set for the church.

It was a joyous and momentous day. Anne looked gorgeous in Anna Karenina-style wedding dress, it was like she'd booked the snow to go with her outfit. And everyone was there, my mum, my aunt and cousins from Wales, the band and all my friends. Culminating, having changed my shoes, in a big party at Lauderdale House in Highgate where we danced the night away. Chalky having lost his best man's speech, much to the relief of everyone.

My honeymoon consisted of two idyllic nights at the Ritz Hotel as I was still in the middle of a Christmas tour. I had to borrow a tie from reception to go in the bar, which looked great with a crew-necked jumper. And the tie was all I was wearing at the freshly delivered breakfast table in our room the following morning. I was just about to tuck into my kippers when the door burst open and room service appeared with a second wave of silver-clad delights. I yanked the table cloth around my midriff nearly sending everything flying. 'Would that be all, sir?' Unfortunately I didn't have a tip about my person.

On the second day of our honeymoon I got up early and sneaked out. I was off to buy Anne a wedding present, a car, a Karmann Ghia, Anne's favourite. One she'd dreamed about ever since seeing her next-door neighbour get one when she was a child. I'd seen one in *Exchange and Mart*, racing green, £1,000, lovely. Only problem was, it was in Luton. Lee came with me, he knew a bit about cars and would kick the tyres and give it the once over. The car looked and sounded great. Dosh was handed over and we were off. The previous couple of days' snow had turned to ice and I'd never driven a car before. Apart from that what could possibly go wrong? Oh, that and the fact the visibility was almost zero, the back window was the size of a postage stamp and the heating in the Karmann normally just got going on arrival at your destination.

Lee, my co-pilot, hollered increasingly desperate instructions as I kangaroo leaped and skidded my way back into town. Fortunately it was Sunday and there wasn't much traffic about.

Finally we arrived at my newly purchased house in Camden Mews. It had been part of the stables for the bigger houses at the back. It was pretty, but tiny. One half of the downstairs was a garage, which we were eventually going to convert. The furniture at this point consisted of one jukebox with one record, 'Cry Me a River' by Julie London. Which did make our house-warming somewhat limited, as did the fact that my mate who'd been in charge of the bar got fed up halfway through the proceedings and locked all the booze in the bathroom (we'd filled the bath with ice as a makeshift fridge) taking the key with him.

After what must have been a twelve-point turn I managed to get the damn car in the garage, tied a ribbon round it and set off back to a bemused Anne at the Ritz.

The years flew and we had two lovely daughters, Scarlett and Viva. The Karmann Ghia became too small and sadly had to go, as did the mews house.

I have lived in North London on and off most of my life, and for the last quarter of a century in the same house in the same street, in, as they say, Tufnell Park if you're selling, Holloway if you're buying. I live in a nice little part of London. Landmarks it doesn't really have none. It's not famous for anything really, except the prison, which you can see quite clearly.

Holloway was exactly that, a hollow way through the woods out of London up to the sunny slopes of Highgate. It was plagued by a notorious highway man called Le Fevre, a Frenchman, who would hang about the Nag's Head, a coaching inn on the corner of Seven Sisters Road. 'Your money or your life, *mon ami*.' Having your chattels removed with menace is one of the few local traditions that survives to this day.

When we eventually settled the family home in Holloway, it was completely by accident. Madness had been riding high, not that we still aren't I hasten to add, but particularly high in the early eighties, we were arguably the biggest band of the decade, certainly in terms of weeks spent in the charts. I bought an enormous place in Camden Square, one of the posher spots in North London. Unfortunately the great god of timing had other things in mind. We had a row with Stiff Records thinking they owed us some money. And in 1983, just four years into our chart-topping career, cracks were starting to appear in the band.

Mike Barson was getting tired of show business. We should have spotted the signs when he turned up at a photo session wearing a balaclava. Then he stopped turning up altogether. In 1984 he left, and the magic started to evaporate. The band was born in his bedroom and without him it wouldn't be the same. And it wasn't: things went downhill. If we'd had the knowledge we have now we would just have taken a break. We'd been working to the same model that bands of the 1960s employed. One album and three singles a year, the rest of the time was spent on the road. Not that we didn't have a great time, cause we did. Going round the world playing music with your best mates.

We really never stopped laughing, and if it looked like we were having a lot of fun, that's because we were. But at this point we were all newly married with young kids and we were very rarely at home.

After the first four years or so, we needed to spend time apart. We split up and it was only on reflection that we realised we should have had a rest. Up to that point there was no sense that you took time off. In fact there was a real terror, not from the band but from the people around the band, that if we stopped even for five minutes then we'd be usurped by somebody else.

We should have had more confidence in the fact that we'd had twenty-odd hits and Madness wasn't going to go out of fashion all of a sudden. But it was only when we came back in 1992 that we realised the enormity of what we'd achieved.

A lot of people say the best music is written by bands when they're young, and that is often the case when you think back to all the great bands. But I think Madness has transcended that a bit, and with *Norton Folgate* we made a really great album, as good as any of the stuff we wrote when we were young. That's partly because we learnt to re-energise ourselves by not doing it all the time. Also it helps a lot for playing live. We now do twenty concerts a year and that's enough for us to keep it exciting for ourselves and not get weary. If I do any more than that I find the music starts to become abstract noise, and you can't really feel it much any more.

But anyway, here I was, newly married with two young kids and a band that was fast falling apart. At this point we also had the recording studio and record label, both of which were draining whatever resources we had accrued up to this point.

It was time to sell up and ship out. The big house had to go. It was a sad day when we moved, and there was nothing fun about moving out. But the house went for a great price, Anne found a lovely Victorian terraced house just down the road in Holloway and we were back in the black.

Strangely, I remember the day we moved was the day of Live Aid. It was a hot day and the concert was blaring out of every open window in the street. 'Feed the world, let them know it's Christmas time . . .' But the words ringing in my ears were, 'What's that Bob Geldof ever gonna organise?' Which is what we replied when asked if we would like to take part in an earlier photo session.

We've been living in our house for twenty-five years, and now the kids have left we're rattling about in a place that's a bit too big. We keep talking about moving, but we never do. The kids are only down the road in Hornsey. I call them kids, they are of course grown women, and beautiful people with it. They're round every other night, decimating our fridge. And we always have Sunday lunch together in this funny old house that's witnessed the majority of our lives.

When the girls were about eight and five respectively, we had topsy-turvy day, something Anne had read about in a Swedish children's book. Adults and the children reverse their roles for a whole day. First off was a trip to the supermarket so the girls could do the shopping. As we waited at the till, Scarlett inevitably came down the aisle pushing a trolly loaded with sweets and fizzy drinks. Half-way down she had a second thought and started unloading handfuls of sweets onto random shelves and replacing them with tins of tuna, bread and salady things. So for lunch we had tuna sandwiches, sweets and lashings of pop. The kids spent the after-noon eating sweets and watching cartoons on the video. We had tuna salad for dinner and then the girls disappeared downstairs to see our lodger, Mo. Mo was a lovely girl who had come with the

house, which gave us a great baby-sitting option. After an hour or
so of Soul II Soul blasting out of the basement I went downstairs for
a look. Mo and Viva were dancing round the room as Scarlett leapt
up and down on the bed sloshing a glass of shandy, her cheeks as
red as apples. 'It's 7.30, time for your bed,' she happily announced.
Which it was in topsy-turvy world, we headed upstairs. 'I'll come
up and read you a story in a bit.' About an hour later she did come
up. The colour having drained from her face. She stuck her head
round our door. 'I'm sorry I can't read a story, I feel sick.' As she
headed upstairs to her bedroom we could hear her saying to Viva,

'I don't like this bit about being a grown-up.'

This house has seen the lot. The fighting, the parties, dancing
on the kitchen table, all of them pet funerals, exams, the ceilings
falling in, rows about the hedge, the loving, the ups, the downs
and indeed the sideways.

And here we still are, in our nice little terraced house. Scarlett and Viva's names still written in the concrete path with their
fingers, the odd letter the wrong way round.

THE LIBERTY OF
NORTON FOLGATE

When I heard of the Liberty of Norton Folgate it just sounded like a great song title, something Syd Barrett might have come up with in his psychedelic pomp. Madness hadn't made an album for a couple of years, the previous one having been an album of covers of the kind of music we started out playing in the pubs and clubs of North London in the late seventies – ska, reggae, some Motown stuff. We recorded it under the pseudonym 'The Dangermen', and the idea was that a return to our musical roots would be a great way to revive and rejuvenate the reason we made music in the first place. We launched the album at our ancestral seat, the Dublin Castle in Camden Town. We ended up staying for a week, and it was enormous fun playing that great old dance music again in a sweaty pub, and, boy, was it sweaty. On the third night I half-heartedly asked the owner, Henry, son of Alo, the guy who'd given us our first break in 1978, if there was any air-con. 'Air-conditioning!' he bellowed, 'I've been turning the heat up!' A chip off the old block.

The Dangermen project went great and ironically became a big hit in France. The whole thing was rejuvenating and revitalising, and now we were back in the mood it was decided our next record would be a dense British pop record, basically a great Madness album, utilising all of the influences that have informed the band for nigh on thirty years. The word 'concept' was being bandied around, a word that up to this point had always engendered thoughts of fellas in capes playing twenty-minute synthesiser solos in a swirling fog of dry ice. But our conversations got as far as the idea of a concept album about London. Despite the observation of my esteemed colleague, guitarist C. J. Foreman, who remarked, 'What?, we thought the majority of our songs *were* about London.'

We were all brought up in London and it has informed most of our work. I'm not saying London is any better than anywhere else, but it just happens to be the place I was sitting in as a budding songwriter, as the world of inspiration strolled by. I'm sure someone who was brought up in Paris, New York, or wherever might feel the same way about his own city.

I've written songs about the characters and indeed the areas of London I've known over the years. I tried once to write a song about London as a whole, inspired by Peter Ackroyd's great book *London: The Biography*, in which he tried rather successfully to capture the personality of this vast metropolis. But I was defeated. For me, the subject was just too big for a song. Ackroyd had hundreds of thousands of words to play with. A smidge too many for a pop song. North, east, south and west, there's just too much diversity and local history in this vast collection of what was once small villages to fit into three verses and a couple of choruses. But chatting to Mike from REM in a bar one night an idea that had been fermenting in the back of my mind for some time resurfaced. We were talking about where I live in North London and he was fascinated to hear how and when the street was built, the layers of history that lie beneath London's pavements. And it got me thinking about that, going down through the pavement through those layers of history in one small area, all the comings and goings of the various migrants who make an area their own, before sometimes moving on. That might be a way, a small way, of painting a picture of London as a whole. A song about a street or an area in its full historical context. Not looking side to side. Not just a song about now. But a song that starts from then, right at the beginning, and takes us to now, via all the various generations of people who've come to this great city to make their way in the world. An X-ray view, going down through the street surface of today's city, peeling back the layers of grime and history, shrapnel and shoes, broken pots and broken dreams. I started to do some research on my own street, and in the process came across a book called *This Bright Field*, written by a chap called William Taylor, which had the intriguing subtitle of 'a travel book in one place'. Words that couldn't have been more appropriate to what I was hoping to convey in this as yet untitled song. Taylor discovered an area of Spitalfields known as 'The Liberty of Norton Folgate'. Originally a rubbish tip, it later became a refuge for actors, writers, thinkers, louts, lowlifes and libertines – outsiders and trouble-makers all. Sounds like our kind of place, does it not?

Which fitted perfectly into a concept the band had had for some time, about making a concept album about London. The city we'd all grown up in and the city that had made us what we were. One by one songs were written which seemed to fit the concept, so the album of *Norton Folgate* began to come together.

We started out in an 8-track studio in Hackney called Toe Rag, trying to capture some of the feeling of our early records. All of us in the room together, recording live. Chris, the guitarist, had left the band during the Dangermen stuff, but decided to rejoin halfway through so we moved to a bigger studio for the second half of the record.

It was hugely critically well received, more than we could ever have imagined, and was a big hit. Once again we were back in the frame of current musical acts. None of our previous records had ever been reviewed like that. It felt as if people were looking back retrospectively over our career and realising we'd added a bit more to the pot of British pop culture than they'd originally assumed.

Old Jack Norris, the musical shrimp and the cadging ramble,
A little bit of this, a little bit of that, but in weather like this you
    should wear a coat, a nice warm hat,
A needle and thread, the hand stitches of time, it's Battling
    Levinsky versus Jacky Berg,
Bobbing and weaving an invisible line,
So step for step and both light on our feet,
We'll travel many a long dim silent street,
Would you like a bit of this, or a little bit of that,
A little bit of what you like does you no harm and you know that,

The perpetual steady echo of the passing feet, a continual dark
    river of people,
In its transience and in its permanence,
But when the street lamp fills the gutter with gold,
So many priceless items bought and sold,

So step for step and both light on our feet,
We'll travel many a long dim silent street, together.
Once round Arnold Circus,
Up through Petticoat Lane,

Past the well of shadows and once back round again,
Arm in arm with an abstracted air, to where the people stare
*   out of the upstairs windows,*
Because we are living like kings and these days will last forever.

Cause sailors from Africa, China and the archipelago of Malay,
Jumped ship ragged and penniless into Shadwell's Tiger Bay,
The Welsh and Irish wagtails, mothers of midnight,
The music hall carousal ends, spilling out into bonfire light,
Sending half-crazed shadows dancing up the brick wall
Of Mr Truman's beer factory, waving bottles ten feet tall,

Whether one calls it Spitalfields, Whitechapel, Tower Hamlets
*   or Banglatown,*
We're all dancing in the moonlight, we're all on borrowed
*   ground.*
Oh I'm just walking down to,
I'm just floating down through,
Won't you come with me, to the Liberty of Norton Folgate.
But wait, what's that? Dan Leno and the Limehouse Golem.

Purposefully walking nowhere, I'm happy just floating about,
On a Sunday afternoon, the stallholders all call and shout,
Avoiding people you know, you're just basking in your own
*   company,*
The technicolour world's going by, but you're the lead in your
*   own movie.*

Cause in the Liberty of Norton Folgate,
Walking wild and free,
In your second-hand coat,

Happy just to float,
In this little piece of Liberty,
A part of everything you see.

They're coming left and right, trying to flog you stuff you don't
*   need nor want,*
A smiling chap takes your hand and drags you in his uncle's
*   restaurant,*
There's a Chinese man trying hard to flog you moody DVDs,
You know you've seen the film, it's black and white, it's got no
*   sound,*
And a man's head pops up and down right across your wide-
*   screen TV.*

Cause in the Liberty of Norton Folgate,
Walking wild and free,
In your second-hand coat,
Happy just to float,
In this little piece of Liberty,
Cause you're a part of everything you see,
Yes, you're a part of everything you see.

Cause it's steady old fellows, pickpockets, dandies, extortioners
*   and night wanderers,*
The feeble, the ghastly, upon whom death had placed a very
*   sure hand,*
Some in shreds and patches, reeling inarticulate, full of noisy
*   and inordinate vivacity,*
Which jars discordantly upon the ear and gives an aching sen-
*   sation to both pair of eyeballs.*

In the beginning was a fear of the immigrant
He made his home there down by the riverside,
They made their homes there down by the riverside,
The city sprang up, from the dark mud of the Thames.

And here we are again with the latest album, *Oui Oui Si Si Ja Ja Da Da*, as well as a fantastic new management team. I always felt like *Norton Folgate* was a bit like an episode of *Star Trek*. We were being dragged towards a sort of black hole of eighties nostalgia, and *The Liberty of Norton Folgate* was warp factor 10 and we'd got ourselves out of the black hole, and were now in search of distant planets, of which *Oui Oui Si Si Ja Ja Da Da* is one.

People often ask where the title came from and the simple answer is we couldn't actually decide on a title. Lots of them were being bandied around, but we were arguing, as we often do. The only thing we could agree on was to go to Peter Blake, the great British

pop artist, to do the cover for us. Of course he did the iconic *Sgt. Pepper's Lonely Hearts Club Band*.

We'd already been negotiating with his wife, Chrissie, if he'd be interested in doing our album cover when she asked if we'd like to play at his eightieth birthday party at the Albert Hall, which was a great honour and an enormous amount of fun. It was duly arranged to meet him in his studio, so an excitable delegation was dispatched. What a place! An old warehouse down an alley, Fulham way, with two floors of the most weird and indeed most wonderful. Stuffed squirrels playing snooker watched on by a life-size waxwork of Joe Louis, Max Miller's shoes, Tommy Cooper's fez, huge collections of model cars, boats, trains, fruit machines and paintings covering every surface.

After the most fantastic guided tour of the place with the great man, we settled in the kitchen. 'To tell you the truth, lads', he said, 'I'm always a bit wary of doing album covers'. We looked deflated. 'Because the band will often come up with a title', Peter continued, 'only for the bass player to ring me two weeks later to say they've changed their minds.' We looked at each other in the full knowledge we weren't quite sure what the album title should be. 'No, no, that won't be the case here', we said confidently, 'this record's gonna be called *Circus Freaks*.' In fairness it was the most popular title we had at that time.

'Great', he said. On the tour of his studio, amongst the many other wonders he showed us was, of all things, a marvelous montage of circus freaks. 'I'll get going right away.'

Two weeks later we rang to say we'd changed our minds. With the sound of montage being binned he said, 'Right, what is it now then?' and so it began. *Men of Steel*. No. *Deolali*. No. *Dial 'M' For*

Madness. 2Pop Music. Ten Commandments. Wait, we've got it, *The Rake's Progress.*

'Right', he said. 'I'm just going to write down all the different titles you have suggested to me, and cross them out one by one until the album is ready for release. And did we change our minds again? Oui oui, si si, ja ja, da da, indeed we did.

In deference to Peter Blake, and his original idea, and to celebrate the deluxe, limited edition version, Cathal had the idea of re-doing the cover in the spirit of Peter's idea and bringing the various rejected titles to life. As you can see, Lee Thompson is 'Circus Freaks,' or is he? Chris Foreman is 'Deolali,' Mike Barson is 'Man of Steel'. Cathal Smyth as 'The Rake'. Daniel Woodgate as 'Dial 'M' for Madness'. Peter Blake is Moses in *The Ten Commandments* and me, I am of course 'Zoltar' the fortune-telling character in The Machine on the Pier, who, when Tom Hanks asks if he can be big, prints out the ticket which just says . . . yes.

UP ON THE ROOF

So we turned up on Sunday afternoon and everything seemed quite normal, like a municipal park with a few tents in it. We could hear a bit of music drifting out behind us, Elton John and the like. Next minute we get a call to go and rehearse on the roof. We jump in some golf buggies, and it was like a scene from *The Matrix*, the Mall eerily empty and silent as we entered the gates of Buckingham Palace. Policemen saluting us, Household Cavalry unflinching as we waved and smiled and drove through an arch into Buckingham Palace proper.

We were then escorted by two heavily armed policemen up the stairs, and took a lift that led to the servants' quarters on the fifth floor. There was a corridor, like a hotel, with lots of open doors and mini staff parties going on in the rooms. We were invited in to a few, but we had our own dressing room. It was No Smoking, but I opened the window and had a cigarette, and could have sworn that I felt a red laser dot on my forehead – there were definitely silhouettes walking around on the roofs opposite.

Then we're called to do our rehearsal and we climb up some rather rickety wooden stairs and out onto the roof. We realise at this point that it's pitched, not flat, so we have to scrabble over the guttering. Around the corner they've built us a flat platform out of scaffolding and planks, and it's jutting over the building so the audience can actually see us. It's quite precarious and I'm not great with heights.

But before I get the chance to feel vertiginous, I look up and it's the most extraordinary sight. I realise that the whole of the London skyline was built around the view you get from Buckingham Palace. The Queen must have ordered it so. It was literally like the Post Office Tower there, the Gherkin there, Big Ben there, the London Eye. Every single landmark was displayed in order. And then the realisation that I'm actually standing on the roof of Buckingham Palace looking down the Mall, which let me tell you, was an extremely odd experience, to say the least.

Then of course it started to rain. I mean really started to rain. And didn't stop raining. But we rehearsed the songs, which went fine, playing 'Our House' and 'It Must Be Love'. I resisted the urge to sing a few lines from The Beatles' 'Get Back', especially the one about 'California Grass'! The next day was the Jubilee Pageant and I went down to see a friend of mine, Eduardo, who has a houseboat in Chelsea Harbour. It didn't stop raining and it looked like the whole weekend was going to be a complete washout. I saw the poor old Queen going by, in a flotilla of people looking like they were freezing and getting pneumonia.

So the prospects for the Sunday, the day of the concert, weren't looking too good. But when we got there in the afternoon it actually stopped raining. It's a mad phenomenon, but in the last ten years or so every time Madness play, no matter how wet the festival or the occasion, it seems to stop raining when we turn up. People are actually now paying us to turn up at festivals, not to play but just in the hope that the rain will stop.

It was a very jolly atmosphere backstage, we did our rehearsal, and then the day drew on without anything really dramatic happening. We just sat around waiting. The call came just as it was starting to get dark, about half eight, and we basically followed the same procedure as before. We got in the golf buggies, went up the staff entrance, as it were, so to speak, and once again up the rickety ladder. But of course it was a completely different view when we got out on the night for the concert itself. To be greeted by the sight of I don't know how many people. They'd built an auditorium around the Victoria Monument, and you could see right down the Mall and it was the most extraordinary sight. That's when it really hit home what the hell we were doing: standing on the roof of Buckingham Palace.

I remember there was an audible gasp when the graphics we'd arranged were beamed onto the palace, via seventy-five projectors, which made it look like it had fallen down and been replaced by a block of flats. It was more than a little ironic, seeing as how we'd all spent a considerable proportion of our lives standing on the roofs of blocks of flats. In fact it was a similar view up there from the top of the flats I used to live in in Clerkenwell. The reaction to our performance was incredible, and the whole thing went in a flash, as things of this enormity seem to do. The next thing we were piling down the stairs and they told us they wanted the band to join the finale with Paul McCartney, singing 'Ob-La-Di, Ob-La-Da', not anyone's favourite of all The Beatles songs, but at least the lyrics weren't too challenging.

Then it got even more bizarre because we were ushered into a tent where we were due to meet the Queen, and it was at that point our keyboard player, Mike, started having a bit of a moment. He was going, 'Look, there's Stevie Wonder. There's Paul McCartney.

And there's the Queen. What are we doing here?' It all started to get a bit much.

'Hang on in there, we're nearly there.' The surrealism was becoming overwhelming for all of us, and then the Queen came along the line and was suddenly standing in front of me. I didn't really have a clue what I was going to say. I just spontaneously said: ''Scuse me, ma'am, but are you still into football?' She said, 'Not particularly,' and I replied, 'Can I have your Cup Final tickets then?' Quick as a flash she said, 'That's Tommy Cooper.' Although it's a famous moment from an old Royal Variety performance, it was extraordinary that she could remember, it must have been fifty-odd years ago. I refrained from sticking a tea bag in her top pocket and saying, 'Have a drink on me.'

Then Charles came along and he was very nice. I've seen him around a few times, at various Prince's Trust dos. And then Camilla came along and she was very charming indeed. I said to her that in all honesty I thought Charles made a great speech about how proud he was to be British and how proud he was of his mum.

In fact I had dinner with Prince Charles shortly after that – it's like I've suddenly become a friend of the royal family. I was doing a bit of my one-man show and giving out some awards for Business in the Community which Prince Charles is involved in and I got a missive asking whether I'd like to have dinner with him afterwards. A most bizarre situation. It was during the meal that he asked how I prepare for my one-man show, and I asked how he prepares for a speech like the one he gave at the Jubilee concert. He said people give him miles of notes and he just throws them all away. He goes on a walk or has a bath and it all comes to him instinctively, which inspired me on stage to tell the story about when Madness played at the first-ever Prince's Trust Awards, and our saxophonist, Lee, was dressed as Gary Glitter. Prince Charles came down the line and Kid Jensen was before me. Kid Jensen?

Anyway, Charles got to Lee and he said, 'I say, you look great. Who have you come as? Batman?' Of course this was a time when you still could dress as Gary Glitter, silver cape and all, amongst a group of kids.

So we got to meet the Queen, and then we got invited to a party in what they call the Bow Room. There were lots of princes wandering around, and princesses with slightly more hair. And as I say, Stevie Wonder, Paul McCartney, Elton John, Grace Jones and all those iconic figures. Our families, my wife and kids. It was big enough, but not too big to feel like a crush. Fantastic champagne and canapés were flowing and flying. But it was a roomful of people all being elbowed by their wives to go and say hello

And who have you come as? Kid Jensen?

to other people being elbowed by their wives to go and say hello to other people being elbowed by their wives. A room full of people saying hello and not much else.

My two daughters, Scarlett and Viva, spotted will.i.am and said, 'Dad, you've got to go and say hello to will.i.am.' He was talking to William, so I strolled over there. Prince William turned on his heels and walked straight away, so I flapped around trying to chat to will.i.am, not knowing a huge amount about what he does. I looked round to see my daughters had also run away. I don't think he was particularly chuffed that I'd ruined his conversation with Prince William. I skulked away.

I had a plastic cup I'd brought from the dressing room and I unconsciously dropped it on the floor, completely oblivious to the fact I wasn't in my dressing room. Princess Beatrice picked it up and said, 'You can't do that. This is my granny's house.' I was dropping litter in Buckingham Palace. The party was over by half twelve. It was a very jolly occasion.

The impact of our performance was immense and the next day my record company said, 'Suggs, we'd like you to go back and do some interviews while the media is still there.' My management were worried none of the other artists would turn up, it would be a bit quiet and I'd be on my own. The BBC had arranged to meet me outside Marks & Spencer's on Piccadilly. When I arrived I realised the ridiculousness of what had been said. We're going to meet somewhere quiet, I know, Piccadilly Circus! What they also forgot was that the Queen actually had another parade down the Mall, so in fact there were thousands of people there.

I ended up in this rather strange situation of trying to get across the Mall to where the BBC's outside broadcast was situated. The police made a break in the fencing and the crowd let me through and burst into a spontaneous chorus of 'Our House'. As I tried to cross the road suddenly the Household Cavalry appeared careering down the Mall, so I was stuck in the middle of one's street. They had closed the gates behind me and I had the cavalry charging towards me with thousands of people singing 'Our House' on either side. What an unassuming and subtle entrance.

Our performance on the roof of Buckingham Palace had a weirdly strong effect on people and seemed to have more impact on the general public than almost anything else we'd done. I think it was the combination of singing 'Our House' and turning the palace into a block of flats, and maybe because we sang 'It Must Be Love'. I mean, nothing more, nothing less, love is the best. Who's gonna go for that? And yes, the lead is still intact.

CLOSING CEREMONY

Shortly before we'd been asked to play at the Jubilee we got a call asking if we'd like to play at the closing ceremony of the Olympics, whatever next? We went down for a meeting at Three Mill Studios in Hackney. It was all top secret and hush-hush, and we had to sign all sorts of bits of paper saying we wouldn't divulge any of the things that we'd learnt. And in their office was a huge mock-up of the set of the closing ceremony, which was a sort of wonky version of London.

They explained to us there'd be a huge traffic jam involving lorries and Minis and vintage cars, and then Michael Caine would go 'I only told you to blow the bloody doors off,' at which point there'd be a huge explosion with trucks blowing up and people flying in all directions, and street parties emanating out of the backs of all these lorries, and on one of these trucks would be us and we'd be playing 'Our House'.

They wanted this song because of the street-party vibe: they were keen to create the notion that the whole world had been invited into our house. It all seemed terribly exciting, although we weren't sure what was happening before or after our bit, cos it was secret, as I say. So that was all great, and it was about two months before the ceremony itself.

But we'd already agreed that we'd play 'Our House' at the Jubilee. What other song would you be singing on the top of Buckingham Palace? We tried to proffer the idea of doing 'House of Fun', but the fact that it's about a teenage kid buying Durex in a chemist's probably wasn't the best celebration to the end of the Queen's party.

So then we had a bit of a problem. The people at the Olympics were getting really fed up because they'd already got us to do 'Our House', and they were a bit worried that the Jubilee was going to upstage the final ceremony of the Olympics – would people want to hear us playing it twice? We ended up compromising by playing half of 'Our House', going into 'It Must Be Love' on the roof of Buckingham Palace, and we agreed that we'd do the whole of 'Our House' on the back of a lorry, driving in and out of this traffic jam.

The next thing, we actually had the dress rehearsal. We presumed it wasn't going to be in the Olympic Stadium, cos by now the Olympics were already in full flow, unlike the opening ceremony, where obviously the events hadn't begun – it would be very difficult to sneak in and out of the main stadium whilst the games were in progress.

We were given an address in Dagenham which turned out to be the old Ford factory. It was a bit like a scene from *The Avengers*. We got down there, and there were lots of circus tents and marquees approximating the kind of buildings that would be utilised for the backstage area. In the middle of the car park of the old factory they'd marked out an exact scale replica of the Olympic Stadium and the running track.

We had the most bizarre experience of pretending that we were in what might possibly be the most glamorous setting in the world rather than in the car park of a disused car factory, with a motorway running along beside us. So we just wobbled round the outer perimeter on the open truck singing 'Our House'. The only thing we did know was that we were going to come right past the Queen and, Lee, our sax player, was going to take off and fly, à la 'Baggy Trousers' all those years ago. He was threatening to wear a kilt.

We knew the Grenadier Guards were going to play 'Park Life', The Pet Shop Boys were going to play and there was to be a top-secret, superstellar guest before the whole thing transferred to an enormous concert that was going to take place in Hyde Park. We also knew there would be some sort of formality in handing over the Olympics to the Brazilians, but we weren't sure what form that would take. So the whole thing was a rather intriguing and exciting affair.

We were all discussing what we were going to wear, which seemed a rather important thing considering 75 billion, or something, people were going to be watching us, and there was a thought that we should all wear grey suits and black turtleneck jumpers as we had on one of our album covers. That obviously fell to pieces, as it always does with the band trying to organise anything collectively. I thought: Yes, I would like a grey suit. I'd like a really nice grey mohair suit. I thought: Yes! what I'd like to do is represent the best of British tailoring.

I went to see Gresham Blake the tailor, and they had this fantastic three-ply grey mohair, and there I was again, wearing a mohair suit. Not aquamarine this time, but paired with a fantastic Vivienne Westwood tie with a very subtle sort of punk exploding Union Jack on it. Then I waited to hear what the hell the rest of the band were going to wear.

TELEVISION CENTRE

The closing of the Queen's Jubilee party, the closing of the Olympic Ceremony and now the closing of the BBC, well, Television Centre. Jesus.

'It Must Be Love' recently replaced Whitney Houston's 'I Will Always Love You', as the song of choice at weddings and indeed funerals, and it would now seem Madness are the band of choice when it comes to the closing of institutions.

We've been described recently as 'National Treasures' and, more incredibly, as a 'National Institution'. Acceptance, you may think, might have alerted us to the fact, now very obvious to the naked eye, that we are in the business of closing 'National Institutions'. Your local hospital, the post office, Cyprus, the EU. What have you got? We're cheap, and open to offers.

When the BBC in their wisdom, started moving huge chunks of radio and TV from the greatest city on the planet, much to the consternation of most of its ten million inhabitants, to Manchester, the writing was on the wall for TV Centre in White City.

With the announcement finally made, the inevitable Mad sign appeared over the skies of North London. We got a call from Mark

Cooper, the head of music, a jolly nice chap we'd worked with over the years on a number of shows, including the best music show on TV: *Later with Jools*.

We liked Mark, and more importantly, unlike a lot of execs at the BBC, he liked us. He phoned to ask if we would be interested in playing at TV centre, on the night they (the men in grey) came to close the place down.

It was a beautiful, typically British spring evening, at the end of March, as we shot from the Mad Cave under our waterfall, headed for the Westway.

Our branded, pimped up Bedford van, sailing above the smoking chimney pots of Notting Hill, up and over the three-lane overpass to the west.

The rain and sleet lashing horizontally across the windscreen as the swirling wind buffeted our over-loaded van in and out of the oncoming traffic.

Hilarity, fear, bravado?

We had fortunately just handbrake turned off the Westway, skidding to a halt in the desolation of what was once the *Blue Peter* garden. We piled out the back of the Mad Mobile, mad, ready for retributional action, the wind slamming both van doors behind us.

We fanned out across the car park ready for anything. Anything.

No discernible enemy approached.

But, as we unlink our arms and begin to relax . . .

. . . our stage has not been erected in the *Later with Jools* studio as presumed, but in the car park in front of us.

Jesus Christ! The whole thing is about to take off.

From a gaggle of cameramen and crew done up like eskimos, Mark enthusiastically bounds towards us. 'What do you reckon, lads?' His words barely audible as the wind whips them away, 'Great, eh? looks like a spaceship.'

Which, we had to admit, it did. The only problem with our space rocket stage, was it looked like it was really about to take off. With us on it.

At six o'clock *The One Show* was going live. A series of interviews from the great and the good, past and present with tales of the old goings on at TV Centre down the years, in which Cathal and I were to be included. The set was laid out in the faux-living-room format beloved of all teatime TV. Potted plants, shelves with comedy nick-nacks. A coffee table set with newspapers and empty branded mugs. Around which, two sofas were placed at right angles. One for the hosts, Chris Evans and the Welsh girl, Alex, and one for the guests.

And yes, if you haven't already guessed, the whole thing was outside. Brilliant! Pot plants flying about all over the gaff, script pages whirling about in a mini tornado. The Welsh girl's hair at right angles. Chris manfully shouting at the wobbling camera.

Cathal and I were in the corridor, taking off our coats, ready to weather the storm. Standing in front of Sir Michael Grade and behind Sir Terence Wogan in the queue of anecdotalists. Terry was not best pleased, to say the least, as he was plunged out through the swing doors and onto the disintegrating set, his hair blowing about like a horse-hair mattress on a bonfire.

On the set the only thing we managed to hear was the Welsh girl shouting, 'Will you shut up!' Terry and I grumbled cheerfully at the ridiculousness of it all. Amongst the flying nick-nacks.

Sir Tel was still ranting off script, oblivious to any questions, at the stupidity of closing Television Centre, as Cathal and I were ushered toward the stage to perform our first number over the closing credits of the, now completely out of control, *One Show*. 'The night they closed the old BBC down, all the people were singing . . .'

On stage it could not have been any colder. (Well, that's not completely accurate, we did play at Edinburgh Castle on New Year's Eve once, up to our ears in snow. As the bells heralding the new year rang, the first words heard on live radio in 2009 were, 'Fuck me!')

The last band ever to play at the BBC Television Centre!

Flashbacks a go-go, the stuff which hummed through school playgrounds for the entire lunch break. Bob Marley, with mini locks and Peter Tosh and them bug-eyed specs and bobble hat; 'Concrete Jungle', The Sensational Alex Harvey Band, Next, Roxy Music, more bug-eyed specs: What's her name? Virginia Plain! With Whispering Bob's horrified face appearing in the middle of the frame, whispering, 'If this is the future of rock and roll, then I'm off.' We all cheered. David Bowie, Star Man, indeed. Slade, blow-up banana drum sticks. Cum on feel the noize! Cockney Rebel, bowler hat, Judie Teen. Dexys with the back drop of 'Jocky Wilson'. The Jesus and Mary Chain, backs to camera. Millions of the things all colliding together like a technicolour steam train. Almost every thing that ever meant anything to me, happened here. Tommy Cooper, Max Wall, Krapp's Last Tape, *Match of the Day*, for Christ's sake!

My spirit was suddenly filled with every show I'd watched in fifty-odd years, broadcast from this building, from *Nationwide* to *Morecambe and Wise*. I urged the people on the top floor to get out before the Daleks got them. I was getting right into it, as the memories flashed past my eyes like a drowning man. The first time we came here as wild-eyed, hollow-cheeked teenagers to perform on *Top of the Pops*, WHAT!!?!! And the millions of appearances since.

But never mind how many times we'd appeared on these hallowed premises, how many shows have we been banned from? Well from immediate memory: *The Terry Wogan Show*; *Tiswas*; *Children in Need*; *This Morning* and, from *Top of the Pops*, about eight times. We'd cock something up or mime irreverently and we'd get banned.

As our spaceship set strained at the guy ropes and the sleet lashed our faces, the trumpet player had his instrument frozen to his lips. Nobody else had any feeling in their fingers. But off we went, the buoyant crowd of Madness fans and now ex-BBC employees raised the spirits. People were hanging out of the top-floor windows and waving from passing buses and tube trains. The atmosphere was stoic, British and brilliant . . . then my trousers fell down.

The echoes of all this are still reverberating. We've played to the biggest global TV audience as part of the Olympic Games closing ceremony. I think back to those seven fresh-faced young chaps from North London who thought they'd made it when they got a residency at their local pub. What an extraordinary adventure we've all been in together since those naïve and chaotic days as The Invaders. And I realise I'd rather be surrounded by my noisy, frustrating gang of fools than anybody else. Madness have always, from the early days, been a sort of surrogate family – with all the frustration, the annoyance, the aggro. A fucked-up, chaotic, ridiculous, argumentative, impossible . . . unbeatable lot.

Thankyou, goodnight.

Hello I must be going,
thank you all so much for showing.

I got high cos you lifted me
we had a laugh we shed a tear,
we shared a glass, or two of frothing beer
(and oh what an
atmosphere)

Hello, I must be going.

INDEX

ACKNOWLEDGEMENTS

Madness. Dave Robinson, Paul Conroy, Rob Dickins, Kellogs, Matthew Sztumpf. Garry, Katy, Jam, James and Nathan and all at Anglo Management. Hugh, Mel, Tony and Gareth and all at Hannah Management. PBJ. Colin Young and all at C.C. Young & Co. Chris and all at Another Tongue. Robert Kirby. Richard and Josh and all at Quercus. Patrick Maguire.